The Purposes of Education

What are the purposes of education and what is the relationship between educational research and policy? Using the twin lenses of *Visible Learning* and educational philosophy, these are among the many fascinating topics discussed in extended conversations between John Hattie and Steen Nepper Larsen. This wide-ranging and informative book offers fundamental propositions about the nature of education. It maps out in fascinating detail a coming together of Hattie's empirical data and world-famous *Visible Learning* paradigm with the rich heritage of educational philosophy. Additionally, it explores the inevitable questions of the purpose of education and the development of students in a learning society.

Part clash of cultures, part meeting of minds, always fascinating and illuminating, this intriguing book will inspire teachers, students, and parents at all levels of the educational system – from kindergarten through school to university.

Conversations include:

What are the purposes of education?
Does educational data speak for itself?
What is the role of the teacher?
Is learning a visible phenomenon?
Is it important to teach and learn specific subjects?
What is the role of neuroscience research?
What is the relationship between educational research and educational politics?
What is the role of the state in education?

John Hattie is Laureate Professor at the University of Melbourne, Australia, and his *Visible Learning* series of books have been translated into 23 different languages and have sold over 1 million copies.

Steen Nepper Larsen is Associate Professor in Education Science at the Danish School of Education, Aarhus University, Denmark, and has published numerous academic books and journal articles. He is a critic connected to the Danish newspaper *Information*, among other organizations, and has worked on several popular philosophy programs for Danmarks Radio, P1.

The Purposes of Education

A Conversation Between John Hattie and Steen Nepper Larsen

John Hattie and Steen Nepper Larsen

Routledge
Taylor & Francis Group

LONDON AND NEW YORK

First published 2020
by Routledge
2 Park Square, Milton Park, Abingdon, Oxon OX14 4RN

and by Routledge
52 Vanderbilt Avenue, New York, NY 10017

Routledge is an imprint of the Taylor & Francis Group, an informa business

Cartoons by Sarah Firth

British Library Cataloguing-in-Publication Data
A catalogue record for this book is available from the British Library

Library of Congress Cataloging-in-Publication Data
A catalog record for this book has been requested

ISBN: 978-0-367-41663-8 (hbk)
ISBN: 978-0-367-41664-5 (pbk)
ISBN: 978-0-367-81556-1 (ebk)

Typeset in Bembo
by Apex Covantage, LLC

Contents

Contents

★ the magnifying glass icon and the use of a bold typeface in the text indicates that the word/phrase concerned is included in the glossary with a brief explanation.

Introduction

Having a conversation is the essence of respect, learning, and coming together. There is a long tradition of conversation in philosophy, with perhaps the high point being Plato's writings of his many conversations. We only know Socrates through these conversations. When we listen to others, we can question our own beliefs and assumptions. When we demonstrate to others, we have heard what they have said, we have shown remarkable levels of respect. Then through conversation we can agree to agree, disagree, we can clarify and critique, we can grow to become more nuanced and sophisticated, and we can be led to more exciting thinking.

Since publishing *Visible Learning* there have been many discussions about this work. For many, it was a breath of fresh air; for others it upset core beliefs, it was too quantitative; and for others it was plain wrong. Over the subsequent years, there have been many systematic interventions in schools based on the *Visible Learning* story – one of the earliest and most comprehensive was in schools across Denmark. At the same time, the political agenda in Denmark was upsetting many of the traditional working conditions and using claims about *Visible Learning* to defend these changes (some wrong and some right attributions). No surprise there grew a backlash, a community of critics, and a turning up of the heat.

Academic ideas thrive in the primordial ooze of critique. Academic models need to be tested, falsified, and rebuilt; we grow via critique, and critique presumes that our understanding of the world is not perfect but can be improved. We can integrate and use many ideas from other disciplines, we can be diligent heirs to history, and can relate many ideas, but only if we are amenable to open conversations with experts in other domains. Unlike many public conversations, and certainly unlike many online fora, the aim is to critique the ideas, not the person.

Steen Nepper Larsen sent John Hattie a copy of his critique of *Visible Learning* and politely asked for comment. The reply was lengthy, and Steen called it "harsh," which was far from the intention – an example of misunderstanding that conversations via email can engender. John claimed that he "fundamentally objected to the quality and nature of your argument. It is too much argument by innuendo, by ignoring and misreading my corpus of work, not considering the actual impact of the work in the many schools near you. . . . I would be happy to have a conversation through a rewriting and while I would respect your viewpoint at least a subsequent article would be a critique of what I said and not what you would want me to have said." Whoops, perhaps it was harsh – but Steen rose to the occasion and invited a more in-depth conversation.

Steen replied that the fundamental questions he was addressing were: "What is the ontology of the learning effect? Can learning be grasped and understood as a visible phenomenon? What happens to schools and pupils when the VL evidence credo/'package' is being implemented by international, national, and local political and educational managers? The first two profound questions are philosophical of and in nature – the third deals foremost with *Bildung* concerns, and obvious threats to freethinking, and the disappearance of autonomous schools."

Already there are two cultures evident – the world of a philosopher and the world of an educational psychologist and psychometrician. We had much to learn about each other's heritage and language. Steen also sent a wonderful exemplar of a conversation between the musician Daniel Barenboim and professor of literature Edward Said (www.youtube.com/watch?v=HWQCy6_TU3A) and suggested we may grow each other's views via such a conversation. Book versions of conversations are not uncommon in philosophy but are rarer in education. In *Resonance Education*, the sociologist Hartmut Rosa talks with the pedagogue Wolfgang Endres about the basic features of learning that are individualized and sustainable, and how the idea of 'resonance' can be applied to the areas of school and education (Rosa & Endres 2016). But such conversations do not happen via email, which soon can move to "I say, no, I said" with little interaction or clarification, and too often such exchanges harden positions with little listening. It can look harsh too quickly. Sherry Turkle has written superbly on the flight from conversation into the world of communication without eye contact, the reaching for the keyboard not noticing the nuances of facial movements and eye gazes, and how too often we are now alone together (Turkle 2017). We also note the powerful quote from Michael Foucault (1984): "Thought is not what inhabits a certain conduct and gives it its meaning; rather, it is what allows one to step back from this way of acting or reacting, to present it to oneself as an object of thought and question it as to its meaning, its conditions, its goals. Thought is freedom in relation to what one does, the motion by which one detaches oneself from it, establishes it as an object, and reflects on it as a problem." So, Steen commented that he had "an idea brewing in his mind": Why not come together for some weeks to converse?

He outlined some key ideas: Let's talk about the purpose of education, there are many more than curious to come to know answers far beyond the *Visible Learning* paradigm and results – and most are now in this book. He wrote, "We could challenge and irritate one another and it is likely that our intellectual exchanges will force both of us to invent and ventilate self-critical and former unknown perspectives on education. We could talk about the purpose of education, why does mankind need education, the legacy of *Bildung*, autonomy in education, the relation between research and politics, the concept of learning, the (in)visibility of learning, the role of education in society, the future of education, e-learning and alienation, and so much more."

We comment about current issues, although note that time can change, governments and ministers change, and this may need to be considered.

Steen packed his eleven-speed bike (so much thinking happens on the bike), and flew to Melbourne, where we spent a few weeks in conversation from May to June 2018. We recorded, then transcribed these conversations, and then worked, reworked, had more discussions, reordered, explored, and created this book. It was a labor of much love as both profited from learning the other's language, ways of thinking, and – we trust you will also see – different perspectives.

If there was ever an example of thinking aloud, this book aims to capture this phenomenon.

Let me introduce the conversationalists: Mr. *Visible Learning*, John Hattie (b.1950) meets Mr. *Bildung*, Steen Nepper Larsen (b.1958).

I. THE ENCOUNTER

WELCOME to OUR CONVERSATION

John: Welcome to Melbourne, Steen. You'll discover, over the next two weeks, that I'm curious about most things. I know some things reasonably well, some things hardly at all. I do not claim, like you can, to be an expert in philosophy. . . . And, as I think I've mentioned to you, I had the luxury, when I was a graduate student at the University of Otago, to sit in classes on the philosophy of science. We had a brand new professor of philosophy who was a philosophy of science expert. And he was this young guy from England, Alan Musgrave (Musgrave 1993), and he was a brilliant teacher and promoted a notion I have loved – theories should make novel predictions – so that in *Visible Learning*, the underlying explanation and theory should make predictions that were not used in the construction of the theory, but should follow from it. Many of us, including me, snuck into his classes. During that time, his mentor, the Austrian-born English philosopher Karl Popper, came on sabbatical to New Zealand. He was then in his 70s, but wow what a thinker – he was one of those rare academics who 'thought aloud'. Have you ever heard Popper speak?

Steen: Only in radio programs, but of course I have read him.

John: The way he lectured, in his very thick, Viennese voice, he read every word. He never looked up once, and as he read it, we were spellbound. He had this thing at the time. He hated social science (and smokers), but he wouldn't talk about it. "It's not a science."

Steen: I know.

John: And so I had to sit there, obviously, as a young 20-year-old social science graduate student, spellbound by this man. You can imagine, he had quite an impact.

He was working on his three worlds paper (Popper 1979). His messages about making bold claims and then attempting to refute them was impressed upon us and became important through my career. I have often cited his claim: "Bold ideas, unjustified anticipations, and speculative thought, are our only means for interpreting nature: our only organon, our only instrument, for grasping her." This was, he argued, because bold ideas propose and predict much, and thus are more easily refutable. I made some "bold" predictions about the underlying story in *Visible Learning* – of course others can refute them, of course they are conjectures and tentative, of course they aim to explain a lot, make new predictions, and of course they are open to counter arguments, falsifiability, and I hope they lead to new ways of seeing the world and they lead to new research. I know there's a lot of criticism of him and he's almost forgotten in many ways now. I don't know if that's true, but many people see him as a figment of history.

Steen: It depends on where you go. But you are right, his 1953 lecture *Conjectures and Refutations* (Popper 2002/1953) is still a classic worth consulting if you want to reflect upon how to learn to ask critical questions to scientific theories and falsify their results.

Visible Learning – working out the story is the hard part, the data is the easy part

John: Yeah, but then, my background, as you know, I'm a statistician in measurement. I have a life in that world and, in fact, up to 2009, the whole *Visible Learning* has been a hobby. It's been a thing I did in my spare time.

I did it all myself, it took me 20 years, but the data part is not difficult. **Meta-analysis** is a straightforward method, calculating effects is not hard, and overall this data side is easy. The data's trivially easy. Working out the story is the hard part.

The 2009 book kind of worked (Hattie 2009). It got attention. The *Visible Learning* books sold half a million copies, so something went right. But it is the story that is most critical.

Steen: And it got translated in all kinds of languages.

John: Twenty-three to 24 languages. But it was my tenth book. What happened to the other nine?

I love this story. It may not be true, but I still like it. My first book on **three-mode factor analysis** is still in print, published in 1984, because they printed 500 copies and they haven't sold them all yet.

Steen: They are probably valuable objects for collecting.

John: And so, the whole *Visible Learning*, it's taken over in a way. I still work at the measurement area, but not as much now as *Visible Learning* has become more dominant.

In fact, I counted it up the other week. For 21 years, I've been a dean or head of school in three universities, and deputy dean at another. As you know, that just takes the life out of you, but I loved it. In fact, I was deputy dean here last year for a year, after a 10-year break from these kinds of duties.

Steen: Okay, but your *Visible Learning* programs also transformed into a business program, I guess. You seem to have been all around the globe, and many different schools have adopted your way of looking at and evaluating things. But have you made and handled the data here in Australia?

John: Yes and no. What happened is that, when I went back to New Zealand in 1999 (I'm originally from there but left in 1974), they were in an interesting stage politically in that one political party said they wanted national testing like America has, like England has. The other party said, "No way." The latter party won government.

And then they said, "Oh, my goodness. We haven't a clue how we will now know what is going on in the schools."

So, they put out a bid for a large amount of money to create a year five and year seven test in reading and writing, the usual nonsense. I was quite opposed to this. I think national testing's a disaster.

We put in a non-compliant bid and we won, and so we built the New Zealand Assessment Scheme and I want to show it to you as it is quite a different way of thinking about assessment (Hattie 2006).

And what we're most proud of, it's voluntary. No school has to use it. Eighty percent of schools are using that assessment tool 17 years later. Very successful.

Steen: That's very different from the European system.

John: Totally.

Steen: The OECD-invented PISA test system was launched in 2000. The idea was to compare and hopefully strengthen the pupils' skills in different nations, and from the school year 2006 to 2007 Denmark has used a mandatory national test program.

John: The NZ system is not mandatory.

Steen: The PISA program was implemented via a so-called voluntary coordination program (see my colleague Krejsler et al. 2014). The different ministers of education and their staff gathered and coordinated their test programs. It thereby turned out to be more or less mandatory, and now they're putting out the figures for all these countries and for every 'stakeholder' to read.

But are you basically critical against all these national competitive initiatives?

John: Yes, I am, and I want to show you the alternative, as it is key to claim it's all about the alternatives.

So, we built this system. In about 2008 we had spent six years building it, and we were turning from building it and doing the research to becoming a maintenance-of-a-computer system. I didn't want to do that.

So, I said to the government, "It's time for me to hand it back to you people." And they were very reluctant to take it in the early days. They didn't have the expertise.

Steen: That was for Australia?

John: New Zealand. I said, "It's just not appropriate that I'm running a computer-based company. It's not my expertise. I don't want to do it." They took it back and did a good job from then on running it. And then I had a team and I was like, "What do you do with the team?"

Visible Learning had just come out and I said to them, "You're very good at translating. That's your skill. I don't want to spend my life going out into schools. I'm not very good at it. I talk too much." Schools like when I go and talk but, as I'm sure you know, nothing happens. Next day, forgotten. It was entertainment.

I said, "I don't want to do that."

So I said, "The task I want you to do is I want you to build the resources around *Visible Learning* and implement the ideas in schools." And you can imagine we didn't know a lot in those days as to how to do this. We did it for about six months to a year and it was becoming very successful in New Zealand.

6:34 p.m. one Saturday night, my dean emailed me without consultation, out of the blue, and said, "You have to close it. Close it by Monday. It's too successful. You're killing part of the university that's supposed to deal with this, as the schools are all coming to you, not them." And I was quite distraught, as you can imagine. I was a reasonably senior person in the place, but no consultation.

In retrospect, it was a very good decision because it allowed me to seek other, more compatible homes to upscale the translation into schools. So, various companies came to me and said, "We'll buy these people."

I went to this one place and I was on the board of this company and they said they'd take it. And I said, "I've got these ten people. They're out of a job." They took them.

Steen: Do you run this business beside your university job?

John: No, it is a completely separate affair, and it's a commercial company. I said, "Look, here are the rules. I don't want to be involved in the day-to-day delivery of this. It's not my skill." My terror, Steen, is – and I see some of my colleagues doing this – that I go out and do the same speeches on the research I did ten years ago. I don't want to do that.

And so I said, "I will give you 30 days a year." That's it. They can have me present on those days. "I want you to build the resources." But, on the other hand, I want quality control.

So, I get all the data from their implementation of the *Visible Learning* model in schools. There's about 100, 200 of them around the world now. I worry about quality control. My argument is, if I don't see an impact on student learning, it's not working. And three companies have gone because they couldn't show that.

Last year the base of the commercial operations switched from New Zealand to a U.S.-based company (**Corwin**). Also, as I start retirement from the university, I'm seriously thinking of giving extra days because I'm quite happy with how they deliver *Visible Learning* across the world. I've been very happy with what they've done and, as I'm sure you know, it's not easy as they had to undertake translation, adapt to the local circumstances, and hire local professional developers. There's lots of things to learn from it, but it's going extremely well as I see from the evidence on the students.

Like, I've seen all the data from the **Skanderborg** schools in your country. It's pretty impressive.

Steen: So, are you working with the Danish professor Lars Qvortrup, the leader of National Centre for School Research at Aarhus University?

John: Yes.

Steen: In his old days, he was a Marxist, and then favored a system theoretical approach inspired by the German sociologist Niklas Luhmann, and now he is very much in favor of a so-called empirical turn in educational research, implying that he's also relying on and producing educational statistics. That's quite a big transformation.

John: I know, it's crazy how we change over our careers. So, as you know, I'm a statistician and, yes, I never imagined that the *Visible Learning* book would ever be of interest. I wrote many versions of it. One version was over 500 pages. It was resplendent with graphs, numbers galore, it had every detail you could imagine, all the moderators, you name it.

My wife looked at it, she said, "Who would ever read this?" and I realized maybe two people would. So I threw it out and she created those dials to provide some flow. When she looked at the next version and she said, "Maybe ten will read it now, as there are still too many numbers." So I made more revisions to make it less measurement-like while aiming to retain the evidence in a more interpretative style.

Janet is a professor of evaluation here at the University of Melbourne. Where are you based – at Aarhus or at Copenhagen?

Steen: In Copenhagen, where we, among other subjects, have Educational Psychology, Educational Philosophy, Educational Sociology, and Educational Anthropology. These four departments all possess substantial prefix-hyphen words ("Educational . . ."; in Danish: *Pædagogisk . . .*) in their names. It's actually pretty interesting, but I actually belong to the department Educational Sciences (in Danish: *Uddannelsesvidenskab*). Besides, I am a critic, for example, reviewing books for research magazines and the Danish newspaper *Information*.

My wife, Ida Winther, is a professor of anthropology. When it comes to educational anthropology, it is both possible to study social processes in formal school institutions and informal learning and depict how students are building up their horizons for themselves. And how do they interact with one another in families that split up and how do different migration background themes "pop up." Educational Anthropology is a very interesting program and it invites the students to do very broad and diverse investigations while they do field work.

II. DOES EDUCATIONAL DATA Speak for ITSELF?

Steen: "This is a world where massive amounts of data and applied mathematics replace every other tool that might be brought to bear. Out with every theory of human behavior, from linguistics to sociology. Forget taxonomy, ontology, and psychology. Who knows why people do what they do? The point is they do it, and we can track and measure it with unprecedented fidelity. With enough data, the numbers speak for themselves" (Anderson 2008).

So Chris Anderson (b.1961), the British–American writer, entrepreneur, and editor of *Wired* (Magazine) wrote in the famous article "The End of Theory: The Data Deluge Makes the Scientific Method Obsolete" way back in 2008, proclaiming that the Big Data revolution will change everything.

Before we start to discuss the effect problem in the field of education I wonder if you agree with Anderson when he claims the numbers speaks for themselves and states that we should get rid of science. But first of all, did you read this article?

John: Yes.

Steen: And is it correctly understood that you are simply against his idea that data are able to interpret themselves and contain the truth when they are piled up?

John: Yes, I am totally against this simplistic way of understanding.

Steen: I agree, and you seem to favor a kind of thinking – and theorizing – while doing research, but at the same time you tend to follow the principle that data must be deprived of context, subject, and the situation in which they're collected to be "real" data.

John: No, it's the opposite. They are empirical questions.

Steen: Empirical questions?

John: Yes, interpretations need to be tested, evaluated for context moderators, those kinds of things.

Steen: The strength of your approach is immediately impressive, that, even though a critical remark could be that there are tremendous differences between mathematics, poetry, and social science or sport or whatever, your approach is so strong that it can cover all dimensions in one program. It has apparently been designed not to be dependent on the substance of the learning matters.

John: Not completely – as it is an empirical question whether the substance of the learning matters. That's the question that I've asked. Does the nature of the content mark a difference to any overall interpretations? I struggle to find any evidence that it does.

Steen: Or that it doesn't.

John: No, that it does. My argument is that it's an empirical question about if what works best in math is the same as what works in English. Is what works best for 5-year-olds the same as what works best with 15-year-olds? They are empirical questions, and, at this stage, I struggle to find any evidence that what works best differs by content domain (mathematics, English) or for age.

I want to be very careful here, as of course children are unique, the subject is unique. The conclusion is not that we treat each child the same irrespective of age, subject they are studying, etc. The conclusion is that the various strategies that combine to have the highest impact seem to work best for children regardless of their age, the content, etc.

The evidence, as I interpret it, puts the onus back on those who argue for models of individual differences, as I struggle to see evidence for this model. Yes, we need to adapt the overall strategies depending on where the student is in the learning cycle, the nature and trajectory of their progress, and the challenge in the success criteria – but the same core principles outlined in *Visible Learning* apply to most students.

Steen: My idea is that, if you will defend more subject-oriented didactics, you will maintain that didactical ideas can be a kind of rival to the abstract claims of objectified evidence.

John: But here's my question back to you. Why is it, then, that subject matter knowledge has an almost zero effect on student attainment? The degree to which teachers know their subject has almost a zero effect on student learning.

Steen: I don't think that it covers the rich world of teacher–subject–pupil interactions to state that the teacher has a substantial knowledge of the subjects themselves.

John: But, the subjects themselves get translated via the teacher. So, why?

Steen: The subjects do not only – or primarily – get translated by the teacher. The student can, for example, read and interpret literature, or even write poems her- or himself. Teaching and education imply and contain much more than a one-way and top-down communication traffic from the teacher to the pupil or student (Larsen 2015b). Teaching and interaction with freethinking and learning youngsters might open doors to magic art works and to the enigmatic structure of figures and equations in mathematics.

John: I see that, yes.

Steen: You seem to over-prioritize whether the teacher is prepared and making a clear statement of his learning ideals and goals. But I still think that this approach doesn't really hit the nail on the head, while the subjects themselves have kind of a second-to-none influence, and it is very important that we dig deeper into the "logic" of subjects and practical deeds of pupils meeting and interpreting the subjects. Too much school life risks to disappear if you're writing off the subjects.

John: Yes, it does. But here's the view I take. The way I see the evidence and my interpretation of it is that the evidence so far shows that knowledge of the subject, the pedagogical content knowledge, whatever you want to call it, hardly matters, which is why we've spent the last 10 or 12 years trying to understand why it doesn't matter – because it should matter.

Steen: But is it correctly understood that you in the first place had a kind of a preconception, that it should matter, and then you came to see from the figures that it didn't matter?

John: Correct.

Steen: So, what is your interpretation?

John: We did about seven or eight studies trying to understand why subject knowledge had such low effects and they all failed. We looked at explanations such as teachers mainly needed to create great relations with students, teaching was teaching, and others. We then had to stand back and look at the way teachers normally interact in classrooms and there's a lot of "tell and practice."

And "tell and practice" can be a good method. It's worked for teachers for many decades. Another study that we have been doing is we take transcriptions of classes as teachers are teaching and we know what percentage of time teachers' talk exceeds 80% of the talk time, on average.

Again, teachers' talking can work. Further, students above average prefer teachers to talk more – they have worked out the game – listen, repeat, and everyone seems happy!

Steen: These figures, interpretations, and theoretical clues might also depend on what kind of regime you are living in. For example, in Denmark a lot of experiments and alternative learning logics flourish. The pupils and students are giving presentations (mini-lectures), they work in autonomous project groups. They interview people and gather information from all kind of sources. . . .

John: Yes, we need to be careful. The studies we've done are based in England, Australia, and America.

Steen: In German you call it *Frontalunterricht* (teaching top-down, including teacher surveillance face to face).

John: The other thing is that, when you look at the nature of what students do, 90% plus of what they do is content, surface level learning, which is quite frankly indefensible.

Steen: Even though it shouldn't be like that, you might be right, that half of what's going on in the class is reproducing things that the pupils already know.

John: Yes, and that's indefensible but that's what happens. Now, if that's the case, it makes perfect sense why a teacher only has to be one page ahead of the students. But, if you reduce the amount of teacher talk and increase the student talk, if you reduce the amount of teacher questions and increase the student questions, if you change the proportion of surface to surface and deep learning, then we have evidence that subject matter knowledge matters a lot.

Steen: So, what you're actually describing through the use of your figures and statistics are more or less the failure of an old-fashioned system rather than propagating what it should be?

John: Correct. But more important, we are using a finding (the low effects of subject matter knowledge) and trying to find an explanation. We are not saying it does not matter, we are saying why is it that it seems not to matter, and on this question, I think we have some answers.

It is like the low effect for class size. Many critics are furious that the effect is so small – but yes, it is a positive effect so reducing class size does relate to higher achievement effects – it is just that this effect is very small, particularly when the list of claims as to why it should be high are many, convincing, seductive, and 'obvious'. So, why is the effect so small? My argument is that we need to understand why it has a small effect to improve it.

Steen: It also depends on the way you organize it. If you are working as a professor in a modern university, you spend much time supervising student written projects based on freely chosen subjects.

A really effective way to help the students develop their argument is that you read their papers thoroughly, profoundly, and closely in order to give them good advice and ideas of how to strengthen their knowledge of the subject and realize their ambitions. You sit there with the student and the paper between you two and have full mutual concentration on how **to let this scriptural 'third' blossom** (Larsen 2015c). This procedure is very different from having a kind of a one-way directive with an arrow: "I know what you should learn."

John: One of my mistakes, which I'm happy to have made, was that league table of 1–250 influences ranging from teacher collective efficacy as #1 to boredom as #250. Too often, this ranking has been misinterpreted with some saying these top ranked are good, these lower ranked are bad. Some of the lower ranked can be critical but they've just been poorly implemented, not introduced in powerful ways, and we need to understand that. Subject matter knowledge is a perfect example of a low-ranked influence that we must not dismiss as irrelevant or not important but need to deeply understand why the effect is so low – as then we can remediate the reasons and ensure it does matter.

And so, as you'll see in the next publications I'm working on, there won't be a league table.

Now, I do not regret developing the ranking – at least it got people's attention – but the downside of it is that people stop there and a lot of the criticisms of my work are round the rankings. I would argue that quite a few of my critics have never read what I've written about them, they've just looked at the numbers, and that is it. For example, there is a recent blog noting the ranking, then claiming you cannot do this as there are moderators, there is overlap, the average for each is too crude – and clearly, they have never opened a page of the book – which is entirely focused on developing an underlying story based on the overlap, the moderators, and the variability within and across the influences. But that's the price you pay for including simple overviews – they get taken out of context.

What is the ontology of an effect in education?

Steen: If we could turn to a profound question to get behind not only the misleading league table rating and the logic of causality and effect measurement in education, I wonder whether you think or do not think that there is something called the ontology of an effect? Does an effect, for example, possess a value in, of, and for itself? Or is effect just a label or a name for gathering right and wrong answers when they are set in relation to progress or regress due to other measurement logics? But basically – and first: What is the ontology of an effect (Larsen 2015a, 2017b)?

John: As you know, the concept of effects and effect-sizes has been around a long time in statistics – they are simply standard deviation units, related to z-scores. It's simple. And it was Gene Glass (Glass 1976) who used **effect-size** as a core notion in his development of meta-analysis. And in many ways, it's an unfortunate word as effect can misleadingly imply causality. Now, when you unpack the multiple forms of effect-sizes it can be a correlate (e.g., personality to achievement); it can mean a factor that the teacher has control over (choice of teaching method); it can be an attribute of its student, which we may or may not have control over (sex of student).

Effect-size is kind of an amalgam of all those and, therefore, suffers because it has those multiple meanings. In my work I discuss each influence with respect to how we can control and change it or not, but sometimes this is missed by critics who only start and finish with the average effects.

The question is whether we can indeed combine effect-sizes based on various types of influences – the answer is yes, but the story of the moderators, of the different types, is critical.

Now, that's the statistical notion of an effect-size.

Steen: My worry is that in politics and the educational planning scene or from a local government perspective, they want to have value for money, and tomorrow is too late. Then 'effect' becomes more or less equal to the right amount of correct answers to give the questions and progress in marks given, etc.

John: You're right.

Steen: The political and managerial bureaucratic misunderstanding of and reductive definition of the effect is very important and risks leading the educational system astray.

John: It is because it's an unfortunate word to those who have never moved beyond the 'typical' uses of the words *effect* and *size*.

Steen: They think a higher mark is better than a lower mark, that three rights instead of two wrongs is better. And therefore effects get translated to hard 'facts' opening for and legitimizing easy conclusions.

John: I know. I agree with you and I wish there was a different word but, from a statistical point of view, it's a very clear notion. It is an indication of the size of differences – typically between a measure prior to an intervention compared to after the intervention has been introduced, or between the average from an intervention compared to a control group. From an interpretation point of view, it's got baggage – and like most baggage, what is inside is most fascinating.

Steen: So, when you have effect measurements on one side and you have something like status, power structures, multifactor scenes, and several correlations on the other side, how do you know then that the interpretation of the effect, for example, is the same seen from different horizons of interest?

An example could be that due to the amount of resources we have invested in certain education grants, we want to have an effect estimate of the long-term quality of the theses the students 'produce'.

Another could be: What kind of meaning does it give to my life as a seven-year-old that I have to answer questions about my well-being or future life paths and expectations compared to other students my age in other schools? So, can we have something called effect measurement that is independent of the different contexts and vast amount of possible correlations that also might have an influence on the 'result' . . .?

John: You can't have an effect-size independent of anything.

Steen: Okay. So, you have always to contextualize.

John: Totally. And then you also should be looking for the moderators. Does it have a different interpretation and different size of effect with 5-year-olds, 15-year-olds, boys, and girls? And that's a key step in this whole business. And this is the problem with, as you're saying, amalgamating it into one overall thing called an effect-size. But, yes, you do have to look at those things and that's why, as said when we started this conversation, the numbers are the easy part. It's the interpretation that's the hard part – trying to get that interpretation of what those effect-sizes, and their multiple meanings are, and investigating the various moderators.

Steen: Can we talk about a three-step logic? First, you have some complex relations in schools. Then you 'translate' them to figures. And the third step leads you to the meta-level where you go from figures to fixated interpretation of figures. But the first part is not that easy, is it?

John: Of course it's not.

Steen: Is it because you are destined and doomed to instrumentalize and to take a reductionist approach where you must translate very complex contextual, cultural, educational – and different 'matters' of socialization – into figures? This procedure does indeed not seem to be easy, maybe not even possible at all . . .

I wonder if you could also try to relate these remarks of mine to your vivid admiration for **Popper's principle of falsification**. I understand how one can try to falsify research claiming a true relation between a theory and empirical data, but how do you falsify a story (an interpretation, a powerful horizon of semantics)?

John: No, it's not easy to consider the various conditional influences. Some have argued it is indeed not possible to use this procedure, which is incorrect. You can, and I have done it; the correct question is more whether the interpretations are defensible.

Imagine taking two studies and comparing them. They come out with the same magnitude of effect, seems more like they are close replications, then this makes life easy. Now, imagine they have different magnitudes and are based on quite different samples. More attention to these details is critical. Multiply this by many hundreds if not thousands of articles and the requirement for detailed interpretation becomes even more critical. What I tried to do is build some common themes from over 800 meta-analyses (for the 2009 book) and now from over 1,600 meta-analyses. How credible, replicable, valid are the common themes – that it is the question.

I agree, a simple average, a simple story, a simple disregard for the nuances is indeed likely to be misleading. I use the average to set a 'hinge' – what are the common attributes that help explain those influences discussed compared to those beyond this hinge?

I made various conjectures in the book, and continue to refine these major messages. These include inviting teachers and students to work together as evaluators of their impact; asking for transparent and high expectations for influencing all in a school; moving towards explicit success criteria about the content and the deeper ideas; using the Goldilocks principle of challenge (not too hard, not too boring) to impel learners to move to these success criteria; seeing errors as opportunities to learn, which means building high trust and supportive environments to fail and learn; teaching how to hear and maximize feedback (especially to teachers) about their impact; and having a focus on learning with the right proportions of surface (content), deep (relationships), and transfer of learning. These are big picture conjectures that live well above the data, lead to many novel predictions, and can be evaluated by seeking evidence that they are not correct (as Popper would ask). There could, in the future, be new studies that show either these conjectures are incorrect or can be surpassed with better claims that explain the data and make bold predictions about what should happen when these ideas are implemented.

I spend a lot of time now evaluating the implementation of these ideas, work with great designers and educators to implement with fidelity, and am very entrenched with evaluators to ask and seek evidence about the merit, worth, and significance of these claims.

Steen: What a journey of obstacles. First from complex context to figures, and then from figures to interpretation, and then from interpretation to politics . . .

John: Not about the politics yet. I'll come back to that.

Steen: But then you have to operate at one, two, three, four different levels.

John: You're right, and Alison Jones had the best criticism ever (which I've cited in the *Visible Learning* book), and I love it so much. She's a sociologist, a good colleague, and she said one time after listening to me, "John, I am impressed that you can reduce classes to two decimal points."

This joke is so, so right — it is about the quality of the interpretation and not about seeing every study as detailed, exact, and explaining too much.

The related criticism is that the effects I have investigated only relate to achievement. Indeed it is, but I make no excuse that the 2009 book was about achievement and its multiple meanings. Of course, there are critical things that happen in classes that are above and beyond achievement.

There's a team in Germany who is looking at doing what I did but looking at motivation and affective outcomes. I've spent the last three years completing a whole new synthesis on *how* students learn, the learning strategies, which I'll come back to. We have been working for many years synthesizing the effects of child health, nutrition, and physical education. David Mitchell published a superb book on the effects on special needs students (Mitchell 2007). Others have synthesized the many meta-analyses for higher-education students, for technology, and there are many other meta-syntheses emerging.

As a father of three boys, I was driven by Henry Levin's claim that the best predictor of adult health, wealth, and happiness is not achievement at school, but more the number of years of schooling (personal communication, 2013). Thus, I have spent a lot of research and policy space investigating how to make schools more inviting places for students to come to.

All these are important.

But achievement is a key part of schooling, although some of my critics think that I'm over-obsessed with achievement. I'm not. It's just one important part. I'm certainly not going to say it's unimportant.

It's like my view about PISA (see www.oecd.org/pisa/) and NAPLAN (the Australian national school assessments, conducted annually). Reading, math, and science are critical. But I do not want to get rid of these measures. I want more. I want broader. I want schools and systems to value music, art, history, entrepreneurship, curiosity, creativity, and much more.

Steen: Is there full completion around the figures so you can compare different schools and different teachers and even different countries around the globe?

John: Not teachers. No, no, just at the school level. The school is, in my view, the proper unit of analysis, as it is the school leaders who are most accountable for the performance of all in the school (and similarly each system when comparing systems). The problem I have in Australia is that all the averages and much more detail is all on the web. The assumption is that these 'numbers' can be reliably interpreted by parents when they make choices about where to send their child to school, and to hold the schools accountable to the parents.

The good news is hardly any parent ever uses the website, and if they did, most look at the average scores and not the value-added information. As we noted, the average may say little about their child's experience, and many parents are as concerned about the friends their child is likely to have in a school. But the scores from 40-minute tests are published, and then the publication puts all the pressure on schools to look good on very narrow measures of what we value.

My argument is that, like economists, we should have a basket of goods and be concerned about what is in the basket. But, at the moment, the basket of goods is defined entirely by a narrow set of measures – and that's, I think, unfortunate.

There are ways we can even more understand the nuances of classrooms. Perhaps the most exciting advance from a research design in the last five years has been the development of meta-analysis, of qualitative research. I think it's very exciting (Kennedy 2008).

Steen: Qualitative research also presupposes that you talk to people for a long time, to pupils and students, doesn't it?

John: Yes, that's one interpretation. The other interpretation with qualitative research is that the emphasis is very much on the researcher asking the right questions, listening to the right discussions, and making the most valid interpretations. Often, these interpretations are based on small samples and have more depth than generalizability. Yes, interpretation should also be the core notion in quantitative analysis.

How to rate among impact 'influencers'?

Steen: When you have these 130 or 140 influences . . .

John: I'm up to 250, and yes, I could get to 350, whatever. That's not the message. The message is the overlap between them. And that's what took me 20 years to work out. Of course they overlap, and that overlap is what the story's about. The aim was to build the story about the overlap from those influences above the average of all effects (which was 0.40) that differentiate the story from those influences below the average. The average of 0.40 is simply an average of all effects, but too many have mythicized it into something magical. It's not. It's the average of all the current influences. And we have already spoken about some of the important influences that have very low effects and the plea to understand why they are so low (and not throw out the evidence because it does not fit preconceived wishes about them, like class size, problem-based learning, technology, and others).

Steen: You also write that whatever we do there is a certain impact.

John: Yes, that surprised me about this.

Steen: And even if we don't do anything, there is also an impact.

John: Well . . .

Steen: If the teacher enters a room and says, "Well, I have no plan. What are you up to?"
  That also has an influence, I presume.

John: Not quite. It means that nearly every influence that we invent to introduce into schools seems to have a positive impact. That is, raised the level of achievement, so the effect is greater than zero. Therefore, we always seem to find evidence to support our pet ideas, for policy decisions, and for any innovation. Therefore, we need to change the debate from 'what works' to 'what works best'.

John: One of the current dilemmas is that we have few methods for teachers to identify those students who are performing well below their potential.

We cannot use 'achievement' measures to do this – as this would be an oxymoron. It's just not true that every kid is going to become an Einstein. It's just not true every person's going to become a Picasso. This is why I have a lot of time for the notion of intelligence or other measures of underlying skills and potential. We are too one dimensional in what we privilege in our schools, in how we then invite students to see success in schools, and we are likely leaving too many children behind – particularly those with an underprivileged background, which is then used to further leave them behind.

When I was a kid in the 1950s in the South Island of NZ, no one told me we were not rich. The town was small, we had no car, the country had no TV, and the biggest trip was a bus ride into town. Now students are told in every possible way that they are asset-poor, come from impoverished backgrounds, are unlikely to succeed in the world, and these explicit or implicit claims surely are daunting to many – what a crime.

So often, having expectations relative to one's family resources leads to self-fulfilling prophecies; thank goodness for my naivety.

The effect problem once again – between causes and correlations

Steen: Let's change the subject. You probably have some answers to the critique of your work that I presented in the article "Blind Spots in John Hattie's Evidence Credo" in *Journal of Academic Perspectives* (Larsen 2015a).

John: I have.

Steen: My basic argument is that there are some blind spots in your evidence credo, so . . .

John: . . . let's go through them. When you say, "John Hattie never explains what the substance of an effect is." Have we dealt with that already in our conversation?

Steen: We have discussed that, but what is your main reply to my critique? When it comes to the impact scores and you state that some factor has an effect value being more than 0.40, and the better it is, like one-point-something or 0.9-something, then I was having a hard time understanding how different causal and correlation logics hide themselves behind these figures.

John: As I have noted, impact includes much more than achievement, but most important is for educators to triangulate, discuss, and have evidence related to their own notions of impact. Yes, I choose the 0.40 as it was the average of all 250 influences – and then aimed to understand the story for those influences above and beyond this average.

I agree that the terminology 'effect' implies causation and in most cases it is not a causal claim. But the art of reviewing literature (and meta-analysis is but a systematic form of literature review) is to deduce meaning, to test hypotheses as to what relates to the discrimination of the high and low influences.

Steen: I have tried to come to understand the content and the structure of your argument. But it is not easy.

John: Nah, some people just ignore the text altogether. Too many just start and stop with the table of 150 to 250 influences as if there is no context or story behind this table. I created the league table to help bring a sense of big picture to it, but that lead table has too often become the story. The table worked in a way, but as I noted, I regret it in another way because people stopped and started with the table. Some have claimed that such a table cannot be developed, which is nonsense as it has; some have argued the influences overlap and of course they do; some have claimed that it is a category error to create the table, and I would say then most literature reviewing would suffer this critique. They missed the thinking and explanation behind the table.

Yes, the table includes influences that are correlation, from interventions, from context of the student, and right now I am reproducing the table with many more conditionals. I also intend to include measures of the credibility of the data, the quality of the study (as best this can be done given my limited resources and the huge debate about measuring quality), and much more. None of these additions change the 'story' but I hope will reduce the overreliance by some critics who tend to only see the table as the story.

Steen: That's it, isn't it? Effect implies cause.

John: Yes it is. It does, but that the major statistic in meta-analysis is called *effect-size* is an unfortunate notion because as a statistical notion, it doesn't imply cause. The effect-size is simply the number of standard deviations difference between two means.

Steen: Effect in everyday life, in everyday language has another meaning . . .

John: Exactly. Beside the more typical 'causal' notion, effect also means the result of a particular influence.

Steen: . . . and there is nearly always a one-way logic of an A causing a B attached to it.

John: Correct, and you take things like students who have a genetic disorder, or come from families of differential resources. As a teacher, you cannot intervene and change these.

Steen: Another thing that strikes me – while I was reading your work for the first time, around 2010 – was that you always seemed to state the obvious (Larsen 2011). Maybe that's okay but do we need millions of data and bunches of meta-analyses to state the obvious?

John: Stating what becomes the obvious, recasting the narrative. . . . But that's often the job of academics. But care is needed. Nat Gage wrote a great article on why research is not 'commonsense'. Gage (1991) argued that the belief that a research result is obvious is untrustworthy. This is because people tend to regard as obvious almost any reasonable statement made about human behavior. These beliefs may be functional, but that does not make them correct and trustworthy. Surely the questions raised about the frequency and consistency across replications should question common sense.

Steen: Okay, but stating the obvious, like it's better to be well prepared as a teacher than not be prepared before you meet the class, and it's better to see through the eyes of the students than to talk down to them from above. . . . Who in the world would oppose or question these 'findings'?

John: Yes, they are obvious. But there are many major counterfactuals to the *Visible Learning* model. For example, when you go and listen to what their teachers talk about, go to the professional learning conferences, go to look at teacher education. . . . It's all about looking through the eyes of a teacher. It's all about how to teach, about classifying students, about curricula, and about (usually against) assessment. *Visible Learning* is more about the *impact* of the teaching, the curricula, and the assessments.

Steen: You might possibly even say through the eyes of the administration.

John: . . . or the inspectors.

Steen: . . . or the principal or the 'masters of education' (the planners and administrators). But I had this problem that you said to me that it was kind of stating the obvious, and it was at the same time very close to this effect language. That was my top worry. It seems to me that the difficult question of the ontology of the effect ends up in a no answer, just presenting the reader for a self-conforming circularity between the obvious and the aligned figures.

John: Yes, but what do we do as academics? We reinterpret what was. We come up with different narratives to help, or better explanations, or better transformation and understanding. And so I have this comment I often cite with my colleagues: "The day you go home and say, 'Oh my gosh, I'm a fraud. All I do is reinvent things,' you're a true academic." This is the Aristotle argument that there's nothing new under the sun, or the biblical maxim: "What has been will be again, what has been done will be done again." What I tried to do was to create a different narrative about the evidence as I saw it. Recall, literature review should emphasize the RE-view – it is indeed looking back on what we claim to know, it is telling a story about these past claims, it is aiming to move the field forward by recasting through different lenses – this is the work of reviewing, and meta-analysis brings a systematic process to this review.

So in one sense, it is banal. It is obvious. But as you know, you got to make compelling and reasonable straight-forward. As Einstein claimed, everything must be made as simple as possible, but not simpler. And when I read Freire, I can see his narrative, his reinvention of the literature and world as he casts it – and it is compelling (**Freire** 1970/1968). Creating a narrative about schooling allows a way of looking at the role of teachers, and schools, and students. The effect-sizes and their moderators allow me to make these (what I hope are) bold claims, and they are indeed quite falsifiable. I'm not claiming much more than that, but you're right in terms of effect implying cause. They do not, in general (although if the effect comes from the too rare controlled study over time they may be so interpreted, with the usual care). And I hope now we're better understanding that an effect-size doesn't answer the question of why. It doesn't answer the question of what. It gives an indicator of the magnitude of various influences. The hard work is interpreting the overlaps, the underlying story, the narrative, and saying something more than we knew before.

Steen: Hopefully, the political establishment and the bureaucrats in education will come to read this reservation of yours, because they haven't understood a word of that. In politics and administration, cause–effect logic language and thinking seem to be predominant.

John: And they look at that effect-size table and say tick, tick, tick to the top influences and no, no, no to the bottom, and this was never my message.

Steen: And then the risk is that they all tend to favor the highest influences, while they think and calculate that those 'causes' at the top are most important, and the low ones are not important. But that seems to go strictly against your idea. Do you think that we should think more about the lowest ones?

John: Indeed yes, and I have spent some of my research time trying to understand why some the low influences are indeed down near the bottom. For example, I have researched and I am still researching and publishing articles on class size, subject matter knowledge, retention, problem-based learning, and also asking why one-third of feedback can be negative. When you accept the evidence that these influences are low, then the research question becomes why, and from this can we learn how to increase their impact.

Like, who would ever want teacher subject matter knowledge to not count? When you accept the current evidence that it does not matter, then you recast your research eyes to understand why it does not, and remediate these suppressor reasons – and this is exactly why I and my team are asking – with fascinating results. Fighting, denying, or denigrating the findings merely means that we may continue to see low impact from enhancing subject matter or pedagogical content knowledge.

I take a responsibility for the list of influences, as I have said. It works and had a purpose. So I'm not going to say I regret doing it. I don't. It helped bring a perspective to what high and low looked like; it challenges all critics to provide a better explanation for the ordering; and it showed some advocates that their pet influence may, while enhancing achievement (i.e., greater than zero), have had a much smaller impact than many other influences. It emphasized the idea of 'relative effects'. Same with those barometers, and I think I've already indicated to you, my partner invented those, and I'm very pleased she did because it gave a high-level picture and provided a flow-through to the first book.

Yes, it is resplendent with facts and figures and I don't know this, but I wonder at times, given the book sold half a million copies, how many people have actually read it, as opposed to looked at the highlights.

Steen: We have tried to read it, some of us.

John: Oh, I know, I know. Your critiques show this, unlike some. But that's not my point. My point is the high-level messages are much more important than the barometers or league table.

Steen: Yes, it's easier to find a summary of your thesis in some slides for some people who have translated your ideas. But another thing is – just if we are only talking about this effect and correlation question – if we stated that, well, people like to have $1,000 every day they come to school, for example, every Monday, it'd probably have an effect that they will be attending school, getting $1,000 every Monday morning.

John: Actually, there's a good research on that, that shows it's not the case.

Steen: But it could also be the problem that the higher a figure is, the more problematic something is. Or it could be that the lower it is, the more you should invest energy in raising the figure.

John: I know. I said this in the book, that it was critical to understand why some effects are low, and then aim to increase their power. But many critics they didn't see this either. I would argue that a more telling criticism is not the $1,000, but whether you are looking at a narrow or a wide concept (and I raised this in the conclusion of the book). If you're looking at a narrow concept, you're more likely to get a higher effect. If you're looking at a narrow concept like vocabulary, then a higher effect – if you're looking at a wider concept like creativity, then a smaller effect. The width of the outcome is a critical moderator.

Some have tried to make this claim but falsely look at the influences and say some are aiming at lower- and some at higher-order notions. They then say, it is obvious why Direct Instruction, Vocabulary programs are so high and discovery-based and problem-based are so low – but this is very selective choosing – what about the high effects of reciprocal teaching and comprehension programs and the low effects of technology and mentoring?

Now, here's the hard point – the reason why I don't think this narrow-to-wide outcomes is a major criticism of my work. Unfortunately, too many outcomes in schooling are narrow. They don't have to be and maybe they shouldn't be, but given – watching the verbs here – this is what it *has been*, I think the research is reflective of schooling. It does not *have to be*. I think, as I mentioned in Chapter 11 in *Visible Learning* (Hattie 2009), it is a critique of schooling that we have so narrowed outcomes in what it values.

Steen: Immediately when people were reading your work, they were also blindfolding themselves in reading and interpreting it in the wrong way. For example, the teachers' union of Denmark, their spokespeople eagerly stressed – when they read your work with admiration that it's very important that the teachers know their impact, and that a teacher is the most important factor for good schooling – that without unions and very strong teachers, there is no good education. So they could use your research and argumentation for instrumental reasons in the political realm and for a power play.

John: They're kind of right for the wrong reason. Although it is critical to note that I said teachers were the most important *in school* influence.

Steen: But they used your standpoint for instrumental reasons in order to back themselves up in their union fight.

John: Yes, and other unions critiqued and dismissed it because some of the favorite advocacy pieces were not that high (such as class size).

Steen: But in the very same moment, the politicians and the leaders of the school bureaucracy, as you could say yourself and anticipate, they probably began to think in this way: "Okay. Hattie tells us that the most important factor for learning is actually the teacher." A strong 'we' and 'we/they' dichotomy were born, stating that 'we' can see, that the teachers don't really manage to include pupils, 'they' don't teach Muslim students a proper Danish language, and many students don't perform well in the national tests or **PISA tests** or fail to pass exams. When you see the teacher as the most important factor for more or less everything in school it means that everything that doesn't work must be the teacher's fault. So from the opposite end of the political spectrum from the teachers' union, they love the teachers to death while they get nearly too easy and smart legitimation to master-blame them.

John: Yes, exactly.

Steen: Friedrich Nietzsche wisely wrote approximately 150 years ago that if you donate somebody the right to be the holder of truth and the *prima causa* (first cause) as an important byproduct, you achieve the possibility and right to punish them for being morally bad later on.

John: **Nietzsche also said there was no such thing as 'immaculate perception'.** There is no one right way of seeing the world.

Is there a telos of learning?

Steen: Does your approach possess a **telos**? It seems exigent that your attempts to gather distant learning data and your overall ambition of enhancing learning effectiveness should also be addressing the capacity for pupils to think differently.

John: Yes, that's one part, but I'm also very clear that the goal of my work is to enhance the learning experiences and opportunities of teachers and students. I would like to think I'm quite critical of the current state of education which the synthesis is based on. Too often it has less focus on the expertise and the learning of teachers and students; too often it is more about the methods, the conditions, explanations why students cannot or can learn; and too often it is about stuff – knowing lots. But yes, the data I use is based on data from current classrooms.

Steen: Yeah, I know, because when you are addressing primarily already known research, already known piling up of data, it could be very close that you come to defend the present situation.

John: Oh, exactly. And my critics call it rear vision mirror thinking.

Steen: Nice wording, I dare say. Why are they wrong, then?

John: Oh, I would argue that when you drive a car, when you ride your bike, I would hope you do look in the rear vision mirror to help you move forward.

Steen: And to take into consideration that objects may be smaller or bigger than they appear?

John: Exactly, and so I try, maybe not as successful as some of my critics have seen or misunderstood, to say, "This is what we currently know." And yes, I get accused of defending the status quo. Well, I am looking at the status quo. I don't have to accept it. But, also, I'm realistic enough to know that that status quo is in our classrooms now. And a lot of it is, and a lot of it is not working.

Steen: Okay. In my article "Blind Spots in John Hattie's Evidence Credo" (Larsen 2015a), I claim, as you know, that you have to take into consideration that each of the studies in your giant collection of meta-analyses are based on different kinds of material and present very different patterns and correlations. You are basically piling up all kinds of knowledge, of diverse data – but these important differences, they seem to disappear when you go to the next layer. You compare here, what we would say – in Danish – an apple with a pear, or a thunder and lightning with a big tower. And that is apparently the price for piling up and making 'meta-reflexes', isn't it?

John: That was one of the very early criticisms of meta-analysis, long before I came along. But it is actually possible to compare or combine apples with pears. They are called fruit.

And, similarly, when I amalgamate, I try to be careful about looking for those moderators that make the difference. And which are apples, which thunder, and so on. And, again, I got in first. The basic research is quite kind of weak in my view on looking for moderators. They use things that are easy to measures like gender, socioeconomic status, and age, but there are much more interesting moderators such as attitudes, their prior behaviors, but these things are hardly ever measured. That's a criticism of the research and, therefore, of what I do. I acknowledge that. I think a major conclusion is to be smarter in future research to allow for more meaningful moderators.

Steen: So there is also kind of a feedback logic – or procedure – from your meta-analysis back to the research people telling them to look for the factors you have stressed in your research?

John: Exactly, and as I said in Chapter 11 of *Visible Learning*, too much of the research – and I would estimate probably 80% to 90% of the effects are based on narrow measures of achievement (Hattie 2009). Now, I have nothing wrong with narrow measures, but they're not good enough. I also want broad measures. And one of the big things in meta-analysis is that if you're looking for something narrow like vocabulary knowledge, you're more likely to get a higher effect than if you're looking at something broad like critical thinking about words.

Steen: Yes, of course.

John: And that is hardly ever accounted for in the meta–analysis. And that's a criticism of my work. I acknowledge that. But I also would argue that this is a criticism of too many classrooms.

Does educational data speak for itself?
What is the ontology of an effect in education?
Are there blind spots in John Hattie's *Visible Learning* paradigm?
How is it possible to (ab)use data from meta-studies for instrumental reasons?
Would falsification (for example, asking "what evidence would I accept that I am wrong?") work well in schools and classrooms?

III. IS LEARNING A VISIBLE phenomenon?

IS LEARNING VISIBLE?

NOT USUALLY. WE SHOULD make IT MORE VISIBLE.

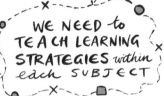

WE NEED to TEACH LEARNING STRATEGIES within each SUBJECT

TEACHERS need TO SHUT UP and LISTEN to HOW STUDENTS are *thinking*

TEACHERS **DON'T** SEE **80%** OF WHAT HAPPENS IN THEIR CLASSROOMS

WE NEED TO KNOW *the* DIFFERENCE *between* SURFACE and DEEP *ideas*

YOU HAVE *the possibility* TO BECOME MUCH WISER WHEN *you* SEE THINGS WITH A TIMELY and REFLECTIVE **DISTANCE.**

The Rediscovery of Teaching

THE AIM *of* VISIBLE LEARNING:

MOVE *from* WHAT WORKS → TO WHAT WORKS BEST

GERT BIESTA *is* AGAINST *the* 'LEARNIFICATION' *of* EDUCATION

TO BE MINDFUL *of* OUR **IMPACT**;

TO SEEK *different* PERSPECTIVES *about* OUR IMPACT;

IF *you* ARE TOLD 'YOU'RE *wrong*', WHAT EVIDENCE WOULD *you* ACCEPT?

Steen: Let's move on to another fundamental question: Is learning visible – or an invisible – phenomenon (Larsen 2019a)?

I would state and claim that in the very moment you learn something, you don't know whether that will have influence or major impact on your life in 10 years or 20 years.

It could be that you think it's very dull, it's very disturbing, it's very irritating. Oh, grammar, what's it good for? Dusty history, endless science classes. Why do I have to care about these subjects? And so on. But in 10 years, 5 years, or maybe in a life perspective, it could be very important what happened that very date or that month or that year (Larsen 2019a).

So, how is it possible to comprehend learning as a visible phenomenon that can be grasped and depicted in the present now?

John: You've changed the conversation. So, let's leave achievement and go to the learning as they're not the same.

Steen: Yes, they're very different. But my idea is that the *Visible Learning* is not instantly there in the moment that it can be measured or exposed.

John: On the learning side, I absolutely agree, and I'll go a step further. I think most of us, as adults, let alone as children, mostly don't have a language for learning. Most of us don't know how we learn. We think we know and, even worse, sometimes we tell people how we learn. But, when you watch people learning, it's not as systematic as that.

You – and because you've been very successful – probably have multiple ways of learning. When one way doesn't work, you have other strategies.

Steen: Yes, I guess so.

John: But, for many students who are not successful in our system, they have a very limited number of strategies. When they don't work, they keep using them. And so one of the arguments – and I spent probably two years ... three years, four years ... trying to come up with a name, *Visible Learning* – is how do you make that learning as visible as you can?

Take, for example, one of the things I would argue. That, by getting the teacher to shut up and the students to talk about what they're doing, you're more likely to hear the strategies they're using. You're more likely to understand how they're doing it. So, the more you can make the learning visible, the more you can have an impact.

Steen: But, basically, if you think that learning has to do with new wiring of synapses in the brain, social interaction, or bodily cunning, then this whole idea of dumping yourself or having an enforced learning agenda could be misleading (Larsen 2013a).

John: Who said it was enforced?

Steen: Enforced strategic idea of people being able to verbalize what they're doing and inscribe it into a personal enhancement and achievement logic.

John: If we want to 'know' our students then we do need to better understand how they are thinking, how they are processing the nature of the task, how they are tackling the problem, what their misconceptions are, where they go wrong, have misconceptions, how they move to success, and much more. This is what we need to be more visible to then know how to teach more effectively. As one example, we have a project going at the moment on creating the 'aha' or 'light bulb' moment, that moment when it just comes together (Berckley 2018). That's not verbal but you can often see it in the student's reaction, eye movements, and sudden changes in how they process the problem. Maybe we need to induce aha moments more often.

Steen: That's correct, but you said before that teachers should shut up.

John: If they shut up and they listen more – for example, as in creating more opportunities for classroom discussion – where they can hear how students ask each other questions, give answers, and then they can hear their impact.

Steen: I see that you promote that the school 'actors' listen much more to each other and not only utter and verbalize sentences and syllables in splendid isolation. But what happened to the bodily aspects of it all?

John: So, let me ask you how you solve that problem.

Steen: My argument is that if *Visible Learning* equals your verbalization effort or your capacity in order to say, "Now I learned," that is just one tiny self-echoing and restricted part of a much larger picture.

John: No, no, I didn't say it was so narrow. I want you as the teacher to better understand myself as the teacher, better understand you, Steen, as the student, how you made that mistake, how you came to that correct answer. I don't just want the correct answer or the mistake. Thinking can relate to the whole person; it is not merely wiring and firing in the brain. Like with the 'light bulb' moment, they can be evidence emotions that certainly can help reinforce the thinking.

How do you get that step which is the processing? I could've called it visible processing, but it was terrible language. And so it shouldn't be that when students are in the process of learning, that they are socialized to silence. Because how can you help them as a teacher if you haven't a clue how they came to their decisions, their thinking?

Steen: Of course, I am also in favor of 'outspoken' communication and pupil 'wordings' in schools. But it doesn't cover what's been going on – or expressed in a more philosophical vocabulary: the epistemology of *Visible Learning* based on explicit verbalization does – so to speak – not cover the ontology of sensing, embodiment, unconscious learning and thinking 1:1 (Larsen 2011, 2018b). My colleague Oliver Kauffmann, a Danish philosopher, stresses that a major part of human learning is invisible and unconscious (Kauffmann 2017).

John: This explicit verbalization needs to be invited, taught, and subject to correction. And yes, there is so much more relating to sensing and so on, as you outline. My claim is a starting towards these less conscious learning notions, but too often now we too rarely 'listen' to how the students are thinking, how they are grappling with connecting ideas, how they are misunderstanding or not, and privileging student talk about their thinking is a powerful beginning. Yes, there is an optimal time to do this, there are skills from the teacher to enable this thinking aloud, and there are conditions of trust, support, and confidence that need to be developed.

Collaborative problem-solving is one good strategy to assist students in thinking aloud. When used at the right time – it is less powerful when students are learning the knowledge or the facts, but when they have sufficient knowledge then hearing how other students relate various ideas, what questions the students are asking, how they go about sifting through the details, watching and participating in the trial and error or making relations – all can be very powerful.

Steen: That's what I try to teach my students when they're doing mathematics, not just to write down the result but to go patiently through the different kinds of arithmetic, including equations, fractions, percentages, etc. Maybe you can get there in four different ways. If you become talented in mathematics, you have the chance to use all kinds of principles to solve a problem.

John: Yes, you're right. As we become more knowledgeable, the distinction between knowing that and knowing how merge more into one process. Take, for example, the work we're doing at the moment; that is, this notion of errors and mistakes. About half the time a student puts their hand up and gives a wrong answer, the teacher corrects it. About half the time the teacher asks another student for the correct answer. About 5% to 10% of the time the teacher uses the wrong answer as a springboard for discussion and deeper understanding of why the error could have been made. Why is it that hardly ever in a class, when a student makes a mistake, it's seen as an opportunity?

Steen: Because, at the same time, the school plays a role for selection and for, you know, power in estimating and donating the marks.

If you receive a very high mark it is likely that you get a good job and a good salary. If you get a bad mark . . . the whole system will not be very friendly.

John: Yes, there are remarkable lessons in ignoring errors for what is valued, what is socialized in classes. When I moved to Auckland in 1999, I used to meet Marie Clay quite often for lunches (Clay 1991). I recall showing her some data I had of the correlation between Concepts About Print (administered to 5- to 6-year-olds) and the same children 5 years later. The correlation between the students' performance at age 5 and age 10 is far too high. Schools have failed if all we're doing is keeping the bright bright and the struggling still struggling. Our role, surely, is to mess up this correlation.

But, when students make errors, for instance, teachers think it's embarrassing, and that we shouldn't upset their self-esteem. Further, as I noted earlier, students above average prefer the teachers to talk. They've worked out the game. They know how to cope. They know there is less chance that they will be exposed about what they do not know. It is a vicious circle that cuts out those who want to know and understand, those who become socialized to silence (but often learn how to look engaged), and reinforces teachers talking more as they know that when they hear a right answer 'all' students understand so they can move on to more talk.

Steen: It's because school is a cultural system, so they know the culture.

John: And they want to be part of it, and probably you and I were very successful at school because we knew how to play the game. I wasn't very verbal at high school, but I was able to assimilate. I was a bit of a sponge of knowledge.

So, how do you get that notion of errors to be seen as opportunities? You go into a Japanese school and watch what they do, and Steen makes an error and then I'll say to the class as the teacher, "Steen made this error. How do you think he did it?" That's making learning visible.

Steen: But in Japan it would be hard because they would lose their face.

John: No they don't, as social issues in class are less critical, certainly, than in Western schools.

Steen: In Japan?

John: In Japan, it's very, very common to do this.

Steen: Okay. I didn't know.

John: No, because it's quite okay. It the norm, the expected, and students expect and want their errors (especially other students' errors) noted and corrected as many of them see this as the best way to learn.

Steen: Maybe that's my prejudice.

John: One of the other ironies, which I think is quite funny, is that when you talk to some Japanese teachers about class size, they say, "How could you have a class size less than 50? You don't have enough students to make sufficient mistakes."

Their culture is that they learn from error. In our culture, error is embarrassing. Now, all learning is error in the sense that you do not go to class to learn that which you already know; learning involves the rectifying of misconceptions, errors, and adjusting our theories of the world.

Steen: A Chinese student came to our program International Cultural Studies at Roskilde University Centre about 15 years ago. She apparently learned from copying. "I found it on the internet," the student said. "Well, you're not supposed to take 1:1 what you find on the internet. You're supposed to present your own argument and to provide the reader with the right references to the quotes you are using in your assessment paper." We've had several incidents of that type.

But let us go back to this question about the visibility of learning. What I do not understand is that you also state that there is very high invisibility of learning, in the practical ground of teaching up to 80% (Hattie & Zierer 2018). How can it be then that people (and not the least politicians and school planners and managers) think that your work and volumes of books have to do with more or less this hurting and stressing of the visibility of learning?

In Denmark (in Gentofte, north of Copenhagen) I have seen giant banners in front of a school where they say: "Our learning is visible" (in Danish: *Vores læring er synlig*; Larsen 2019a). They seem to more or less take for granted that it's easy to get hands on the visible things, even though most of them are invisible and not graspable.

John: You've got to be careful about simplistic labels. Take, for example, Graham Nuthall's work, *The Hidden Lives of Students* (Nuthall 2007). He spent much of his career putting microphones on students and listening to their talk – often over many weeks. One of his major findings was that the teacher did not see or hear about 80% of what was occurring in their classrooms. My argument is that we need to help the teacher see that other 80%.

Now, I'm not pretending it's easy, but we need to help teachers understand how student A is thinking and processing information and how student B is doing it, what they do when they get success or particularly what they do when they get failure. What are the consequences? It shouldn't be invisible if we are going to maximize the impact of our teaching.

Steen: Okay. If I do a little philosophizing about this question, what are the major obstacles to visibility? Is it the lack of a good language, lack of a good perception, lack of a possibility to look into brains or into psychic systems of the pupils? You probably know that Niklas Luhmann argues convincingly that a social system (of communication) is not able to look into the psychic systems, because it is a system obeying a completely other logic (Luhmann 2002). So, what are your major arguments for obstacles towards visibility?

John: Thanks for exposing me to Luhmann's writings; they are indeed powerful. But in the business of education, we need not accept that you cannot make thinking visible, difficult as it may be. You are so right for those in the brain business, and this why I have spent the past few years working with neuroscientists in our Science of Learning Centre here. I went back to graduate school and took courses to better understand their language, their methods, and their findings. I certainly discovered that we know a lot about the brain, the firing, and the wiring. I'm not sure it tells us much or helps us improve what we do in the classroom – as least not yet.

Steen: No, we live in an era of high expectations to neuroscience, but much of this neuro-hype fosters neuro-myths. The brain is not something of which we can acquire control and decide what it should learn (Fuchs 2006, 2009; Larsen 2013a). What should that look like?

John: I think it's going to go the other way. Not from the brain science to the classroom. But we are going to help the brain people understand learning. We know so much about classrooms, but we cannot always explain what is happening, or why. Here is where the brain research may help us to better understand.

Certainly, when you go to observe classrooms, I want to move the debate away from how the teacher is teaching to the impact of that teaching because, at the moment, we're obsessed with teaching methods. Observing the teaching seems hard enough – particularly given the notorious unreliability of so many observation schedules that focus on what the teacher is doing. I am much more interested in the impact of this teaching, which I why we need to watch and listen to the students and their reactions to the teacher and the teaching.

And so, in teacher education programs, I want particularly brand-new teachers to watch the students and understand their barriers or enablers of what's happening. Can we help new teachers focus more on the impact of their teaching on the students' thinking and learning strategies – and make that all the more visible? Not easy, but that is what the teacher education program here at Melbourne is aiming to do.

I am certainly not saying that everything is visible, that's not true. Now, I think the pendulum's almost the other way. Too much is invisible.

And so how do you privilege students' thinking, not because you want the students' thinking to be right or wrong, but you do want to better understand how they go about processing, about what they do when they make errors, how they go about their judgments. In the same way, I want to understand how teachers think and make decisions and judgments about what to best do next. The agenda is similar for how students learn as it is for how teachers learn (and principals, and systems leaders).

It's about how teachers make decisions in the moment by moment. Now, that's really hard to get hold of.

Is it possible to anticipate the quality of learning in a lifetime perspective of the individual?

Steen: Now, here is an additional question. In the quality of learning, and if the quality of this has to do with long-term life experiences with some principle undetermined and not anticipatory processes, how can your team then know anything about the quality of learning for an individual in a deep and broad life perspective?

Listening to you I get the feeling that you primarily seem to stick to the present and let teachers interpret *Visible Learning* data in short-term perspective. My critical question is based on the argument that we first come to know what was important to know and to learn in schools, for example, but also the non–institutionalized informal learning, and what you learn from your parents, in a long-term life perspective.

And it seems to me that your data and what you are relying on in your learning program has more this kind of idea that it's instantly there and that we are able to describe it and fixate it, but my idea is that *Visible*

Learning that the researchers can grasp in an instant movement, and measure and discuss ex post, is just the tip of the iceberg. Most learning is not visible.

In 20, 30. . . 50 years you might have become wiser, but learning is not visible in the very moment when something is said to be learned (Larsen 2019a, 2019b). So how do you relate to this time span and the necessary differentiations between visible and in *Visible Learning*?

John: Yes, so much of who I am not I can see traces back from school. So, sometimes there can be latency, a cumulative effect of many school experiences, and probably certain habits of thinking and doing came from school experiences. But so much we do not learn at school. Yes, *Visible Learning* relates to what happens at school. Many are based on shortish interventions, and of course, all are based on achievement effects. So only part of the whole is included.

I have a lot of interest in seeing change over a shortish time; we use about 10 to 12 weeks to evaluate change – shorter than this you tend to over-assess, and learning is not always linear so there needs to be time for the evidence of learning to emerge. It is likely a 1- to 3-year cycle before you can be more sure of enhanced learning gains, but certainly there needs to be proxies, or some forms of evidence in the shorter term. Waiting 3 years and then finding there is none is a major loss for the student.

Also, some things we overlearn and forget we know it. And if you then tested students on some things that have become so ingrown or overlearned into how they think, they may not be able to articulate the processes of knowing, but that doesn't mean to say they can't go on and use them.

There is also the reverse to your longer-term view: How could you possibly know that what you learned at age 10 in social studies, or history, or English is going to have any predictive path when you're 20 or 30? Certainly the content of what you learned at age 10 in history can also be learned in moments when you are 20 or 30; so there is a lot of defense for focusing on the development of the 'thinking like a historian', but of course this depends on content. This is why I am not so interested only in the 'what' of some subjects (like history – let the teacher choose their passion content) as the development of the 'knowing how'.

The current grammar of content is favored by those teachers and students who are good at memorizing and overlearning facts, but it also increases the gap between the haves and have nots. Not having sufficient subject matter knowledge can be a killer, and maybe too often teachers move to the relations between ideas, the application of ideas, before all students have this knowledge.

This overzealous focus on content is most evident at the upper high school levels primarily because so many of the exam systems privilege content. But this content is usually a reduced canon of subjects – like history, physics, math – and rarely in carpentry, or barista-ship. Why can you not develop excellence in all these content domains? In the early 2000s, New Zealand abolished the traditional high school exit exams – much to the horror of many universities and many high school teachers of the canon. The claim was: let the universities determine their own admission policies but do not straitlace the high school system. The claim was: let us certify what students can do over their last three years of high school.

Yes, there were woeful implementation problems, but in time it settled down. One of the principles later introduced was that any subject where they could devise assessments that could reliably distinguish between students at the excellence, merit, achieved, and not achieved level could be in the approved list of courses. The language teachers and carpentry teachers said, "We can't distinguish so we only want pass or fail." And we said, "Fine. You're out." Within three years, all their subjects worked out how to devise assessments and the country went from 80% of students who finished high school to 93%.

Why can't we prime high school students towards excellence no matter the content? Now I'm nervous here, Steen, because my colleague Pat Alexander argues that it's not the purpose of schools to make students excellent (Alexander 2000). And I have a lot of respect for her arguments. Excellence for me, in the model I just portrayed to you, it's to say we can't demarcate between just doing something at a merit level and doing it above this meritorious level. This is a much more realizable vision than by claiming that high schools prepare students for jobs. Of course, I see no problem if high school helps get jobs, but surely we want more than that.

I look at my undergraduate and probably yours in humanities. It probably didn't help us get a job when we were 20 as much as if we'd have gone into law or business. Today is a different story. You go into law, it's so oversaturated with lawyers, it is hard to get a job. Also, I started in painting and paper hanging, and I would be horrified to think the purpose of schooling is to prepare me for that job as it would have even further restricted my options. I'm not a great fan of the idea that school is about preparing for jobs, but I'm a great fan about how you get people to think in such a way that they know what to do when they don't know what to do. They can go and learn new subjects. They've got the interaction skills with other people. All that stuff we were talking about before. Now I've drifted a long way from your question.

Steen: Listening to your long remark made me think of two philosophical notions. The first one comes from Immanuel Kant, the **reflective**

judgment (Kant 2008/1790). You need this type of thinking when you are in the midst of a former unknown situation and have to navigate and decide in a field with no strict laws or rules to follow. In such a situation, you cannot just rely on classified logic, using the subsuming judgment capacity to order and differentiate between well-known objects. The other notion comes to life in Hegel's view that the **Owl of Minerva**, the symbol of wisdom, waits the whole day to fly out in the sunset (Hegel 1979/1807). Meaning that you have the possibility to become much wiser when you see things in a timely and reflective distance. In a future position, one is looking backwards with a clearer sight to see what happened in a moment in which you once were standing without knowing what happened to you back then. My idea and ambition are now to try to combine the **reflective judgment** of Kantian origin with Hegel's version of Minerva's owl. Kant gave birth to the three critiques of which his third critique deals with the status and specificity of judgment (*Urteilskraft* in German) – and **Hegel is the dynamic, dialectical, and relational philosopher par excellence**.

John: What's your answer?

Steen: Well, the answer is probably not to pile up data and meta-analysis, and neither is it to have an open era of welcoming learning to imperialize all fields of education. But it's probably a combination of different *Übungen*, the German word for exercises; that is, repetitive training and practicing. So my whole idea is maybe with this Peter Sloterdijk, a very inspiring German philosopher, who in 2009 wrote a book called *You Must Change Your Life* in English (Sloterdijk 2013/2009). It deals with so-called anthropo-technical ways of building up man and woman through thousands of years of exercises at all levels, from war, hunt, farming, sport, philosophy, art, love, and education, etc.

His idea is that our primary job as human beings is to practice and be better in practicing, to enter into a world of positive feedback slopes, becoming a little bit better in what we are doing each time we practice.

So my point of view is this: if we have good schools and great teachers, those are the ones who would favor and promote practice without fear. The right to be patient and different without fear must be secured for all exercising practitioners.

If we combine all this with one another, what we should have in the school system could be possible ways of building together those at least four 'things' at the same time: reflective judgment, the Owl of Minerva, the 'exercise-anthropology', and the fostering of a courageous individual.

John: Did you need content knowledge to do all that?

Steen: I guess so. It helps.

John: So why did you, in that last soliloquy, put the words meta-analysis in there?

Steen: I think that meta-analysis is very important but also at the same time hands-on studies. And you have to have a kind of a circuit that creates a dialectic between meta-reflection and concrete hands-on knowledge of the subject.

John: And this dialectic is indeed often not as present in meta-analysis as you or I would desire.

Steen: No, you are right. I have this idea that you have to be very good at painting in a naturalistic way in order to break the scheme and paint in a surrealistic or cubistic way or in a fragmented way. So my idea is to combine skills with the freedom to deviate and improvise.

John: We agree on this matter – and therefore should demand more of schools, or at least a focus on this practice you speak of, learning the skill to see ideas in different ways, and have this higher-order reflection on what we are studying.

Falsification as a way to go

Steen: What have you, inspired by Karl Popper (Popper 2002/1953), falsified – I mean managed to falsify – since 2009 in your own approach? Which of your research results are not valid and durable?

John: I have underestimated the importance of teachers as learners working together, the skills and focus of principals to build the trust and provide the time and resources for this working together to occur, and the need of the system to fund this working together not only among teachers but also among school leaders.

Steen: Okay, you seem to have realized that the team spirit plays a decisive role.

John: I have also struggled with why some of the things at the bottom of the chart are down there. They just didn't make sense to me. Like subject-matter knowledge. Why is the effect of class size so small? Why homework has very small effect in primary school. Why problem-based learning, inquiry-based learning, and such are so low.

Steen: Have you got a better thesis than you had before?

John: Yes, the thesis is ever evolving. For example, when you add the surface-deep dimensions, some of these low effects begin to make sense. Take, for example, problem-based learning. When it is introduced, before students have sufficient content or subject matter knowledge, then the effects are very low – and too often, this is what happens. Teachers arrive proclaiming that problem-based learning is the answer and apply it irrespective of the nature of the task or the readiness of the students to be involved in problem-based learning. The effect is close to zero for learning surface or content information but increases substantially when the students are ready, and the tasks ask for relationships between ideas.

The biggest change for me over the last 10 years relates to feedback and I've written on this too. My mistake was that I focused on teachers giving feedback, not students or teachers receiving feedback, and that was a mammoth aha moment for me a few years ago. And this helps unravel the seeming paradox of feedback where the effect-size is very high but a third of it is negative. And understanding why this is so has taken me a long time. The same feedback can be received (or not) differently by students, hence the key to solving the puzzle of feedback.

We know the power of dialogue but why do we not see many classroom discussions? I'm very taken with the research by another Kiwi, Graham Nuthall. He went into classrooms every day of the year and put microphones on all the students, and every afternoon he went home and listened to their conversations. This was in the 1970–1980s when technology wasn't as good, and in his book *The Hidden Lives of Students*, he noted – as I have already stated – that "80% of what happens in the classroom the teacher doesn't see or hear" (Nuthall 2007). He's the one that showed that students have incredibly strong private vocabularies and dialogues between students about their learning which we need to understand if we're going to have any effect on them. We are now replicating his work using modern technologies, and 20 to 30 years later finding the same – students have much dialogue, most not about the work, but much more on how one might be alert, act correct, and be helpful. Too often, they do not think the teacher's feedback is aimed at them, know how to look on task when the teacher comes to their group or in their gaze, but so much of their dialogue is about just completing the task – often at any level of completeness or quality.

All the current debate about student voice often misses this dialogue between the students, too often focuses too much on students talking to the class, and needs to focus more on teaching students how to engage in learning dialogue. It is not merely students talking for the sake of talking, but knowing when to talk, how to talk about their learning, and how to receive, evaluate, and act on feedback.

Steen: Is it in your view a mandatory part of empirical research that you must have the courage to try to falsify your preconceptions, prejudices, and research results?

John: Yes, as we started, I am a great fan of falsification and if only more worked on this premise.

Steen: You claim that many researchers are just piling up data as evidence for what is supposed to be hard science.

John: Or self-confirmation?

Steen: . . . accumulation, leading to self-confirmation.

John: The usual claim is: "It worked for me last year, but it didn't work this year, so it must be the students." That's a very bad way of thinking.

Steen: You are right. That's a very unsatisfying and wide-spread 'custom'. Many scientists – also from education sciences – do their best to either ignore Popper's falsification claim or they have never heard about or read it.

Hitting the zeitgeist

Steen: *Visible Learning* was your tenth book, and maybe not due to your knowledge, maybe you couldn't have anticipated it, but it indeed really did hit the zeitgeist of the moment (Hattie 2009).

John: As I said to you, I don't regret writing the book. As an academic, I can spend my whole life, and no one would care. The fact that people care is wonderful. But wow, what a responsibility to now get the message as I understand it as right as I can.

Steen: There's very, very big difference between probabilities . . . and strict laws or even causes.

John: Exactly. Yes the book deals mostly in leading to probability claims, and all the effort then needs to be focused on the fidelity of implementation and thence the impact of implementation at the local level.

Steen: I also studied mathematics when I was younger. I used to love mathematics, like my dad, who was a mathematician and engineer. And as we both know there is a very big difference between probabilities and causality . . .

John: Totally.

Steen: . . . and a deduction logic and all that.

John: Yes.

Steen: And that means that, all the reasonable reservations and clear-sighted limitations for the actual use of your studies and work – they seemed to vanish. They were disappearing.

John: Sure, and one of the things I'm doing now in what I'm writing is saying for each meta-analysis and each influence more is needed to delve deeper.

Steen: Great. I welcome that.

John: I am adding a new metric to the database – a credibility index. For example, if a meta-analysis is based on 20 studies, you don't have much confidence. If five meta-analyses are based on 2,000 studies, you had more confidence. For each influence, I am looking at the number of meta-analyses, the number of studies, the number of students, and the number of effects to form this indicator of credibility (see www.visible learningmetax.com/).

Steen: That's one of my critiques, because it can be very hard, maybe even impossible, to see what each meta-analysis covers in your first *Visible Learning* book.

John: Well, it is. That's a very good argument, and so I'm working on that and have since published much on many specific influences, thus delving deeper into the particular meta-analyses.

Steen: So when I called your approach megalomaniac, I was not referring to your person, but to the research attitude in the book.

John: I know, but megalomaniac means an obsessive desire for power, and that I do not have.

Steen: Meaning that if you forget to talk openly about the validity and limitations of your scientific results, they risk becoming megalomaniac.

John: Aha, then we agree.

To help the teacher to see the invisible

John: But here's the problem. I can't stop classroom observation coming, but I can change the methodology of classroom observation. So, I said to our team here, "We need to invent something that has classroom observation, in the sense of what Danielson (Danielson 2011) and Marzano (Marzano 2018) did, to help the teacher see that other 80% (and note, Danielson and Marzano never introduce their matrices for them to be abused this way). We need to introduce not for the accountability. We need to do it in a way that doesn't have another person in the room because they can't see it through the eyes of the students. And their presence changes the nature of what happens in the class. We can't have a video because the trouble with video is, for every hour of video it's two hours of analysis. It's not the best use of teachers' time to sit and analyze what they did – too expensive for the return."

Steen: I know, and another thing is that you might be able to teach or study students, but it is very many years ago you were seven years old yourself, so how can you at all think as a pupil being seven years old? It is not possible to enter the students' minds and to be like them. You're not like them.

John: That's right, so we asked the question: "Can we invent a technology that can help the teacher see the 'other' 80%?" And it had to be scalable because there's no point doing it with 10 or 20 teachers only. We want to change the world, so we have. And it's a free app on the Apple Store, and it's very simple. It is called *Visible Classroom*. The teacher takes out their phone, they either dial a local number or they just turn on the recording app within *Visible Classroom*. There are two options – one to just receive a transcribed script with minimal coding (the free version), or the for-purchase version where a real-time captioner (a person who listens to the transcript and turns it into a written text) transcribes the voice and simultaneously codes the transcript. Oh, there is a third version where this transcript is deeply coded – and we are aiming to use AI as much as possible to do this to reduce costs.

   And if you do it live then within three seconds we can reproduce, on a whiteboard or on the students' iPads, everything you say, with the highest levels of reliability. And for many students, particularly those below average, they're not as fast at picking up what you mean. We know from this research – and we've only done around about 7,000 to 8,000 teachers at the moment – that teachers, on average, give eight to ten instructions for every part of a lesson.

"Steen, I want you to get your reading book out. I want you to turn to page 52. Today, you have to use the blue pen. When you finish the first page, I want you to turn it over, and I want you to color in the picture on the back. And then at the end of this, go and get the book from the library." Now, for the struggling students, they might recall getting the book from the library. The bright students know that the only thing that mattered in that was turn to page 52. The beauty of this technology is the students can go back and review the instructions and get rid of the extras and focus on the important. The beauty of this technology is when the teacher is talking and working with another group, then all students can 'listen in' and read the transcript of what the teacher is saying: "Oh my goodness, that's what I'm supposed to do." I can see it.

The other thing is I can, if you want, ask the students to rate their learning, and we use six items from the Gates–MET study (Kane & Staiger 2012). These items ask about their learning in the lesson. As the teacher walks out of the room, they instantly can get their transcript, they can get it automatically coded for 16 of the variables that really matter, and they can see the students' rating of their learning.

We know that by doing it for five sessions of two hours over two weeks, we can improve 70% of the teachers on the things that matter. They are much more aware of their impact, their levels of language, their talking speed, their proportion of surface to deep, how they teach, and the level and amount of their teaching. Now, my point is that we are informing the teacher more about how they are seen through the eyes of their students, and helping them see how students are reacting to their teaching. And our argument is that if teachers then want to use that as evidence for any kind of performance review, they can. That's their decision, and what then matters are their interpretations of the evidence, not merely the evidence. We need to privilege their interpretations and enhance these interpretations.

Can we ever get 'rid of' the concept of learning?

John: I want to ask you a question. I've just read the continental European educational philosopher Gert Biesta's newest book, *The Rediscovery of Teaching*, and both you and Biesta talk against the present 'learnification' of education, and all that 'learning nonsense', as you call it (Biesta 2017; Larsen 2014a, 2015a). What is your conception of learning?

Steen: I think we should try to get rid of that term, 'learning', in a way.

John: Tell me more.

Steen: My idea is that, at least in Denmark, learning was originally in the 1960s to the 1980s a counter-concept coming from the reform pedagogical and leftist movement, stating that bottom-up and not top-down learning should be promoted and established. Students and pupils should have the right and the possibility to organize their own problem-based group work, and organize their own educational system and study activities from below. But from the 1990s and onwards, the concepts of 'learning' and 'competence' were fused closely together and were becoming governance concepts, stating that we should have learning goals and inscribe them into mandatory descriptions of every subject, every year in the school, every year in a university. It is hard to imagine and to accept that today's universities have learning goals inscribed into their study regulations and courses. By the way, I have also read Biesta's new book, actually during the long plane ride from Denmark to 'down under'.

John: Oh, I can see all that, but then, Biesta's book, he overstates his case against learning and introduces a derogatory term for what he opposes: 'learnification'. But then, what does he propose instead with respect to learning.

Steen: He criticizes the lack of substance in the learning ideology and emphasizes the role of the teacher.

John: Well, so do I.

Steen: Yeah, but where do you disagree with him, then?

John: I'm struggling with his notion of what he's opposing. He is careful to say he is not against learning but more against its over-dominance in the current debate, which means more critical questions about the purposes of education get missed.

Steen: What he wants to do is to defend the Lithuanian-French philosopher Emmanuel Levinas' logic of exteriority against learning regimes and constructivism. Instead of stating, "Now, we tell you guys to construe or to interpret the things you like . . .", **Biesta favors that teaching processes open the door to exteriorities. But basically he is critical against voluntary constructivism.**

John: So am I. I see constructivism as a theory of knowledge. It's not a theory of teaching. I want students to construct language, too. But that doesn't mean that you have a particular form of teaching to do it; but it does mean that more often than not you have to actively 'teach' students how to construct knowledge, introduce them to the valued forms of knowledge you want them to relate and extend to prior understanding, etc.

Steen: **Biesta's idea is that we should deal with things we do not know of – the exteriority, the transcendental questions, ontology, and the impossible** – and embrace dissensus and fight against 'learnification'.

John: Yeah, but you have to know stuff . . .

Steen: Biesta also emphasizes the importance of the capacity to wonder (*Thaumadzein* in Greek).

John: Absolutely, wonder is often the precursor to investing in knowing.

Steen: Yes, here all the three of us do agree. Biesta also states that the students should adopt and live with a concept instead of interpreting the concept. It can be hard to know exactly what that means and implies. But his position concerning the role of the teacher. Pupils and students don't need a teacher to tell them exactly what to do, think, and 'learn'. He favors – like **Sloterdijk – the endless 'second birth'** (Sloterdijk 2013/2009) of a freethinking person and not to forget humble existential being in the world.

John: I agree with that.

Steen: According to the Danish professor in life-long learning, Knud Illeris, who has made a useful definition of the term in *Sociologisk leksikon* (which I have edited together with my colleague, sociologist Inge Kryger Pedersen), learning can broadly be defined as a permanent change in capacities, not only due to oblivion, biological maturation, or ageing. Often – but not always – learning is connected to deliberate interpretation, intention, and handling of the processes leading to learning, as a change in capacities, 'producing' new possibilities to act and think differently (Illeris in Larsen and Pedersen [eds.] 2011: 380–381, see also Illeris 2004, 2018). Learning is not just coming from the outside. Learning is always incarnated in the individual and has a specific expression. But learning probably also contains enigmatic elements that you can never come to understand in your own person or reconstruct 1:1 in theories of learning. At the same time, it is important to stress that learning is a contested concept in modern societies. More or less everyone favors more learning even though not very many people agree to the same definition of the term.

John: Yes, this notion by Illeris is powerful. I see learning as moving from attending to surface to deep to transfer, but this is more a guide for teachers. Illeris' 'definition' goes deeper, more into the meaning of learning. And yes, like most worthwhile claims, it is a contested word. But then I have never been a fan of claims that you have to define a word before you can use it. If this was the case, we could not talk about electricity or magnetism. Our psychological concepts are more rich, more conditional, and nuanced than a simple dictionary definition. Illeris shows this wonderfully.

So can I ask you this? This is a legitimate question. Steen, how do you learn?

Steen: I more or less think that this question is hard to answer because, for me, learning has now been more or less smashed down as a concept and destroyed by its political and bureaucratic success.

John: No. You're not answering my question.

Steen: I could probably learn in very many ways, if I should answer in a positive way, inspired by Illeris' definition. I could, for example, learn through not speaking, listening, reading, playing, investigating, writing, sensing, moving my body . . . and in very many other ways.

John: Yes, you can.

Steen: Listening to a very good speech. Reading a very difficult argument or an enigmatic poem. Bicycle riding, moving the body through the town and landscape, making love, visiting art exhibitions and concerts, experiencing surprising communicative events together with my family, students, good friends . . .

John: This helps highlight a major problem for me – even we as adults do not have a rich or deep language about how we learn; so what chance children? We do not have great access to higher-order cognitive processes. There can be a more active discussion about how we think, strategies, revisit ideas, grapple with the unknown, how new ideas attach to old, and so on. It should not be assumed that students know how to learn, nor that there is one right way to learn, that learning is necessarily fast and easy. This is among the beauties of highlighting the notion of learning. So what's wrong with having a debate about that question, which Biesta seems to be opposing?

What works the best is the most important question

John: Sure, but then I go back to the *Visible Learning* book, and I should've been smarter when I wrote it. There are sections that have been misinterpreted and I could have written these parts better. I said this book is not going to investigate the quality issues in meta-analyses and this has falsely been misinterpreted as I did not care for quality. I said enough times that achievement is but one important outcome in schooling, but this has been misinterpreted as if I am obsessed with achievement and nothing else matters. I spent pages on each influence looking for moderators, trying to understand the variability, but so many just look at the list of influences and imagine that is it. I spent about 30 years (it started in Seattle in 1984) trying to work out the story as to the common denominators for those influences above compared to those below 0.40, but some still question why I just list the influences in a league table. The book was about the research, in that sense, it is a rear-mirror vision, but that is the case with all literature reviews – the literature collections are the data to tell a story for the future. I do believe that it is worthwhile to develop a model, and a model should predict as much as it also aims to explain.

Yes, I have pivoted to emphasizing more 'Know Thy Impact', begging the questions we have talked about relating to educators' meanings of impact. I have worked with teams in thousands of schools around the world and seen the impact – in person, in the words and actions of the students, and in the evidence. We have learned lots, we have written a further 20 books, and we have become smarter in our implementation – and not once have we told a teacher 'how' to teach. In essence, we go back to the reason why most educators entered the profession – to have a positive impact on students.

Most important, I hope to have changed the question from 'what works' to 'what works best'.

It is fascinating and exciting that expertise is a common denominator among the top influences. And given that there are so many educators and schools with this expertise, we should constantly esteem this expertise and ask not how to change the profession but how to scale up the excellence that is all around us.

I get frustrated when I hear educators, parents, and politicians asking for more 'stuff', smaller class sizes, more ability groups, more dense curricula, bring on the tests – and not asking for resources for enhancing the expertise. Yes, it is not cheap to do this, but it is the right stuff.

The core notion is turning students on to a passion of learning, I think that's a really critical thing we should do. And again, it begs the question: learning about what, to what depth of knowing and understanding.

Steen: I have already mentioned one of my favorite living philosophers, the hyper-productive German thinker Peter Sloterdijk, and his view on intergenerational generosity can be paraphrased this way: "We have the capacity to 'spoil' and to inspire one another, to give each other all kind of good ideas" (Sloterdijk 2013/2009).

John: Yes, such caring can be transformative. To paraphrase Einstein, we have come to know schooling as a process of our past thinking. It cannot be changed without changing our thinking.

Steen: It starts when you are a parent, and you have this little kid, and you protect it, give it food, breastfeed it, jump around with it, and play with it in every kind of sense. And we keep inspiring one another because we are unfinished creatures. We are going through a long second birth after we've been born. And we are born with the chance and task to develop our identity as a lifelong process of inter-being and becoming, oscillating between stable and dynamic 'elements', conceptualized by the French philosopher, hermeneutic, and phenomenologist, Paul Ricoeur in his master-piece *Oneself as Another* (Ricoeur 1995a). We have these tremendously plastic brains that can develop and change qualitatively all through life. The utmost enigmatic brains will not be fixated when you are turning 16 years old (Fuchs 2009, 2018; Larsen 2013a). How do you view positions like that when you're talking about plastic biology, you're talking about inspiring possibilities?

John: Yes, we go through dramatic transformations in our brain structure and wiring and firing as we grow. And yes, inspire, I think that's a really great part of it. Now, the difficulty with students is that there's no question they can also inspire each other about the wrong stuff, and that's why we have schooling. Now, with you, as adults, we hope you're at the stage when you have those critical judgment skills where you say, "Not good enough. I don't accept it." But with seven- or eight-year-olds, they don't have those skills, which is why we have to teach them about openness versus indoctrination. We need to build evaluative skills and judgments.

Steen: You also have the famous *Lord of the Flies* novel that tells you that some students might develop all kind of non-moral behavior and even become violent and kill one another (Golding 1954).

John: Sure, but even going back to the research that we're doing now in our team here, listening in to the private language that students have when they're in classrooms and understanding how they interact. They are human beings that are interacting in a private language. It's not the language of schooling. So often, the talk has nothing to do with the lessons. And certainly, we know that if you allow students to talk to each other too early in the learning equation about their work, they could reinforce wrong things very successfully. After they have knowledge, then getting them to discuss can be so powerful to consolidate the learning. So, yes, inspiring, but there is a constraint on inspiring, and that there is good, bad, right, wrong inspiring.

Steen: And the philosophers, they also stress this idea that if you have a little calf, a big cow, in a few months, the little calf is as good in using its capacity to walk and to eat grass as the big cow. And it seems to me that human beings have to have at least 15 to 20 – maybe even 35 years if you come from Italy, wild jokes being that they still live with their parents when they're 35 – before you leave home. So we have a very long period for upbringing mankind, while we do not have enough automatic instincts we can count on.

John: And here in Australia there is a new phase of life from age 17 to 27, which is yet to be named (perhaps tween-teens), but it is quite different from 20 years ago. Many jobs, tertiary education of a multitude of versions, moving in and out of the family home, and there are fewer ladders to get onto, fewer anticipations of longer-term employment, and with more wealth a great social life.

   But returning to your claim, yes, the human has a longer dependency span. We have a long weaning time, and as our brains take quite some time to develop, we have a long post-weaning dependence, with much adult investment.

Steen: Yes, ontologically speaking our being is a being in language and social interaction. We cannot escape this double condition, this double fact.

John: And the cow doesn't have it in the same way that they can learn through a language. And because we have a language, we have more chances of getting it right and getting it wrong.

Steen: That's true.

John: And I think that's a key part of how we develop – the language of learning, how we develop the language of questioning, how we build that on to content so that we know what the right language of questions are.

Steen: It means that, in a way, your answer to this question, "Why does mankind need education?" – which we'll come back to later in our conversation and donate our mutual attention to – is also related to the idea that we should be able to create and generate societies and make social bonding like, for example, the early French sociologist Émile Durkheim wrote about more than 100 years ago (Durkheim 1956/1922) . . .

John: Yeah, we do. Absolutely.

Steen: . . . and social communication.

John: And as you saw in the *10 Mindframes for Visible Learning: Teaching for Success,* I think schooling needs to be among the most civilizing organization in society (Hattie & Zierer 2018). It is, for good or bad.

The statistician as sociologist

Steen: So how do you then come to and up with this interpretation? I agree with you, but you were trained as a statistician, and now you are becoming a sociologist. That's really interesting.

John: I thought you were going to say I'm becoming a philosopher.

Steen: You are closer to sociology than you are to philosophy, or to . . .

John: Am I?

Steen: . . . art, literature, poetry, and so on in your replies here, not to say that it's wrong.

John: No one has ever accused me of being a sociologist.

Steen: No, it is not an accusation. It's more like an observation.

John: One of your colleagues, Hanne Knudsen, interviewed me and somehow decided to title her article that I was a statistician not a philosopher – as if you have to be one or the other (Knudsen 2017). Surely a little philosophy rains on every parade. Like I just said to you the other day, with my own students. My philosophy as a parent is that I want to teach them to give back.

Steen: Okay, I have another theme and question for you because at home, in Denmark, I often deal with architects and people studying architecture in the art schools. In the old days, I would say it was maybe easier to make a kind of a drawing or a model of a construction, or come up to some meeting, and let the drawings talk for themselves or the model talk for itself. But right now, the architecture school students, they go through rhetoric training. They go through talkative procedures in order to present something, to learn to be outspoken. It means that the whole literature or rhetoric and social communication becomes a major part also of being a successful architect. Meaning that you should be able to talk about the purpose of the building, the idea and the narrative of the building. How it fits into the structure of the historical town, or whatever. Could you see a certain parallel here? That from your field, primarily to come up with figures from educational statistics and say, "These data talk for themselves."

John: No, no. Data never speak for themselves, as we have already discussed.

Steen: Okay, now I know it is not your position, but I guess you must also have felt a rising urge or pressure towards coming up and out to perform – like the architecture students – and to be able to build up a stronger and more coherent narrative about the overall purpose of the data on learning impact?

John: I would like to argue that has been the dominant theme for 40 years, particularly as a statistician. I was taught that it was not the data; it was the interpretation of the data. The core question is: Can you defend the interpretation? And it's the Nietzsche argument. There is no such thing as immaculate perception. There is no one right way but there are multiple interpretations. For example, 30 people can look at a mountain. They can see different things. But the mountain doesn't change. And my whole logic as a researcher is: How do you draw common themes? How do you draw a narrative? How do you perceive data? How could you be wrong? I would argue that this approach is throughout my work. I'd like to think even in *Visible Learning* I've made some strong statements that could be shown to be wrong. Even in the book I wrote in the 1990s on *Self-concept* (Hattie 1992a), the whole first chapter was about kind of a philosophy of thinking about how you could be wrong, the purposes and value of developing models, and the need to make bold claims. Bold is not necessarily agreeing with what is claimed to be known by now. Bold is making testable claims that future observations might reveal to be false. I take the risk of being wrong. In the true Popperian manner.

Steen: But it will maybe also soon be stated as a general mandatory capacity (and inscribed into business and policy papers) that every human being should be able to describe him- or herself in developmental terms (i.e., 'developmentalism' as a new ideology, a new 'ism). Implying that one thing is to be a good carpenter or a good architect, but also claiming that it becomes more and more important to double yourself in a narrative practice beside what you are good at. The new ideal is to become a performative and strategic subject wanting to control *The Presentation of Self in Everyday Life*, due to the anticipatory title of a famous book of the Canadian sociologist Erving Goffman (Goffman 1959).

John: Totally. But I want to hear their perceptions of the classroom, or whatever, because it's their perceptions that matter to them. What is their story about what it means to be learning in their class, for example?

Steen: But it could also mean that people are more or less becoming what I call strategic animals, trying to instantiate, and fertilize, and even fuel their ever-ongoing talkative self-doubling.

John: Yeah, but that is why we should be looking for contrary information about our story; that is why we should reflect through the eyes of others.

The question of placebo in the *Visible Learning* program

Steen: Let's move to another question because back home at the university I have a colleague, Kirsten Hyldgaard is her name, and she is a Lacanian psychoanalyst and a historian of ideas. Recently, she wrote a very dense and eye-opening critique of our *Visible Learning* program (Hyldgaard 2017).

John: Okay. I'd love to see it, in English.

Steen: I will give it to you, or rather, I'll ask her to send it to you in an English version. Now I'd like to pose a question that she'd probably love to hear your reply to.

John: Sure.

Steen: And it goes like this: In medicine, the researchers try hard to overcome placebo problems and challenges when they search for evidence, and as you know, they high-prioritize RCT-studies in evidence-based medicine. Is there something called a placebo problem in evidence-seeking educational research, based on *Visible Learning* principles? And if the answer is affirmative, do you see and try to anticipate or even solve placebo problems in the *Visible Learning* program? Is there a placebo problem here?

John: Oh, without a question, she's right, and I've tried to tackle this in a number of ways. Let me start to answer her by looking at a particular kind of placebo, and that's the Hawthorne effect.

Steen: Yeah, I know that, from sociology.

John: And I've been fascinated with that study for many years. In fact, I've gone back and read the original transcripts of the work. Because the argument, as you know, is that people who are involved in a study or in an experiment are more likely to change because they know they're involved in a study and experiment. But if you actually go back and look at the Hawthorne study, it was done in the company General Electric. It was done with these women, who were doing a very tedious task of putting the filaments in light bulbs. My reading of that study is a little different in terms of what a Hawthorne effect is. At the end of each day, they were told how well they were doing. And they knew that they were being compared to another group. So my argument is that the Hawthorne effect is more related to this feedback they received about their progress. And in many ways, and this is too strong, but my answer to your colleague would be: "If that's all we need to do in education to enhance people's ability to improve in light of feedback, I'll take a placebo, thank you."

We do need to do better than in medicine, where a placebo deliberately is a non-effect. It's similar to the question I asked in the early days about the meaning of the 'zero' effect-size – students develop and grow anyway. What's the best estimate I can have for annual growth for students who never go to school? And I did derive an estimate of this growth, not very well. I admit it, because it was hard to get these data. I looked for evidence from countries where students didn't go to school. Nepal, Guatemala, these places. And I tried to look at the development quotient. My best estimate – and it's a very, very crude estimate – was that an effect-size of 0.15 is what you get by developmental placebo, not effects. So you've got to beat that. So in schools the 'placebo' reference point is not zero or the non-effect, but about 0.15.

If you do not do much in school, students are still going to learn. You go to some of those countries, and you look at their 15-year-old students who've never been to school. Their street smarts are incredible. They've obviously learned how to live in their learning society. And so, yes, there is a placebo effect; and any intervention needs to be better than this effect.

Steen: Okay. Seen from the eyes of, for example, the school leaders, you go out there to the countryside, and you meet maybe 50 or 100 school leaders or administrative people. And they have now more or less 'bought' your *Visible Learning* program. Could there then be a placebo effect from the eyes of how they handle it? That they want to be a part of it, they want to show the 'right' figures, they want to succeed, and, last but not least, they want to show that they succeed?

John: Yes, they can indeed, Steen.

Steen: So there can be a placebo from the eye of the administrator?

John: Yes, there can be, and it does happen.

Steen: But this 'noisy' over-confirmative behavior is not scientific . . .?

John: And it drives me mad because I get people saying, "Oh, we've done *Visible Learning.*" When people come to me, as they do, and say, "I want to introduce your *Visible Learning* program," my comment is: "And what is the problem to which *Visible Learning* is the answer?" And too many of them don't have an answer. Merely having a book study, picking the bits you like or are already doing, and then saying you're doing or done *Visible Learning* is absurd.

Steen: They think it's a package that they can buy – order and implement.

John: Correct, but it is less a program, and more of developing a way of thinking. What we do when we start our *Visible Learning* programs with schools is conduct a good old-fashioned needs analysis. We spend a lot of time on diagnosis because we know that if we don't understand the context, we don't understand what's working or what's not working. We ask the educators to do a needs analysis, as it is their interpretations of the evidence that we want to reveal. We argue very strongly that we are more about the *how*, and not the *what*, because *Visible Learning* can be undertaken in any kind of context. We are not so interested in how teachers teach, but the impact on the students. We ask, for example, teachers about their vision of a good learner in their class, and we ask a sample of students. If this is similar then wonderful, but too often students think learning is coming prepared, sitting up straight, doing the work and handing it in, and watching the teacher working. Ouch, therein starts the program.

   We also ask all about their notion of impact. What do they mean, about what, for whom, and to what magnitude? And we teach them how to use artefacts of student work to help answer and reflect on their beliefs about impact, use effect-sizes from tests and assignments, and use student voice about their views of impact. If students do not believe they have progressed then we have a sad state indeed.

Steen: Okay. I'm not a specialist in medicine but, basically, if you take this very, maybe too simplistic logic, you have some cancer medicine, and an idea that it might be curing something. And then you have a harmless and neutral product, you could compare the possible effect to, like a chalk or a vitamin pill. And you blindfold people – both the test and the control group – through all this testing based on the RCT evidence standards. Do you have a similar test logic that you use in educational statistics trying to decipher and estimate impacts and effects of different learning 'interventions', and is there something like a zero logic coming in education, like a harmless and neutral chalk or a vitamin pill?

John: Yes, I do, and yes there is . . .

Steen: I nearly can't wait to hear your answers.

John: . . . I take the view that you've got two ways of looking at the vitamin pill. One is to consider it the 'zero point' and that if students don't grow, whatever that means, then the intervention has not worked. But I think that's too minimal because my argument is that virtually 97% of things we do to students positively enhances their learning. Almost every intervention can beat the 'zero point'.

So I do use an average effect across all influences, which is 0.40. Now care is needed, and building local norms and understandings is critical. Probably the greatest moderator is how narrow or wide the measure is. If it is narrow, it is easier to get higher effects. But the message is to decide on some locally agreed standard and use this. For example, in our program we work with schools to build some local standards from their past tests. We also compare the impact across various years, subjects, and sub-groups of students. So my 'placebo' is much greater than the zero, or absence of an intervention.

Steen: If you were really a trickster, you could be building some wrong ideas in your own offer and see if the smart people would ever find out.

John: Yes, you can.

Steen: And you could build in some quotations, measurements, algorithms, whatever, that'll completely fool people to see whether or not they could be able to falsify your program.

John: Yes, but the students are harder to fool, if they are not progressing in their learning. So we need to ask more comparative questions, ask what works best, determine one's personal best and beat this.

You could get dramatic changes in schools by focusing on very narrow things, and that's a worry, but that's something that we're very, very aware of.

But I want to go back a step. If your colleague Kirsten Hyldgaard is asking about whether we need more control over placebos in the same way as doctors, then my measurement self has no trouble with randomized controlled trials (RCTs) in education. I've been involved in conducting some RCTs in England right now. I just don't think that RCTs are the gold standard. I think that's a major, major mistake when you privilege a method as the gold standard.

Steen: And what are their prime faults, or the prime mistakes they're doing?

Is there a blindness of seeing in the *Visible Learning* paradigm?

John: First, let me give you a higher principle. The higher principle is, I think, beyond reasonable doubt (promulgated by Michael Scriven, see Cook et al. 2010). This is kind of like a jury, where you have to put up a case as to why you're going to do this program rather than this program, with the evidence, with the context, and so on, and the aim is to convince, beyond reasonable doubt, that this is what you as a researcher and teacher should do. This begs where the evidence is.

If you use good methodology, you're more likely to go beyond reasonable doubt. I wrote this review of a report once about a particular group of randomized controlled studies that were criminally incompetent. The studies were based on very few students, were very poorly controlled studies, but they were randomized controlled studies. And they were privileged in being published and well cited – primarily because they were RCTs. There are poor as well as good randomized controlled studies. I think there is something like 150 reviews of educational interventions in the US What Works Clearinghouse. What's the average number of articles each review is based on? Two, because those are the only articles that passed their criteria (Lortie-Forgues & Inglis 2019). And their argument is: "On these two, we can make these conclusions, but of course we need more research." On the basis of this poverty of RCT articles, the average effect-size across the 141 reviews is 0.03. So if schools are forced to choose intervention from these sites, they are doomed to failure. They review some influences where there are oodles of evidence that are not RCTs, and they have much more robust findings that can led to powerful interventions. It is criminal to claim any higher order of truth, and that's the problem with the medicine model where they've privileged methodology, and, hopefully, in education, we'll never privilege methodology. We'll privilege a way of thinking, and this is where beyond reasonable doubt is so powerful. We, as researchers, needs to have compelling evidence and a narrative or story about this evidence. Of course, for the teacher or the person who needs to be convinced, the option is to say, "I don't accept your evidence." And I, as the person convincing you, have to listen to you and understand how you think so I can marshal the evidence and narrative so as to convince you. But in doing this I may find contrary evidence, or you could advance contrary evidence – hence the development, enhancements, and refinements happen – or it could devastate and kill the story. But that is how we advance. That's how we can contribute to a learning society. I wonder how you and your colleague, Hyldgaard, will react to these reflections?

Steen: Well, it sounds like a good critical consciousness 'loaded' with carefulness is needed when you deal with such difficult questions of statistical validity and evidence.

John: Yes, of course, it is.

Steen: Some of my other colleagues in Denmark, Søren Christensen and John Krejsler, differentiate between what is evidence based and what is evidence informed (Christensen & Krejsler 2015). In education and pedagogy, they favor the search for and spreading of evidence-informed practices.

John: Yes, but I don't make that distinction.

Steen: Why not? Let me pose you a question even though – you know – I am very skeptical towards evidence 'thinking' as such, and especially within the field of education (see, for example, Larsen 2019b). Do you see your results produced by the *Visible Learning* programs and your correlation tables based on all the data and the meta-analyses you have piled up as a provider of evidence-based global knowledge? Or 'only' as an attempt to help the teachers to work as evidence-informed professionals, strengthening their expertise?

John: No, that's far too narrow a concept of evidence. If I'm a teacher, and I've been teaching 20 years, why are you denying that evidence?

Steen: Maybe because of your 'elaborated' and cunning experience is much more than just immediate and vanishing experiences.

John: Yes. Such experience can be construed as a form of evidence.

Steen: Well, in Denmark one of the worst, most insulting things that have been said about teachers is that they are 'hit by their own experience', meaning that they don't want to listen to real science but only to believe in their own limited horizon of subjective experience …

John: Yeah, but experience is evidence, and of course subject to the rules of evidence – can it be validated, triangulated, convincing; and how does the narrative the teacher pronounces fit with this evidence? It must be contested and subjected to falsification – by other teachers, by students, by artefacts of student work, by interpretations of test scores, and so on.

Steen: . . . some researchers, politicians, and school administrators claim that the teachers are too much flavored by their own experience (in Danish: *erfaringsramte*, hit or struck by experience in English) and they have to wave the experience goodbye to become evidence based and effective.

John: Of course not. No, no, no. I want the same standards of enquiry, and interrogation, and deductivism for your experience as I want for the research out there. I want to question your evidence. I don't think your evidence is right just because you have it. I want to say, "Show me the evidence." You could bring along evidence that when you did this, these students did this, that, and the other. That's evidence.

Steen: The idea is, among these colleagues of mine, that instead of finding an evidence-based logic test to be mandatory, you could be informed by different types of evidence . . .

John: Oh, you can be.

Steen: But it all depends on the content, the subject, and the context (Larsen 2011, 2014c, 2015d, 2017b, 2019a, 2019b). Your *Visible Learning* paradigm risks to 'produce' a blindness in seeing if it does not integrate questions concerning the content, the subject, and the context in its approach and procedures for investigation and examination.

John: I think evidence should include the research studies. It should include teacher experience. And they both should be subjected to the same evaluative and falsification notion. What is your narrative, and can you defend your narrative? The evidence doesn't do it. It's the interpretation of the evidence. I want to know how you interpret that evidence.

Different perspectives on the same 'thing' must be provided

Steen: I would then like to ask you a question. Because it seems to me that you are always coming back to this question about the interpretative strength, the strong narrative, the strong interpretation of data, and the critical question examining of arguments.

John: Yes, the key question is: "What evidence would you accept you're wrong?"

Steen: And how do people build up that capacity? Does it come through reading and training?

John: That's the point of schooling.

Steen: Yeah, but as a statistician you have an approach, but as a sociologist, a philosopher, and a historian, you apply utmost different ways of reflecting.

John: Yes, and there are statisticians who don't think this way.

Steen: I guess so. So your idea is now that this capacity for interpreting can be trained in very many different ways?

John: I think it's the fundamental purpose of education, to give you different perspectives of the same thing. Recall the mountain story – there can be many perspectives, and you need to start by understanding the person's concept of the mountain.

Steen: I once was a teacher in a, what do you call it, People's Folk Academy (in Danish: *Højskole*), which has a long history in Denmark: more than 150 years of self-organized schools in the countryside with a lot of so-called practical and theoretical subjects, ranging from art programs to physical activities. These schools have a high autonomy, they get state support, you don't pass exams or get a diploma or a certification there, and you don't get qualified for specific jobs within the societal division of labor. And in the 1990s I 'ran' this philosophy course, or workshop, about theories of acknowledgment, actually, epistemology. It was called "Why a bottle is not just a bottle?" It was a pretty smart title because you could take a simple and utmost concrete beer bottle, and start to discuss what it is. It could be seen as a phallus symbol, a potential weapon, and suddenly it awakens the long time forgotten memory of your drunken favorite uncle's long-term 'suicide', etc.

And the beer bottle can be a part of a modern artwork, labeled 'Danish Culture'. Put a nail through it and hang it on the wall of a modern art museum. It could be deposit, worth one Danish Krone (Crown), and could be seen as a container for all kind of fluids. It could be an object of a color. So there were so many interpretations of just a simple bottle. So my idea was, of course, to give all these kinds of ideas of how we can interpret the world differently. But it seems to me that both this bottle example and your defense of multi-perspectivism provide the open and ever-changing interpretation logic with a much higher and more important role than a stricter scientific deductive logic. But how does that relate to your credo to be a good deductivist?

John: You sound like a modern creativity test – how many unusual uses can you think of for a tin can? Yes, there can be multiple interpretations, but just because you have made an interpretation does not make it true, valid, or replicable. The interpretation is the first part of the narrative. You can even enjoy the narrative, but this is insufficient to be a valid theory. It needs evidence, it needs a counterfactual, it needs a search for contrary evidence. You could, for example, line up all the competing theories for the data in *Visible Learning*, but then the fun begins. And if only others would put up competing theories. Indeed, in education we need more competing theories.

To go the abductive way

Steen: In most method books around the globe, you are normally also introduced to two other ways of scientific thinking and reflecting: induction and abduction.

John: I'm a great fan of abduction.

Steen: So am I. Abduction is quite often being seen as a deviation, because you have to be inventive while you do research. You have to dare to meet the challenge and honor the ambition to combine things from different worlds, even though they are not combined themselves, and to qualify and master different ways of reasoning,

John: My friend Brian Haig has written on abduction in factor analysis and research design and I find him convincing (he also was my prefect when I was in High School, and then my tutor in first year university; see Haig 2014, 2018). Like in *Visible Learning*, there is the bringing together of multiple data sets to be analyzed (for means, variation, moderators, regularities) and then the search for meaning occurs. A key step in abduction is detecting empirical phenomena, which is more than just data – they are the relatively stable, recurrent, general features underlying the data. Then we construct plausible models of the relations between the influences, and these are tested against rival claims aiming for high levels of explanatory power and generalizability. A good theory provides a better explanation of the evidence than its rivals.

Hence, in *Visible Learning* there is no shortage of data, and my task was to detect the general features underlying the data – particularly advance plausible models as to what are the underlying relations between those influences above and below the average. From this, I developed the big themes, then reversed the process to seek contrary evidence, alternative rival claims, until I was sufficiently satisfied the model was defensible. Others now can provide alternative explanations, and I continue to add data, which could well reverse the evidence for my claims. Bring it on.

Steen: One thing that worries me is that if you happen to be a teacher, and you have this class, and it's full of problems, because there are all kind of problems among the students or the pupils. And you have more than enough to do without handling all these different learning goals, and all these different human beings, all these different conflicts, and all these different tensions. And then there will be somebody – like you or one of your international colleagues – coming in with an advice, stating, "Well, this is more than 0.40. This is 1.80 or 0.80 effective. 'Know Thy impact!' Change what you do, and how you think." Would you understand a teacher who states, "I have enough to do, and I cannot use the *Visible Learning* program because it will not help me in this very specific situation, in which I have to invent my own ways of handling all these tasks and conflicts"?

John: My first reaction to that is teachers, in general, have the same time, they often have the same kinds of students as their neighbor class, the same curricula, the same school leaders, the same political press – and some have higher impacts than others despite these similarities. Some teachers do prioritize learning and maximizing impact on their students and others aim to get through the curricula, engage students in interesting and engaging tasks, and see success as having all hand in the work, on time. Also, I'm quite happy for you to say, "I don't need to learn all this *Visible Learning* stuff." But I still think there's a moral obligation on you to demonstrate to me, as your principal, or as the parent, or as the student, or to the community of people, you have got evidence that you're having a reasonable, appropriate, and desirable impact on these students – and again can defend the domain in which the impact relates to.

What I'm trying to do in the *Visible Learning* work, particularly our programs in schools, is not to privilege any kind of teaching. We are neutral on how one teaches. We say, "We will come in, and we will help you understand your impact." Because I know, as teachers, they have very strong theories of teaching. They may not be based on the research. They may not even have heard of Heidegger or Rousseau, but they have very strong theories about what works for them and their students. If you go in and change what they do without changing how they think about what they do, you haven't got a good chance. But there are not many teachers that we have met who aren't interested and keen to learn more when you help them understand their narrative and their impact and, sometimes, the inconsistencies between those.

And most teachers, not all, absolutely want to have an improvement agenda. They don't want a change agenda, they want an improvement agenda. And if they already have sufficiently high impact and can defend the worthwhileness of their content, challenge, and coverage of all students, we simply say, "Permission to keep doing what you're doing. Why would we change you?" Why would we make them use any particular, no matter how desirable, teaching method? To the contrary, the majority of professional learning and education works on the assumption "Steen, you are not doing a good enough job. Come, and I'll improve you or change you. I'll watch you teach and show you how to teach better." I think that's insulting, particularly for those already have high impact.

'Know Thy Impact' on more or less everything?

Steen: Okay, then let us try to approach another topic and raise a new debate. Is it possible to translate this logic of teaching, and schooling, and learning to other branches of human interaction? For example, if you 'have' a lover or a wife: "'Know Thy Impact' on 'your' woman!" Or 'lifted' into another sphere: "'Know Thy Impact', if you are an artist, on people looking at art!" Will all these different domains obey same logic that you should strengthen your impact?

John: No, no. Sometimes we should accept beauty and wisdom and give and receive the love of others. Not everything is an experiment, we do not need to think abductively all the time, sometimes we should just smell the roses.

Steen: Because my concern is now that if it is the most wanted clue to come to know your impact, it is a kind of thinking that places you in the very center of the narrative. And the question here – the counter question – could be: Why do pupils and students let you have impact upon them?

John: Well, because it's compulsory. But also we want to make our classes and schools so inviting that students want to come and be impacted. This is why making learning interesting, and challenging and showing the students they progress are so critical.

Steen: And there must be different systems at and in play here. One for love, one for art, one for education . . .

John: Why not. I don't want to go into art and love because they don't have the same moral issues about being responsible for people who are yet to be responsible for themselves; and in the process of being taught responsibility – which entails knowing, understanding, etc. These other domains don't deal with development of human beings.

Steen: So you think that this whole logic is also embedded in this Kantian notion of the pedagogical paradox (Kant 1971/1803)?

John: Yes.

Steen: We are, when we do schooling, forced to let people be liberated in a position where they cannot liberate themselves.

John: Correct. We need to teach them to be liberated in the Freirean notion. Absolutely, yes, and hence the importance of developing knowledge, critique, evaluation – to allow them to be critics of what they have received through their schooling.

Steen: And that's very different from a love relation or an art relation.

John: Yes, and for parenting, for sport, etc. We are working in our team on *Visible Learning* in parenting and coaching in sport. Because in parenting and in coaching you've got the same kind of moral imperative in a different way about the responsibilities for people and the paradox, yes.

Steen: Okay, but where to find the limits for that narrative? Because I can see it in sport and parenting. But what else could there be . . . leadership, for example?

John: Of course, you can relate the *Visible Learning* messages to leadership in schools.

Steen: Yeah, but not in love?

John: No, there is a fuzzy boundary about applying notions to the education domain.

Steen: Not in art?

John: No.

Steen: Not in belief systems? But you have had fathers or preacher men, big leading church authorities, telling you how to believe.

John: Yes, but they cannot address the core scientific question about what evidence would they accept that they were wrong.

Steen: But it's just to know what you think about whether these basic principles of 'Know Thy Impact' can be transported and translated to other spheres.

John: But that's not fair, Steen, because you talked about 'Know Thy Impact' in terms of the narrow notion of knowing thy impact on others. Then you went to belief systems. When you go to belief systems, yes, I do think there is some generality in terms of how we question, how we accept negative evidence, how we are aware of our confirmation biases in every area. But that's a different part of it. And I think there are rules, procedures, and understandings about methodology in religion, art, love, etc. But in terms of having an impact on other people, that gives us an extra obligation in our discipline of schooling to be very aware of the moral imperative. And it does, as you have said 1,000 times, and I'm agreeing with you, beg that moral purpose question much more. In art, is there a moral purpose question? No, or not in the same sense. You can invoke one through art, you can develop a narrative, but you do not use evidence, abduction, seeking negative evidence in the same way. Beauty transcends in this case.

Steen: Maybe the students and the students also allow you to impact upon them when you show them that you 'incarnate' and demonstrate a certain quality in what you're talking about.

John: Yes, they can indeed, and this is a very powerful notion.

Steen: And you possess knowledge of what you're talking about. And they cannot foresee or anticipate what you would say in five or ten minutes. The quality of teaching should not let them fall asleep, and it invites their intellects and attentions to sparkle.

John: You're absolutely right. Education as sparkle – it sounds great. But there is a legal requirement that they're forced to go to school.

Steen: Yeah, so the rules are here, but not in Denmark. Teaching people to learn something is mandatory, but not to go to school. That's different in Denmark. You have the right and the opportunity to homeschool and to go together with other parents and establish state supported so-called free schools (in Danish: *friskoler*).

John: Oh, you can do homeschooling here. But they have to attend some form of schooling.

Steen: In my home country, students do not have to attend a school. You can organize schooling yourself or together with other people. But they have to, in the end, to pass exams.

John: Oh, okay. So there's requirements on pupils and youngsters to do certain things.

Steen: Yeah, but you don't have to go to school. So that's what people didn't understand, while we were riding on our racing bikes 4,200 km through Europe – Spain, France, and Germany – with Albert, our 12-year-old son, back home from Malaga far down south to Denmark far up north in spring 2012. "How could you take him out of school for so long?" We just answered that we had taken the responsibility over him for two months, and he'll come back and take the exams. But that's the Danish way.

John: In New Zealand you can be fined and even jailed for taking your child out of school for an extended time without prior permission. Yeah, but the notion that the society forces schooling on students gives us an even higher level of responsibility than many of us ever realize.

Is learning a visible or invisible phenomenon?

Is it possible to anticipate the quality of learning in a lifetime perspective of the individual?

Is there something called a placebo problem in evidence-seeking educational research, based on *Visible Learning* principles?

How can abductive thinking qualify educational research?

IV. IS IT IMPORTANT to TEACH and LEARN specific SUBJECTS?

SHOULD SUBJECTS BE TAUGHT?

PRIMARY teachers love CHILDREN

SECONDARY teachers love SUBJECTS

AND ACADEMICS love THEMSELVES

YES! THERE IS PRECIOUS KNOWLEDGE

THE FROG

AND A DOG

IN the EARLY YEARS we NEED LANGUAGE PLAY

SAT on A LOG!

WITHIN the FRAME of language PLAY many ASTONISHING THINGS are POSSIBLE.

know thy impact

- WHAT do you MEAN by IMPACT?
- HOW many STUDENTS are IMPACTED?
- IMPACT on what?
- WHAT is the MAGNITUDE?

THE MORE DATA YOU COLLECT the FURTHER away YOU GET FROM the PEOPLE involved.

So META-META-ANALYSIS COULD be renamed DISTANCE ANALYSIS.

ALL WE NEED is to pay ATTENTION to QUESTIONS of CONTENT, PURPOSE, and RELATIONSHIPS.

GERT BIESTA

LET DIFFERENT VIEWS of THE WORLD CLASH

WE NEED to TEACH parents THE LANGUAGE of TEACHING.

Steen: Okay, let's go back and discuss this question: Is it important to teach and learn specific subjects?

John: It's an empirical question about whether the subject topic makes a difference to the effectiveness of various teaching methods. But I struggled to find evidence for this differentiation. That does not mean subjects aren't important. Absolutely we need content to then make relations between the content and transfer our thinking to new problems; we need the subject matter vocabulary; we need to understand what others have found in developing new ideas and relations between ideas in the content domain. Over the past 30 years, I've been writing about the Structural Observations of Learning Outcomes (SOLO; Biggs & Collis 1982) taxonomy, which demarcates (loosely) between surface to deep, and the premise of this model is that you need content (surface) to then move to deep (relationships). It is sad, however, that too often in schools both teachers and students prefer to think in terms mainly of content. Of course, that's a problem.

Steen: We also ask our colleagues whether they are math teachers or literature teachers . . .

John: Exactly. But the question is whether the most effective way of teaching languages is similar or different from the effective way of teaching welding, from teaching chemistry? And the evidence seems to say, "No, it's not." So subjects, yes. Different teaching methods for different subjects, no.

But don't get me wrong. Knowledge is important. I'm a great fan of Michael Young (Young & Muller 2013), the English sociologist, who talks about 'precious knowledge'. I am sure he is asking about 'which' knowledge as we cannot have everything. And knowing things is important to know. We privilege people in our society, like you Steen, who know a lot. And for you, who know a lot, the distinction between knowing a lot, and capabilities, and thinking is very small. People at the other end of the distribution, who do not have the knowledge, often are penalized as they also cannot see the relations between ideas as readily, often have fewer strategies of learning, so it is easier to separate this content, relationships and thinking, and strategies, and sometimes we overplay the learning capabilities for these students instead of developing content as well as capabilities. We have a new rhetoric about the 21st-Century Skills and demand all students have these skills (Griffin & Care 2014) – but they need knowledge, too. And my worry with 21st-Century Skills (like resilience, resourcefulness, reflectiveness, and collaboration) is that you're going to teach young students to be critical thinkers, and we're not going to privilege them. We want both.

Steen: I think you have a good point in stating that these medicine students couldn't do problem-oriented work the first year. If we go to young students and say, "Well, now we have an innovation program." Then they will probably say, "What should we innovate, and why?" Before you can innovate, you have to know the tradition and feel and discuss why old ways of doing things might not function any longer.

John: This is true, but going to the early childhood area, I get very frustrated when they talk about play. 'Play without language is not good play'.

Steen: Students are developing their language while they are playing. Ludwig Wittgenstein depicted the intimate relations between life-forms, language games, and the ever-ongoing socialization (e.g., via hard discipline; **Abrichtung** in German) to follow language rules (Wittgenstein 1953).

John: That's an assumption. We did an evaluation of 3,000 early childcare settings, in Australia. Home care, government preschools, kindergarten, private settings (Tayler et al. 2013). We followed these students for several years from age three up to age eight or nine. When you come up with measures of quality of those early childcare centers, particularly in terms of the ones that help students get ready for school, and you ask the question, "How many quality centers are there, in Australia, for students below average socioeconomic status?" The answer is exactly zero. Too many are obsessed about play, and they don't use play for language, they use it to keep young children occupied. Of course, using play for language can be powerful. But they were obsessed about play; not play to develop language.

Steen: Yes. I haven't made observation of that type. But I just listened to my own students, and those two girls of mine, and while they were playing they were developing their own linguistic communicating capacity – and of course also developing physical strength and social interactions skills. For example, they were pretending that this is the mama, this is the father, and this one has this capacity, and so on.

John: Look at the most famous study (Hart & Risley 2003, which is hotly contested; see Sperry et al. 2018) – and take your five-year-old daughter and compare her to a five-year-old kid from a lower socioeconomic status family. How many more words has she been exposed to? That is, how many more words has she heard – not unique words – than that kid by age five?

Steen: Okay, 30 times as many.

John: 30 million.

Steen: 30 million? That is a wild and nearly ungraspable figure.

John: Now, I am obsessed that these students need language via play. I have nothing wrong with play. But it's not the end, and too often we hear early childhood people think it is. And I'm working at the moment on my next project relating to developing an assessment scheme from zero to eight. You can imagine how provocative that is for many. I recall at a previous university, there was a seminar why researchers should never use quantitative methods in early childhood – absurd beyond sense. We can find ways to better diagnose, understand, and progress these young children. It will be fun trying, and most of the sector here in Australia are keen for it to happen.

I am also writing a book with my son called *Visible Learning for Parents*. It's not very parent friendly yet. So I'm getting others to help make it friendlier to parents. The whole message is based on three themes: language, language, and language.

Steen: In a way, it's very interesting to hear. We could also debate the German philosophical hermeneutic **Hans–Georg Gadamer** and his concept of play, which is in German *das Spiel*. He uses that also to analyze our encounter with art in his grand work *Truth and Method* (Gadamer 1989/1960) . . .

John: Oh, sounds fascinating.

Steen: . . . and literature. Because he says that in order to understand art, you must be played by the art – ***gespielt werden*** in German.

John: It's the same being a researcher.

Steen: And that means to open yourself to it and to give interpretations of it in a dialectical logic.

John: That's not anything different to what we're doing today.

Steen: You are completely right. We are being played by educational philosophical language, we are playing in language and with language, and hopefully we are inventing new language. And that's exactly this fertile hermeneutical approach. Within the frame of language many astonishing things are made possible.

The content and substance of learning

Steen: Let's turn to another question. If learning differs, as I claim, in quality due to the content and substance of the learning process, how do you ever come to know whether or not a student has learned to do and partake in autonomous reflection? That means, stating the obvious, understand, reflect, or interpret, or even think, or criticize? A learning effect plus 0.40 or more does not necessarily say anything of the quality of learning, nor detect whether or not the student or the pupil have learned to think autonomously or not.

John: Let me answer that in two halves.

Steen: So how do we know about the difference between just stating the obvious and then thinking?

John: No, no, no. That's unfair. Let's go to the first half of the question. How do you know whether students learn or not? And then you say, "It relates to the content." I would also argue that it relates to the content. But I also want more than this. This is a fundamental problem here if you interpret me to say that I say nothing about the quality of learning.

A few years back I shifted the narrative in *Visible Learning* from what I talked about in the 2009 book. Too many readers thought I was saying we can rank all effects one by one (whereas there are underlying themes differentiating the top and bottom influences), too many thought 0.40 was somehow magic (whereas I called it a 'hinge point,' discriminating half the effects above and half below this hinge point), and they too often missed the underlying messages. And yes, I take some responsibility for not writing more clearly about these messages. So I nudged the message towards 'Know Thy Impact', the notion we have touched upon earlier. I was surprised when I thought of the idea that it had not been used in this context before. I looked it up on Google, and no one had used it. So I thought, right, this could help focus on the major messages. Asking 'Know Thy Impact' begs the questions: "What do you mean by impact?", "How many students share this impact?", "Impact about what?", and "What is the magnitude of this impact?"

If impact means doing well on multiple-choice tests, well, that's very narrow and certainly then you are right as it may have little to do with thinking. If your concept is that they have an ability to think in scientific or historical ways, I would probably critique that, too Because it's too broad and you leave too many students out – and it needs to also include the content relating to the ways of thinking. The view I take is a much more nuanced notion of what you mean by impact. Depending on where the students are. Where you want to go. How many students are getting the impact. This is where you do need to know your individual students very well and why I talk about the centrality of the student. I want educators to have robust discussions about their concepts of impact, yes informed by evidence (in multiple ways) as that is core to what they are then aiming for in their classes. Wouldn't it be wonderful for this discussion about impact to also occur with the students? I have seen many classes of five-year-olds really get into what is meant by impact, and yes it gets harder as they grow through school as too often they learn that this debate is not their role – this is a tragedy.

And the magnitude related to what you think is 'good enough' growth over the time you are considering? Why should you be in a class where a teacher thinks that growth is about this (JH holds up a finger and thumb to indicate small growth) and the teacher down the corridor has a much larger conception of growth (finger and thumb much wider apart)? That's very unfair on the students in the first teacher's class. And so having a debate among these teachers about what they mean by progress over three months' work, a year's work for a year's progress, is the critical step. I don't answer that. I want the educators to answer that because your answer to those questions about impact has more effect on your students than anything else you do. That is the core of my argument. So that comes back to your question. You would, I imagine (as would I) include more than stating the obvious, you would include thinking about, tackling difficult problems, knowledge sufficient to then make relations between ideas, building skills to transfer the learning to new problems – and such a debate would be powerful, and lead then to asking whether the lesson, the materials, the assignments are structured to make this clear to students, to allow for them to see you value these skills, and then the evidence of success on these work artefacts is part of the ongoing discussion.

Steen: My view is, that a very good teacher is able to tell you how to decenter your own strategic self from the moment. Because if you're always saying to yourself, "Well, do I need this for exam?" or "Will that give me an A or a C?", or whatever, then you are not ever meeting the content, the subject – the poem, botanics, quantum physics – in its own right.

John: I agree with that, absolutely.

Steen: The school's role is also to challenge you in order to open your eyes to comprehensions and interpretations of something you don't know of.

John: Correct, and to critique what you think you know and understand.

Steen: And if you just want to reproduce the already known then the great and daring teacher helps you to forget about short-term behavior and strategy (Larsen 2016a, 2017c).

John: Exactly. Overlearning is a core feature to reduce the load on working memory to then move to deeper concepts.

Steen: And forget about utilitarian approaches.

John: Forget, maybe go well beyond. The more you've got it, the more you don't have to think about it. Those we esteem know lots, but more importantly see relations between ideas, sometimes in ways the rest of us do not. It is this combination of knowing lots and using this information that is critical to development in school curricula. It is not either/or. Yes, too many know lots, and this is esteemed by some teachers, by some exams, and certainly by many students. Ask a high school student who is the best learner in the class and they inevitable say – person x because they know lots, can learn it quickly, and have good recall. Sad but too often true.

How to get knowledge through de-contextualizing and de-subjectifying learning processes?

Steen: Listening to you and reading your books, the *Visible Learning* program seems to de-contextualize and de-subjectify and maybe even naturalize the data collected in order to get and gather real scientific material for production of evidence. The ideal seems to be that the data is not 'polluted' by living subjects in complex school system, and the quest for deduction – and you stated to me that you are a strong deductivist – is based on a large amount of processed data.

My critical remark to you is: The more visible the learning data seems to present themselves, the more reductionist and deprived the qualitative and unique meaning. Seen in a horizon of the first-person phenomenological experience there seems to be a kind of an inner paradox here. The more data you collect, the further away you get from the people involved (Larsen 2015a, 2019a).

You could also state it in this slightly more positive way, that if the *Visible Learning* program and your meta-analysis, and your giant effort here for the last ten years, have also been to do something that's really like the physics of learning or something like that, the kind of empiricist data-collection objective must be to find what we can come to know.

John: Thank you – for the more positive viewpoint.

Steen: Are you favoring a strong realistic type of objectified, and maybe even a positivistic, scientific approach that vast empirical knowledge is the premise for making deductions?

John: Yes, it is.

Steen: That's your vision. So what I hear is a paradox. You have deliberately de-contextualized and de-subjectified the field of education, taken away the substance matter from math and whatever, in comparison with literature and philosophy, and we have in a way also naturalized them and then we're piling all that up and then we are returning to the field and saying, "In this unique situation I have the knowledge to know how to do the right thing"? How can we do that if beforehand we have de-contextualized and de-subjectified all the complexities within the very different fields in which the data was collected?

John: You're right. I would argue there is a knowledge base in education and teaching. I think there are things we know and things we that we know we should not do. I don't think teaching is a craft to the extent that everybody has the right to teach as they think fit just as, in the same way, you do not have the right to fly an airplane as you wish. I think there are things in schools that we do know that work better, and we know things that do not work so well and should stop these.

There is, indeed, a certain level of de-contextualization, but that should never stop the hunt for context matters, for moderators, for interactions between the impact of the teaching and the maximal learning of the student. Sometimes it helps to de-contextualize to make generalizable comments, and then see how these generalizations then work back in the context of the classroom. Remember, literature searching is a rear vision way of thinking, and I certainly have come to emphasize the mantra 'Know Thy Impact' that asks whether high probability interventions work in your classroom, for your students, for this curriculum.

You are right in your notion that dehumanizing, de-contextualizing, and de-subjectifying would of course work brilliantly if we didn't have to teach students.

Steen: In 'my' university right now, the courses are being modularized such that the student program is interchangeable 10-ECTS-point courses, 15-point courses, 20-point courses, 30-point courses, and at the top of all that, the learning goals, as they are called in our department should be expressed in such a way that any teacher can take over instead of another teacher (Larsen 2016c). Because each of the courses should not contain a slight resemblance of what could be attached to a life story or a certain teacher personality or a certain way of reading from some dedicated professor. So that means that when you are de-personalizing the whole structure and construct a modulizing learning goal machine then you're also taking out the life of it. That will be my worry, that you take out also the heritage, the living and loving care for your subject, and that means that in a way you cleanse the university of all obstacles, personal styles, and passion. And suddenly you end up with a too easy, accessible learning program, in which any teacher becomes replaceable with any other teacher?

John: This exchangeable notion is attractive to modern corporate university. I note many US online courses are written by influential academics and then delivered by (often) a very young junior faculty. There is again a probability statement at work – but once again it is the adaptation, the listening to the impact on the students, the revising and re-teaching, and the delving into understanding how students come to incorrect or not optimal understandings – this is the art of the teaching. Devising teacher-proof curricula is like devising student-proof learning. Absurd.

Steen: And that can also be a problem of the *Visible Learning* program that one (e.g., a politician, a school leader, an educational planner, a journalist . . .) risks forgetting the actual subjects carrying and living among the structures of the institutions?

John: That's a very bad reading of my work and I trust it is not the case. We spend a lot of time in our workshops listening to the participants, seeing if they understand the messages, inviting them to try ideas and then evaluate them in their context, and most importantly critiquing and cooperatively working together in a safe environment to debate their impact.
        And you have switched from schools to universities.

Steen: I have.

John: What you're saying is even less likely to happen in a school. But the issues do not have to be a bipolar issue – there can be a happy middle of experts devising the curricula and then working with more junior staff in the teaching – this is the university model I was brought up in, even though I can see more and more what you are saying. And what you are saying is all too often occurring on online courses.

Steen: And if we go back to the history of the university it has been very fruitful to let different views of the world clash. Quantum mechanics and quantum physics were born out of a critique of the acknowledged lacks within Newtonian physics. The university should not be an institution that falls too much in love with its own module arranged learning agenda.

John: Let me give you another example. The University of Phoenix employed Nobel Prize winners (among others) to get the content right and then employed other people to teach their scripts. Or would you recommend that we ask people who do not know the content and then get experts (or novices) to teach it. Which way would you go?

Steen: Well, I would let people try to go both ways and make forthcoming conferences where you could debate the experiences you have gained via two different strategies.

John: I didn't give you that choice. But in that conference would you have people who know this stuff at the conference or people who didn't know this stuff at the conference?

Steen: Of course, you would prioritize the first.

John: But there aren't enough of them.

Steen: But it might also be an idea that you could set up some bottom–up experiments in which the people involved are inventing curricula from below . . . at least as an experiment.

John: In the 1990s, before *Visible Learning* even existed, Herb Marsh and I did a meta-analysis on the relationship between research and teaching at universities (Hattie & Marsh 1996; Marsh & Hattie 2002). And we were not popular when we showed across 46 studies, at a large number of academics and universities, that however you measure quality of research or teaching, the correlation is absolutely centered very narrowly on zero.

Now, it took me a time to work out the story, that if you look at research on the y-axis, and you look at teaching on x-axis, then everyone wants to be in the quadrant where you hire great researchers and you have great teachers. But there are too few of these scholars. My view is that in a good university, you have a mixture of people who are good researchers and teachers, good researchers and maybe okay teachers, good teachers and okay researchers, but no one wants poor teachers and/or researchers. If you look at what a zero correlation can mean, it can include similar numbers in each of these three quadrants.

Further, one of the interesting things that I did in a previous university, as part of an audit system, was a review of all policies relating to teaching and research. We couldn't find a single policy in the university that brought teaching and research together. Not in appointments, promotions, study leave, awards, and so on. Universities are kind of hypocritical when they argue that we are the place where there is a nexus between great research and teaching. I have challenged every vice chancellor and president I met with the same request – be the first university to offer an award for the top researcher *and* top teacher. We offer awards for each but rarely (in fact I have never seen one instance) of them together – which surely epitomizes the nexus.

Steen: I think you are right. And what we are also facing, it's a kind of a paradox, is that the more grants you bring into the university, the more freedom you have not to educate people in the long run and to teach. When your research is supported you become 'free' not to teach.

John: Yes, too often these grants lead to reduction in involvement in teaching! In a previous university, there was the rule that no matter how many millions you won, there was still a minimal course load for all academics. But they also provided high levels of support for such successful grant getters. We know that those who gain large grants are a small percentage, so they are often coveted – in part because they bring the cream to the cake (in nearly every university, the preponderance of income is still via teaching; but many can teach whereas fewer can attract grants).

Steen: And that is, of course, the hidden contradiction in this whole logic. Turning to Denmark, for example, it's stated in the university manuals that if you want to hire people, you should also look upon their teaching experience and not only at their peer-reviewed article production. And that teaching skills should be estimated as high as the academic quality. But it's not really what's going on right now. It's still the academic merits that count much more.

John: Another major change over my career is also the larger number of part-time and casual academics within universities.

Steen: Yes, that's of course correct, and that's also what goes on. You have part-time teachers not having a right to do research. They are called the precariat among sociologists, and they are coming in and out of university all the time.

John: But how do they pay the mortgage?

Steen: Yes, they have a hard time getting a decent salary and way of living.

John: And I am certainly aware of some universities where over half the staff is on one-year contracts. Moreover, 80% of academic jobs in Australia are taps on shoulders. We hardly advertise as it's easier and safer to take the person you know. We tend to not invest in the longer-term development of academics, and too often new academics are expected to earn their salary almost immediately. I entered at a different time, and there was no expectation to earn my salary via grants, and indeed did not get my first grant until my 17th year within a university. Yes, I taught, supervised, and published (and played golf, lived on a farm, had students, etc.), made many pushes into different topics, and learned the academic ways and standards. It was more gradual than expected for a newbie today. The immediate expectation of grants, high-level publications, massive teaching, one-year contracts is not conducive to building a future cadre of great academics. This is not the university I was raised in. It's time for me to retire.

Close content contact

Steen: In the aforementioned book *The Rediscovery of Teaching*, Gert Biesta says, "Unlike the language of learning, a language of education, all we need is to pay attention to questions of *content, purpose*, and *relationships*" (Biesta 2017: 28). That's where you basically differ, I guess, because you think that we can rely on giant content-less meta-studies and unify millions of data to general clues versus Biesta's and my view. We maintain that the language of education has to deal with content, purpose, and relationship in an utmost concrete and specific way.

John: Not completely, each original study had a content of some sort, and each meta-analysis deals with one or many content domains. Then the nature of this content becomes a moderator worth exploring by the meta-analyst. This is a core notion and value of meta-analysis. Too many critics think that meta-analysis is just the summary effect-size measure and miss Gene Glass' major contribution – how to systematically ask questions about moderators to the effect-sizes (Glass 1976). Larry Hedges just won the Yidan Prize (https://yidanprize.org), and one of his major contributions is decomposing the variability within meta-analyses and again asking loudly for identifying moderating influences (Hedges & Olkin 1990). And one could be content – it turns out empirically that many of the teaching methods, for example, do not differ markedly depending on the content – but this finding does not mean we should then ignore the possibility of content interacting with the method. The data in *Visible Learning* are far from content-less, devoid of nuance, and simplistically summarized to the second decimal point.

You can't have content and just say, "Here's the content, Steen." I've got to have a process for helping you understand the content, get the knowledge, get the facts, get the relationships, get the extension of those ideas. What's that process? And what does Biesta call that?

Steen: He is embedding this problem field in what he calls the three domains. You've probably heard about it. In his earlier books he depicted these domains as qualification, socialization, and subjectification (see, e.g., Biesta 2013). This tripod might be clarifying but I see a problem in his way of thinking because it seems to be so, that qualification is the same as coming into contact with the content of education, but a formal qualification is not Hamlet (as a text of a play), the law of Archimedes, or man's genetic heritage . . .

John: It seems to be a consequence.

Steen: Or can qualification be the same as substance, matter . . .?

John: Yeah, good question.

Steen: I will argue that it is completely wrong because a qualification is qualifying you to do something in the world – for example, to perform in and on the labor market and maybe to possess or to take care of a function. Now you have the qualification of being a blacksmith or a nurse.

John: It's a consequence of learning.

Steen: But I think that content is much more than giving you a qualification.

John: Well, I do too.

Steen: So, I guess Biesta has a serious problem with the first of his three concepts. At page 29, he promotes "a *meaningful balance* between the three domains" (Biesta 2017: 29). But that doesn't really solve the problem.

John: Exactly. No, it doesn't.

Steen: But I agree with him, when he writes, "In its shortest formula the issue here is that the point of teaching, and of education more generally, is never that students 'just' learn, but always that they learn *something*, that they learn for particular *reasons*, and that they learn it from *someone*" (Biesta 2017: 27–28; Larsen 2016a). Do you?

John: Yes, in the same way when I talk about impact, I then ask about what, to whom, to what magnitude of improvement. It is always learning about something, typically as a consequence of someone.

Steen: I guess, it is difficult not to use it. But to say learn is not to subscribe to the ideology of learning, nor to love 'learnification', or to be convinced that the *Visible Learning* program can make all that's going on in the class and in and among the pupils transparent. But please notice that *someone* is the teacher, and that Biesta a few sentences later stresses that "the question of purpose is in my view the most important and fundamental question" (Biesta 2017: 28), meaning that Biesta enters our stage where we discuss the purpose – and the *why* – of education.

John: That's fine, I'm happy with that.

Steen: And the *something* is more or less being the exterior.

John: But, again, he jumps and does not want to use the words 'learn' and 'learning' even though he does it several times in his own sentences.

Steen: Good observation, but me too, I am basically not a great fan of the concept 'learning'. Instead I would turn to inspiration from – among many other philosophers – Ernst Bloch's *The Principle of Hope*, Theodor W. Adorno's *Negative Dialectics*, Hannah Arendt's *The Life of the Mind*, and Maxine Sheets-Johnstone's *The Roots of Thinking* and invest my attention in the concept 'thinking', which is – by the way – much more important and ambitious than the dominant phrase 'learning' (**Bloch 1986/1954– 1959; Adorno 2004/1966; Arendt 1971; Sheets-Johnstone 1990**).

John: You're not a fan of 'learning' as it's used to compartmentalize knowledge and a reductionist notion of . . . that's what I'm hearing you say.

Steen: Yes, and the learning concept is also used as a kind of self-confirming **teleology** – learning is directed towards itself . . .

John: Correct.

Steen: And as a process term at the same time . . .

John: So when I get up and I say, "I would rather switch the focus from teaching to learning," you'd have troubles with that?

Steen: I would have serious problems because I still think that the essence of teaching also implies that you get the chance to be set free to come up with a critique of the teacher's offers and not just to accept what you are taught. That's where I differ from Biesta. I will say that when you get really trained, you can learn to make a critique of the teacher's teaching you something, and gain a kind of transformative and transgressing talent to question, delegitimize, and even – if it is necessary – to smash down bad arguments that are used to maintain and defend societal power structures. You do not just live with and honor concepts. As an autonomous thinker you are free to reconstruct them, make some new, or even throw them out.

John: But what about the cliché: "I have successfully taught, but the students have not learned"?

Steen: Yes, Biesta's stressing that all the time, that you can teach without learning goals.

John: He also says you can learn without being taught, which I absolutely agree with.

Steen: Yes, of course, you can. Or else you couldn't play with your friends, come to sail a boat, ride a bike, and play soccer, or whatever.

John: As you know I read the book. I like what he said, but I struggle with the core notion of 'learnification'. And so quite at the moment, it's not going to rank high on my list of things to worry about because he's got a massive gap.

Steen: Biesta is in a way disturbing me a little bit, posing this either/or logic. Either you have a strong teacher, or you have your free right to interpret and to comprehend – and this voluntary constructionism, he doesn't like. And he even states that comprehension and interpretation, they are always there for constructive reasons, and I think that's wrong (Larsen 2017a).

In **hermeneutics**, one of the key problems is to understand and conceptualize how artwork might speak to you. If you are involved in understanding the artwork, you get in a dialectical movement where you are 'played by' the artwork and not in center of your own sovereign interpretation of the artwork. I think he simply misunderstands that. He sees only hermeneutics as a constructive logic from the subject's side. He seems not to know that hermeneutics is critical towards the subject-centered idea of interpretation, at least in the philosophical hermeneutics, that Hans-Georg Gadamer has given us. Have you ever read his most profound book: *Truth and Method* (Gadamer 1989/1960)?

John: No, I haven't read it.

89

Steen: If you had, you would probably agree with me that Biesta is not really contributing to a hermeneutical understanding of what goes on in education. He is lacking the dialectical approach to the dynamic interaction between text and interpretation, and he does not revitalize the concept of *Bildung*. His focus is different.

Why do we teach subjects?

John: I struggle with the answer to this question. Why do we teach mathematics, and science, and English? Why don't we teach completely different things like interaction styles, video games, other topics? How do you defend the canon?

Steen: I am not defending a canon nor do I have a straight answer to your question but I will try to offer you four different and hopefully qualifying replies to your important 'interrogation'.

The traditional answer is that we always have, ever since public schools were invented and designed their inner 'logic'. But that's not really an argument to refer to tradition. Besides that it is a practical division of labor and respecting the mental capacity of both teachers and pupils not to teach everything at the same time. Then follows the point of view that every subject in school has created an important world of its own that we ought not to cancel if we don't want to risk to lose our societal coordinates and mutual communicative substance.

On the top of these three points of references comes a more practical and functional credo that, for example, without mathematics, you get lost because people will cheat you when you go shopping, or you don't know how to build a house.

What do you have to say to these four 'offers'?

John: We have always taught subjects, yes, but they have changed quite a lot – with the demise of Latin and now geography, the rise of computing and coding, and environmental studies. I do not think that the limitations of teachers to teach many subjects is convincing as a reason for any particular subject dominance (e.g., it could as well be asking them to go deeper into video gaming or tiddlywinks, but this is not an argument for the teaching of these subjects). Yes, I can see your claims about risks to "our societal coordinates and mutual communicative substance" and this is the claim that many dictators have used to justify their choice of content in schools. Finally, I can see the need for defensible levels of competency to not be cheated, and so on, but this requires about a 12-year-old understanding of mathematics and English – so why the high school subjects?

Steen: Yes, but of course most of us use mathematics all the time and also sciences, at least at a low level.

John: Well, it's very low levels. Most adults use very low levels of mathematics. Especially when you compare the depth taught across the years in high schools.

Steen: Yeah, and you do some accounting when you check your bank account. But you could say that's a very poor argument. Isn't it?

John: Well, it's not a very poor argument. It's an argument about why you shouldn't go beyond about an age 10 to 12 level of mathematics.

Steen: Another argument is present when it comes to teaching and learning English language. For example, from a Danish point of view, if you don't know English or another big 'world' language, it is rather complicated to travel, and you risk not being able to interact with many people in the global world. Besides, you have a hard time understanding media, international politics, and tensions and conflicts in the world outside Denmark.

John: Well, yeah. I mean, you're not very convincing, Steen. I travel a lot and know no Danish, Mandarin, and so on.

Steen: So that's what the normal argument would be.

John: I know, and I agree with that because you're talking about the minimum level to survive. Look particularly at high schools, where a lot of the stuff I learned in mathematics and I'm sure you learned in mathematics we don't need to survive as an adult.

Steen: You needed it because you became a statistician.

John: In my area, I know I need this depth. But in terms of surviving as an adult, you don't need it.

Steen: No, but I think that we cannot reduce the raison d'être of all subjects within education to pure survival.

John: Yes, but surely that is the excitement. I hear the claims that we need to do x subject because by understating x we learn the beauties of x and learn why it is that x is worth learning; the claim that there is precious knowledge we should be exposed to as part of being an educated citizen. And so I wonder how you philosophers solve this problem because I can't.

Certainly, too many justifications for why these and not those subjects are tautologous – they start with the subjects and they support and justify their existence. Then typically, what is there already is defended and nothing new shall venture into this canon. Just look at the subjects privileged in admission to university and thus often exit exams from schools – what does this tell students – there are privileged subjects and others – meat and vegetables!

I see the argument that students should be introduced to different types of thinking, experience, and knowledge, but in a time-limited program this does not answer the question, why this and not that? I hear the argument that by subjects that lead to students knowing the answer why this and not that are favored – but to me that justifies ping-pong and computer games.

I hear the claims that we should develop the multiple intelligences (Gardner 1983), have students develop critical analyses, read Freire's critical pedagogy (Freire 1970/1968), but I still wonder why we choose the subjects and content we (still) teach in our schools. Surely there are multiple ways to be excellent, and the answer for a student who is to become a barista, painter, or water polo coach is not high-level mathematics, chemistry, history, or music. Maybe some degrees of, but that is not what is privileged in so many of our upper levels in high school.

Steen: The American philosopher Richard Rorty was right when he said that philosophy was important to **strengthen the eternal communication of mankind** – and of course to make it possible at all (Rorty 1989, 1999). And I think that mathematics, literature, language, and all the other subjects, they all contribute to this communication credo. Besides, Rorty did hope that close contact to literature could prevent us from being cruel. A kind of a moral defense of ethics of *Bildung*.

John: If you mean the ways of thinking via reasoning, critical thinking, and other argumentative manners from a more philosophical perspective, yes – that is, teaching the 'knowing how' but there is a 'knowing that'. Maybe, what I hear you saying is that we need to have a deep dive into religion?

Steen: You also have to know about religion in a scientific way, not in a confessional way. But we don't need confessions in school, if you're not attending a Catholic, a Hindu, or a Muslim school, and have chosen this more or less voluntarily.

John: No, no. That's fine.

Steen: Basically, if you are in kind of a state school and get educated in a municipality somewhere in the country, you do not expect to listen to or honor confessions. That should be your private faith and not a part of the state apparatus.

John: I agree with that.

Steen: In theocratic totalitarian regimes, religious faith is a mandatory 'discipline' (think, for example, of Iran). And if a country like Turkey wants to become a part of the EU, the Turkish president has to ensure that freedom of expression and religious freedom – even the right not to believe in any religion – exists and is protected by the state apparatus.

     The school subjects have changed through the times. Beginning in school in the mid-1960s, the girls were sewing and knitting as the women they were supposed to become, and we boys were doing something with trees, saws, and hammers, brought up as a little men and potential carpenters. And in the very old days, you had the seven liberal arts in the universities. The subjects have indeed changed.

John: Oh, they have. Like I told you, I'm not a great fan of curriculum debates. I'm delighted people do, however. But it's because I know too little about it and I see that most of the arguments are cosmetic around the edges. And most of the arguments are "How do you put more stuff in?", because the requirements of schools now are dramatic.

     I also know Michael Porter's work on curriculum alignment across US states and districts (Porter et al. 2009). On a scale from 1 (perfect) to 0 (none) he rated the many math and reading curricula and the average was 0.10 – what one district argues is precious knowledge is not the same as the next district – and in all cases the math and reading people proclaim that their curricula is right – it expressed the core, necessary, and right sequence – but there is no such notion if the alignment is this low!

Steen: What I don't understand now is why we don't have a very strong sociology subject in school. Because sociology deals with social bonding, how you receive recognition, how you contact and maybe even provoke or irritate other people, how we have proximity, distance, closeness, norms, habits, etc.

John: Yes, I can see this claim, particularly given what is happening across the US.

Steen: I think that we all have to know and to discuss how we respect and secure rights, equity, the environment, etc. How we protect the welfare state and how we embed our ideas and visions in institutions and all that, it means also a basic knowledge of social interaction, social communication, social skills, and interacting – and how to perceive conflicts between cultures, and to handle conflicts between individuals. Basically, you ought to have a much stronger sociological training and maybe also sociology as a major subject in school.

Maybe we should still maintain (some of) the subjects so the youngsters get the chance to gain a vivid access to society's understanding of itself and at the very same time fertilize the option that they dare to transgress it in new and formerly unseen ways.

On the road to 'pedagogical nihilism': has the dogma 'learn to learn' become more important than to know something substantial?

John: No, I want both, and see the nexus is strong between learning to learn and learning something.

Steen: In my country, some university and school leaders start saying, "Well, it's not important what we learn. It's important that we learn to learn." That's what I call pedagogical nihilism (Larsen 2016a).

John: I don't agree with that. This is going back to Michael Polanyi's distinction between 'knowing how' and 'knowing that' (Polanyi 1962). I know how to ride a bike but I may not know the physics of how I ride it (the 'knowing that' part). Similarly, I want students to have multiple strategies of learning, and apply these learning strategies to knowing that.

In many senses, this is akin to some of the first reviews of my book that said I did not take into account the sociological, social cultural nature of the classroom (Snook et al. 2009).

Steen: That's also my critique.

John: Although, I said at the start of the *Visible Learning* book that I wasn't going to deal with all these questions but focus more on the achievement questions. But many were not happy, demanding that I write the next book on the sociology of learning and similar claims. My answer is that others can and are doing this and the reader can balance their reading across disciplines (particularly when I am far from qualified to write a sociology book on achievement, but an avid reader of these claims).

The power question and the role of the parents

Steen: So how do you view, in this respect, the claim of Michel Foucault – the famous French philosopher and historian of ideas, who was born in

1926 and died of AIDS in 1984 – that whenever there's knowledge, there is power? In the French language the two are audibly interrelated: *savoir* (knowledge) and *pouvoir* (power) (see, e.g., Foucault 1980).

John: Exactly, expressed with a **pleonasm**: Power is powerful in schooling, and ever present.

Steen: Does this imply that there is nothing called pure knowledge isolated from the question of power in schooling?

John: Yes, and I have no trouble with power as long as it's transparent, understood, and appropriate. And to say that teachers don't have power, or to say that supervisors don't have power, ignores the obvious and gets you into huge troubles. The student doesn't have the same power as the teacher, which is why we have an obligation to be even more moral, just, fair, and accountable for the nature of impact we have on our students.

Steen: I think you're right here, because there has been a period, in which there was, maybe, so much doubt and even self-hatred among teachers that they would not even acknowledge that they themselves played a part of the power game.

John: In the same way – and this is one of my frustrations with teachers – they are the best, of any profession I know, about denying their expertise.

Steen: And they deny their own role in the power play, too. How can that be?

John: Partly, I think this is because teachers are engaged in a nurturing profession, that they are kind and nice people, and they want to give the credit for their impact to the students. The students invested, the students engaged, the students critiqued, the students completed this fine work.

Steen: You're also very often playing the role of a social pedagogical worker, a nurse, or a standing helper. Maybe even a parental substitute . . .

John: Exactly, it is part of my being as a teacher to say to my student, "Wow. Look what you do. Isn't it great you have agency to do what you do. Look at what you learned." And we never say, "I caused that."

Steen: Nope.

John: But they did cause a lot of this learning. A fundamental message of *Visible Learning* is that teachers can be powerful change agents – they do cause change and improvement. By denying it we create an enormous political problem, because every time we deny our expertise, we give away that power, and others then circumvent us and abrogate the power to them (we decided the curriculum, the assessment, the rules of schooling). And teachers are bypassed. My fundamental platform here in Australia is to reintroduce the power of educator expertise back into the equation of influence.

Steen: I have another argument to add. If you are a professional dentist or what can we say . . . an automotive mechanic repairing a car . . .

John: . . . or an electrician . . .

Steen: Yeah, you'd never ever ask people to bring in the parents to sit in and tell you what to do with the dentist work or with the combustion engine. But the teachers never seem to be able to get rid of the 'customers' – the students and the parents – and as a schoolkid you quite often have to bring your dad and mom with you to school. And now and then, the students' parents, they 'play' what you would call in volleyball, 'social volleyball', meaning they don't know even know how to play basic volleyball. They just think they can enter the track and play volleyball. But volleyball is a very technical game, and you have to know different lifting and smashing techniques. They tend to forget or underestimate real expertise in volleyball – and in the school. So they think that they can go beyond that and just have meanings and points of views, giving bunches of ideas to these teachers, telling them what to do, because they are engaged in their children's upbringing. I think that one problem – even though it, of course, also could be necessary now and then – is that we have invited the parents too frequently into the schools, so that the expertise is always challenged from the 'consumer' level, meaning by the parents. What do you think about this problem?

John: I wanted to ask you a question back on that because, unlike the electrician and the dentist, education doesn't stop in the school.

Steen: You're right.

John: And so, there is a role for parents. We know legally that the notion of 'in loco parentis' that we had years ago is now not the driving notion of teachers. We have an obligation to parents, but sometimes we involve parents in not so productive ways. We did a study where we looked at parents involved with homework, and the more the parents are involved in homework, particularly in a surveillance role, the less the effective the homework.

Steen: Not in the higher middle class, because it will only the help the kid to help him- or herself and stimulate the development of critical and autonomous skills.

John: Yes, there can be wide variation in homework help. Too many higher middle classes enact 'homework help' by employing tutors that often end up doing the homework for the students.

Steen: What?

John: They employ tutors, and tutors, as we know, do the homework for the students.

Steen: Yes, this happens, I guess. And the private enterprise for educational homework services is growing wild.

John: That's why my view is that there is an expertise in teaching that tutors and many parents don't have – and that is expertise in teaching. Here's my fundamental problem, why should students be advantaged and dis-advantaged because of the skills of their parents to be teachers for their children? And there is a moral dilemma. If the parents can, then I'm delighted. When they can't, we a have a responsibility.

We worked with the five poorest schools in New Zealand, and we followed them and their students through four years (Clinton & Hattie 2005). They went through 100 different interventions, and the one that worked the most effectively was placing computers in the homes. At the end of the first year, we said to the five schools, "Placing computers in the home is not the answer." They were angry with us to the point where we close to being fired as evaluators. But we said, "What happened is you hired ex-teachers to go into the homes to teach the parents and the students how to use the computers." And the effect was the parents learned the language of teachers. They learned how to talk to teachers. It could've been tiddlywinks or volleyball. It wasn't the computers. It was learning how to interact with teachers. Many of these parents did not have such good experiences or memories of their own school days, and talking to teachers (many of whom were from a different class level, were quite disciplined in their teaching and selves) was a frightening step. And what do you talk to them about, how to phrase the discussion and interaction, and how to query, delve deeper, and understand their answers and jargon. This broke down by speaking to the teachers in the home about the computers.

We also interviewed every single one of those parents as the students started school at age five, and one of the questions we asked them was "What is your ambition for your child when they leave school?"

The majority said, "When they leave school, we want them to go into university." We interviewed those parents when their students went from primary school to high school, same parents, same students, and every single one of them said, "I want them to get a job." You cannot tell me, across those 5,000 students, that some couldn't have got on to university. We have taken away those parents' ambitions, and it is a major role of parents to have those ambitions. Our job is to support those ambitions and not constrain them. But those parents did not know how to help their students, although every one of them wanted to. They trusted us to do it better than themselves, and in this case we failed them.

Is it important to teach and learn specific subjects in school?

How is it possible to learn without being taught?

Has the content-less dogma 'learn to learn' become more important than to come to know something substantial?

How can parents play an important role in school life?

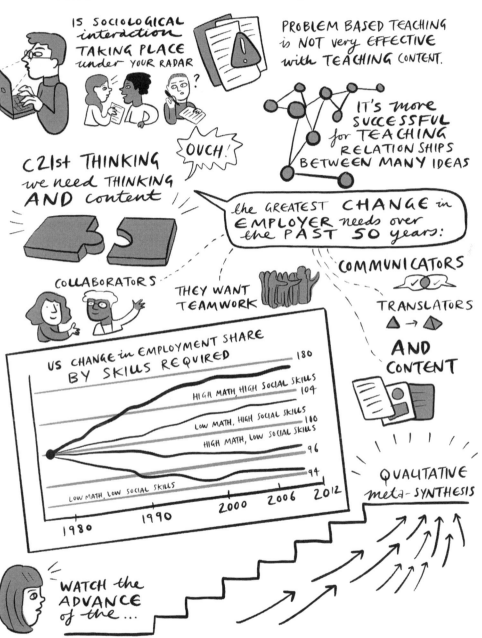

V. HOW NOT to OBJECTIFY
the STUDENTS and PUPILS you are STUDYING

IS SOCIOLOGICAL *interaction* TAKING PLACE under YOUR RADAR

OUCH!

PROBLEM BASED TEACHING is NOT very EFFECTIVE with TEACHING CONTENT.

IT'S *more* SUCCESSFUL *for* TEACHING RELATIONSHIPS BETWEEN MANY IDEAS

C 21st THINKING we need THINKING AND content

the GREATEST CHANGE in EMPLOYER needs over the PAST 50 years:

COLLABORATORS

THEY WANT TEAMWORK

COMMUNICATORS

TRANSLATORS

AND CONTENT

US CHANGE in EMPLOYMENT SHARE BY SKILLS REQUIRED

180

HIGH MATH, HIGH SOCIAL SKILLS — 104

LOW MATH, HIGH SOCIAL SKILLS — 100

HIGH MATH, LOW SOCIAL SKILLS

96

94

LOW MATH, LOW SOCIAL SKILLS

1980 1990 2000 2006 2012

QUALITATIVE *meta*-SYNTHESIS

WATCH the ADVANCE of the ...

Steen: When I read your work, it's like you have the teachers here and you have the students there. But what goes on in the class, or around the class, before and after the lessons, is also a question of manifold social interaction in a group of students. And it means that this whole sociological aspect, socializing the group, socializing people, moving in and out of the classroom, informal learning taking place outside the school's threshold must be taken into consideration. You may get more or less recognition for your correct answers or for your ability to criticize a teacher, or even to come up with another expectation that he or she doesn't know of so that you might be transformed to a supplementary extra mini-teacher; that is, a pupil helping the teacher (Larsen 2017b).

So, there are all kind of things, or maybe alternatives or other authorities, all these different logics, all these sociological logics, that you have to reflect upon doing your *Visible Learning* studies and theory. Is sociological interaction taking place under your radar?

John: No, not at all. I tried to do a meta-analysis of the classroom observation research, but I did not succeed, as it was hard to define the outcomes and effect-sizes. But I have completed a more traditional review of this literature. It is no surprise to note that the dominant mode remains the teacher in front of the class. Teachers talk, teachers orchestrate, teachers are dominant. Is that desirable? It's not necessarily bad at all but it's not the only way. At the moment, I am part of a big project where we are looking at innovative learning environments (Imms et al. 2016), which used to be called open-plan classes. In fact, my son is a teacher in a class of 90 students, three teachers, and I'm fascinated with these classrooms and when that works, it's beyond stunning in terms of what happens, the kind of interactions you're talking with. It is almost impossible to stand at the front and talk, orchestrate, or be dominant.

You have to learn to work with and trust other teachers planning, working together, and not 'owning' students. The 'we' more than the 'I' dominates. They need to create more collaborative tasks and activities; teach the students to be more interdependent but know when best to seek help; construct opportunities to go into the pit of now knowing and how then to work out the right problem to be solved; and enable students to become more aware and reflective of their own learning progress.

The innovative learning environments are certainly not the norm, about 10% to 15% of schools at best are like that. Not all teachers can cope, or have learned to work together, trust each other's planning, and we should never underestimate their skills to use pot plants, filing cabinets, and bookcases to create their own cocoons.

My interest in those classes is the nature of how students go about learning, what they do when they make mistakes and, quite frankly, it's a heck of a lot more exciting than the traditional classroom, whereas, as you said, most students know by age eight their place in the classroom. They turn straight to the teacher.

Steen: And then you have problem-based project studies and group work, prescribed by the institution and self-organized by the students. When I started studying at Roskilde University Centre in 1978, we also had these kinds of internal evaluation sessions where we were reading the other neighbor project group's work, and they were reading ours and it was, like, a school in exercising public criticism.

John: Exactly.

Steen: And we were developing all kind of paper writing and student activities besides the class, far overrating the program.

John: It's no different for my PhD students. They read each other's stuff before I see it. Wow, what a community this helps create. I find it fascinating that even at the PhD level we rarely teach them the skills of critique of others – and they will need it if they become academics marking assignments, commenting on these drafts, reviewing articles.

Steen: We were organizing it ourselves.

John: Okay, so, let me ask you a question. Why is it, then, that project-based learning has a 0.15 effect-size?

Steen: Do your figures really 'say' so? Well, I cannot understand nor explain that 'fact'.

John: Yeah, but that's my point, Steen. We need to understand why it is so low, as it doesn't make sense.

Steen: It doesn't make sense. You'd think it should have a higher effect.

John: It should have a higher effect for all the reasons you say, and my frustration is that educators talk about what should happen and confuse it with what did happen. Project-based learning is our most notorious failure, and so my interest is why it doesn't work and that's what we've been working on.

Steen: But, first of all I don't know if your effect 'machine' is 'catching' all that counts and takes place in mutual project study groups. Besides, I think that the cultural settings of the late 1970s and the late 2010s are very different. Forty years ago, many students were reading and dreaming about and working for radical changes of society (Larsen 2017c). Right now, nearly no one thinks about the radical change of capitalism in my country, even though we have to face all these sustainability problems, climate crises, rising inequalities, financial crisis, ruthless and fierce capitalist exploitation, harsh nationalism, and heavy migration (refugees, asylum seekers, poor people looking for a better life . . .), etc. But people are as, for example, a social group of students, not a counter block of resistance.

John: I have a different opinion although I'm sure you're right.

Steen: One dominant tendency is that we see individuals competing with one another to get success in the limited labor market with fewer jobs than there were before.

John: Correct, and too often these competing skills are learned in the classroom.

Steen: And computers have come in, and the algorithms, and big data. So, it is estimated that approximately 800 million jobs will be gone in 20 years worldwide. I think that, when we were living in those days, in the late 1970s, fond of this self-organized study process, we probably also thought gradually more of the power bastions of society would be taken over . . .

John: And maybe you should have.

Steen: . . . and made to dissolve and disappear but it really didn't happen.

John: No, that's not going to happen. How are we going to keep mum and dad in the workplace and not have merely professional babysitting?

Steen: Of course, you have to have professional babysitting.

John: And we have to make good use of that time. But let me come back to problem-solving and, again, part of what we do here is we say problem-solving should be successful. But we don't need to do another study to show it's pretty much a failure.

And so what we looked at were the reasons why it doesn't work, and we developed this model from our Science of Learning work, of seeing learning as involving moving from surface to deep to transfer.

By surface, I mean the information, the ideas, the facts, the content, and by deep I mean the relation between ideas, the higher-order understanding, the bringing together of many ideas, and seeing patterns. At the deep level there can be strategies for self-monitoring and self-regulation, and extending and transferring the ideas to apply in new situations or contexts. Both are powerful, and the deep very much depends on acquiring the surface, so it is a matter of proportion and when to focus on one or the other, and when on both together.

And what I did is I looked at the effects of problem-solving at the surface learning and at the deep learning phase. And the breakthrough came through Filip Dochy and his team's work in Switzerland and France (Dochy et al. 2003). What he showed is that problem-based learning in first-year medical schools has an effect-size of 0 to negative. But problem-solving in fourth-year medical schools has an effect-size of 0.40 and that was the clue.

And what we found, and published, is that, if problem-solving is about the facts, the content, then it's a failure. If it's about the relationships between the ideas, then the effect-size rises to about 0.50.

Here's the problem. So many people who introduced problem-solving often do so with a religious zeal, claim it is the answer to everything, introduce it far too early, and never teach or check to see that the students have the content that they will use to problem solve.

So, it can work, it does work, and we need to better understand *when* in the learning cycle it works.

Steen: Actually, my argument is a little bit parallel because, being not quite as old as you (born in 1958), in retrospect I am also quite critical towards what happened to the 1968 movement – as we call the movement and the quest for radical cultural political changes in Europe 50 years ago – when they got success. Self-organized project work, problem-solving, and self-learning became parts of the university structure at the so-called progressive institutions, which did not always pay respect to deeper knowledge and the important role of teaching. But of course we have to know something on the basis of which we could do experiments and engage in self-organized study activities.

John: My criticism of the current education system is that it is too much focused on the content and knowing lots. I would argue 90% of the tasks students are asked to do in classes can be successfully accomplished by knowing lots – it is still too much about the facts and the content, as it was 200 years ago. Indefensible.

Now, here's the problem for you as a philosopher. For people who succeed in our society, knowledge and processing are inter-related. For people who don't succeed, they don't have the knowledge to succeed.

The other thing that stunned me is . . . there's a graph, I saw recently of employment rates for math and science graduates in the US from the 1980s to today (Deming 2017). The employment rate has continued to grow for those students with high math and high social skills. Similarly – no surprise – low math, low social skills, it's a disaster.

Here's the fascination. Lower math and higher social skills are employable. Higher math, low social skills are not.

The biggest change over the last 20 years is employers saying, "If you don't have the ability to work in groups, to translate, to collaborate and communicate, I can't teach you those things. I want you to have math or science skills but also the social skills to work in teams."

And what I find fascinating is how we take these students who are lower in math and we track them into the lower streams. But they are employable. We take these students with lower social skills but higher math and put them in the higher tracks, they're not employable.

Makes you seriously question the value of ability grouping. Makes you seriously question the tasks and assessment we give to students that privilege individual success. Makes you wonder why we don't see students with higher content knowledge working with others, learning how to teach others, and developing social sensitivity skills to work in teams.

And so my question is, when I go into your school in Denmark or my school here in Melbourne, and look at upper high school math and science and I look at what students are doing – do I see them working alone, do I see them doing assignments alone, do I see them doing a test alone, do I see any translation, do I see any communication to peers about what they know and understand, do I see any collaboration, particularly with non-math or non-science people? If not, it is likely these students are not employable.

We're killing these students because that tradition of the last 30 years focused on knowing lots, separating out those who know lots and privileging them. This is so dominant in the current system and it's killing these students. Worse, too often these students love the content. Nothing wrong with that. Just not enough. We need to privilege building these social skills as well, entitling those who may not be the highest content students to be exposed to higher math and science, and change how we structure tasks and assignments to bring both higher content knowledge and higher social sensitivity skills.

Now, I'm not a fan of treating these social skills or capabilities as separate capabilities. I'm not a great fan of all these 21st-Century Skills stuff. I'm not a fan of what Korea and Singapore are doing, introducing them as separate curricula area. It's got to be done *within* the context of the content.

I'm very much a traditionalist in that sense.

How to maintain the quality of education at the university

Steen: I don't know what happened here, but in Denmark, for example, some of the very good ideas, like the progressive feedback interaction between students, disappeared. So did the written and thorough evaluation of your master dissertation made by your supervisor and the external censor. Many very good things from the old system simply disappeared. As another example, oral defense of your dissertation is not possible any longer at Aarhus University, where I work.

John: Not here either.

Steen: And until one year ago it was possible. So, for example, if you write a master's degree paper, you've written 80 to 100 pages, and it was normal to go to an exam for one hour to defend it. Dense and challenging questions, real academic discussions, and good talks. I remember that many of those exams were at a very high level. But it has disappeared. All to save money.

John: So, we have – you're right. The efficiency claims. We still have an oral before you submit.

But I have to confess . . . and I put my head of school hat on. The major reason we do that is to make sure the supervisors have done their job.

Steen: Ah yeah, to control the supervisor.

John: The biggest problem in academia is supervision. It's not students. Twenty percent of academics supervise 80% of the students. We have a lot of people here . . . and in most universities who don't supervise. I need to ask, though, when do we train a person to supervise?

Steen: No, you don't do it. More often it is supposed to happen 'naturally'.

John: For so many their only training is their own experience as a thesis student themselves.

Steen: I love supervising.

John: So do I! You know, I'm very proud, this year my 200th thesis student graduated.

Steen: Yeah, I saw you had 191. . . now it's 200.

John: My biggest contribution in academia are my students. What a weird and wonderful world it is – they pay to come to complete a thesis, they deeply and intensely study an important topic, they teach you about work you might never have seen yourself, they write and publish, they work with you to critique your and their own ideas – and I get paid for this. Luxury, indeed.

Steen: Yeah, but they reduce the number of hours that you're supervising. They want us to supervise people in groups, which is stupid.

John: But the trouble is prescribing how to supervise. Why would you prescribe it? Some people do brilliantly in groups. I do not. I prefer the one by one. Even though the students work out how they work in groups, how to critique each other's work, and given moral and personal support to each other.

But I've worked out how to do it . . . go back to my son. He taught five years in a regular classroom and then he came and said to me one day, "Dad, I don't want to be a better teacher . . ." Which is kind of not the thing you say to me.

I said, "What are you getting at?" He said, "I don't want to be a better teacher in that kind of school." So he went to a brand-new open-plan school, and he has now been in two of them for the last four to five years. He works with 90+ students and two other teachers and his argument is, "Don't tell anyone," he said, "I do a third less planning."

He has learned to trust others, to work with other experts, and to share the thrills of teaching in a tram.

Why is it a secret in education that you can be efficient? I have another person I'm shadowing at the moment and she's in her second year in a regular classroom. She spends every waking minute writing resources, creating materials, marking students' work. And I know in a couple of years' time she's probably going to leave teaching, arguing that no one supported her. How come she thinks being busy is being a good teacher? Where is the support for collegiality in the job?

I think Larry Cuban, he is a superb historian of education, I think he's got it right. For the last 200 years we've become more and more efficient at being busy (Cuban 1984).

Steen: That is a great description of the present paradoxical madness. And the school teachers are destined and doomed to create something that looks like an ex ante and ex post business plan and to feed the system with their educational data (Larsen 2019b). In Denmark, the system is baptized 'the learning platform' (in Danish: *læringsplatform*).

John: Yeah, but my fascination is that when teacher teams work, it's stunning. But it inevitably fails. I recall a recent case in an innovative team school.

Three teachers, they had 90 year-one, year-two, and year-three children in one class. Brilliant. It just . . . it was a model to esteem. Then they appointed a new person to the group who didn't like that kind of teaching. And she destroyed the team work almost instantly. All you need is one solo player and it's over. That class has now gone to rack and ruin.

And, that's the problem, the traditional model of solo business dominates. Teachers love to share what they do, how they work, as if this is the way for all. They love to be on committees to create and modify curriculum, and too often they end up adding more and more to the curriculum as they each add their own content, barely negotiating to remove or replace much.

It's like when people ask me to go on curriculum committees. I refuse unless the minister agrees to allow the committee to take half the stuff out.

As a consequence, I'm on one curriculum committee right now (in one of the European countries). But unfortunately, the minister has changed and the new one wants to put more stuff back in again! We don't need half the stuff.

And my classic question is: What did you learn in history or English when you were ten?

Steen: It was a really bad education system we had in those days.

John: You aren't answering my question.

Steen: In history, we were learning about kings and queens and, you know, Danish history.

John: My point is, you could have learned anything in History, and you'd still be who you are today. You could learn about those kinds and queens now in moments. But I bet those teachers would argue black and blue that what they were teaching, the content, was critical to your future!

Steen: Probably, but in those days, they just did what they did without much reflection.

John: And has it changed today? In too many classrooms and systems, over 90%, students can be successful by just knowing lots – becoming Mr. Google or Mrs. Siri. Really, is this the purpose of education?

Steen: But when Mr. PISA himself, the director of OECD's office for Education and Skills, Andreas Schleicher, in the prologue to the important policy paper *Four-Dimensional Education, The Competences Learner Need to Succeed* (see Fadel et al. [eds.] 2015) proclaims that we don't have to know things today and we'll not be celebrated (or hired) if we do, because the machines know everything, we have to cry out loud: No, it is not true. First of all, informational machines do not know anything, only people do. Besides, only people who know how to interpret, create, and criticize knowledge can understand and change the systems in which they are living. Knowledge, thinking, reflections, and autonomy are interrelated concepts and normative leading stars in and for education. Therefore, I guess, I cannot completely subscribe to your critique of 'the knowing-lots', even though you often might be right in criticizing established top-down infusion of old and dead packages of 'knowledge'.

John: But I agree that among those who become proficient in a domain there are high levels of overlap between the surface and deep, the knowledge and the strategies of learning. Indeed, merging them could be seen as an aim of schooling, but in developing this knowledge and skill there is a pathway from gaining the knowledge, to relating the ideas, to extending or transferring to new problems or situations.

How not to objectify students and pupils

Steen: But concerning the danger in objectifying students and pupils while you are doing empirical research, my basic worry is not yet vaporized, so I dare to maintain my question. Why did you never talk to pupils and students about their learning experiences? Why do you first and foremost want the teachers to know their impact, but you choose not to listen to or reflect upon the other important actors in schools and institutions: the pupils and the students?

I have a worry that every time you go into upscaling in data you risk losing control over the ideographic moments, and you make these nomothetic generalizations (Larsen 2017b, 2019a).

John: Well, no, wait a moment. We spend an inordinate amount of time talking and listening to students and then notions of what they understand by impact, their notions of what it means to be a learner in this class. But if you are asking about the meta-studies then yes we could have started with the students' views about impact. It just turns out there is very little research asking the students, which is a massive gap.

Steen: Yes, that's what I think.

John: I'm a great supporter of the student voice notion even though I think it's become a little bit too grandiose, where people think student voice is legitimate because students said it. Student voice needs prompting, needs scaffolding, needs teachers who can show they are listening and understand what the students are saying, need to be taught and developed with the students. Student voice and agency involves teaching students to have the meta-cognition to know how to use various learning strategies; to be assessment capable learners; to understand how to give, seek, receive, and understand feedback; and to learn where best to move next in their learning. This requires them developing their voice and agency in these processes, evidence with an increased investment, a curiosity and joy of learning, and progress through to achievement

Steen: But it seems to an important part of the whole story to acknowledge that students and pupils indeed have a voice and can tell us how the learning processes function and are 'felt' and how the 'learned' get inscribed in and 'donate' meaning to their existential-ontological perspective (Batchelor 2008).

John: Oh, yeah, and I think it's critical we understand their voice. One of the major points of education is to give the students a narrative about learning, and what they've learned, and the vocabulary of understanding. An important question for me is "How are we to build a narrative of learning?" Is that also what you ask?

Steen: I don't really know, John. As you know, I'm not a great fan of the learning concept per se (Larsen 2014a).

John: But I love to build a narrative of learning and understanding. But that's not where I started because that's not where the literature was at. I wanted to look at how you synthesize what we know. And there are huge gaps in the literature, and one is about student voice. Yes, there are researchers now working on this topic, but it is pretty underdeveloped.

   Of course it is a limitation that I did not in *Visible Learning* look at classroom interactions or at what the students do. Not because it's not important. Because I didn't do it. Others can do that. And I want to stand on their shoulders. My whole argument is about how we can impact that learning. How can we recognize that some teachers are very good at causing learning?

   I am not a fan of the notion that the teacher is a guide on the side or is a facilitator because many students need expertise to learn. They need deliberate interventions. And we have many great teachers doing this. My interest was, "How can we best look at the influences on students?" As I say in the book 10, 15 hundred times, the biggest source of variance is the students, not the teachers. The biggest source of variance that any of us have any control over in the school are the teachers, and that variability is of special interest to me.

Steen: It probably also has to do with your overall method that you want to pile up knowledge of already existing research.

John: Yes, it is research based on meta-studies. There are many other kinds of excellent research that can complement, contest, and be used to build bold theories about what best influences students.

Steen: And on behalf of this meta-research concept and on the basis of all this data on 250 million students – or how much you have collected by now – you claim that you have covered the field.

John: And as I've critiqued myself in the book – in my jocular moments, I call it distance-analysis because I'm a long way away from the kid. There are so many influences, although the 200+ that I have identified are a pretty good coverage. It is understanding the interaction between them that will never stop.

Steen: Why is the *Visible Learning* program primarily directed towards rating and stimulating the teacher's efforts and not centered on the students – their lives and learning activities?

John: No, no. Be careful.

Steen: I sense a risk that the pupils become objectified. Is the role of learning subjects in *Visible Learning* research to become objects?

John: No, no. The *Visible Learning* program is different from the *Visible Learning* research. And if you look at the program, absolutely it's focused on students. It's the triangulation of teachers' information about students' growth, students' estimation of their own growth, and interrogating the artefacts of what they do. So it's very much focused on students – but the *Visible Learning* book is about a synthesis of research.

Steen: So you tend to make a differentiation between what other researchers are doing and collecting – and how you and your team gather knowledge in order to find possible correlations.

John: Sure, but I now have 15+ books based on the original *Visible Learning* research – most aiming to show the translation we have accomplished in classrooms with real students and real teachers. We have worked with over 100,000 teachers around the world, and the team has deep understandings of how to implement in various contexts with a myriad different type of students. I work with this team and get the data from what they do about implementation of these ideas.

Steen: But my worry is that if you objectify the pupils and students – and that must be a part of the *Visible Learning*, at least the book that you're writing, you call it distant learning or distant metered learning – or distant correlation logic building, or whatever you can call it.

John: Well, that's correct. Yeah, you're right.

Steen: And then you also know that can be open to criticism?

John: Of course, it is.

Steen: From, for example, **phenomenology, critical theory, hermeneutics, and theories based on the importance of agency and reflexive subjectivity** (Larsen 2015b, 2017c)?

John: Absolutely. No question. And my argument is that if you think that what I wrote was everything, it wasn't. I was quite specific. I'm looking at achievement. I'm not looking at emotion, or motivation, or satisfaction. I'm not looking at physical health. Those things are critical also.

Steen: Or the precious capacity to think, search new knowledge, and the will to become wiser (Larsen 2018b)?

John: Absolutely, and this is why we completed a meta-synthesis relating to this capacity to think.

In favor of qualitative research

Steen: I wonder if you have respect for and interest in qualitative research even though you primarily rely on quantitative data?

John: Of course I have incredible respect for this method, and some starting and fascinating interpretations are often present in qualitative research.

Steen: Great, and again it may be prejudices, that you have a somehow bad reputation, but among the Danish readers of your work, I know – researchers, students, and teachers – it is typical to think, "Hattie is not interested in qualitative research, for example, not in anthropological fieldwork. He's not listening to phenomenological life stories. He's reading people like things, objects, and figures."

John: I have one lifetime. I would love others to write those books, and I'll read them. I do.

Steen: Yeah, but do you think that'll build up your knowledge properly?

John: Sure. My biggest struggle is relating to the normative issues. We often privilege qualitative stories because they're written, and that's not good enough, particularly if they do not explain, lead to next best steps, or build models. It's like asking Nobel Prize winners why they became Nobel Prize winners. They may be wrong about why they got there. There may be other alternative views of how they got there. There is still an obligation to interpret. I know this is not the right approach, but with qualitative research the participant's stories and so on are the 'data' from which the interpretations are thus derived. Yes, there is more induction that I tend to like, but I can still read and see the author's story.

Steen: You are probably right. Everybody seems to be blind to their own life path.

John: I see little value in merely writing stories in the terms of 'this is what happened'. The greatest advance in literature reviews in the past ten years has been the advance of qualitative meta-synthesis. One of my favorite authors, Mary Kennedy, has some stunning deep, fascinating, and powerful interpretations from such methods; and this method also mitigates a deficit I often see in qualitative research – here's how to stand on the should of giants (Kennedy 2005). Too many qualitative studies do not know how to use prior qualitative research to sharpen their own research – as if this group is so unique, we have to start again.

Steen: There is also this Hegelian notion that the **owl of Minerva** is very clever at sunset, because then it thinks it knows all. But it couldn't know what would happen beforehand, and there is also a Kierkegaard quote in which he states that you have a better chance to know what your life was looking backwards to what it was, not while it was happening and you looked forward, but looking backwards, when it was lived (Hegel 1979/1807).

Is it important not to objectify in educational research – or is it an inevitable necessity?

Is the price for upscaling quantitative educational research that the individual pupils and students disappear?

Which ethical considerations do educational researchers have?

Is it not enough to come know a lot, but much more important to learn how to learn?

VI. WHAT is the ROLE of the TEACHER?

KNOW THY IMPACT BEGS moral PURPOSE QUESTIONS,

ASKS deeply ABOUT the CHOICE and VALUE of THE CONTENT,

and INVITES a BROAD RANGE of STUDENT OUTCOMES

'If A COMPUTER can REPLACE a TEACHER, get RID of THAT TEACHER.'

ARTHUR C. CLARKE

THERE are MANY LEARNING PROGRESSIONS to SUCCESS.

why TEACH HISTORY rather THAN MATH?

LET'S NOT JUST LOOK for ONE WAY, then HAVE MANY STUDENTS DERAILED because they WALK A DIFFERENT PATH.

EDUCATION is about 'LEARNING'

 HOW TO EXPERIENCE,

 HOW to BE CURIOUS,

 HOW to INVEST in MORE LEARNING.

THE COMBINATION between

COGNITIVE SKILLS,   SOCIAL SKILLS,
embodied THOUGHT,   UNCONSCIOUS embodiment,

AND MAPPING of THE WORLD

WE CREATE CULTURE EVEN when WE ARE IMMERSED in CULTURE; teachers CREATE CULTURES in THEIR CLASS.

SOME STUDENTS ACCEPT it and SOME rebel AGAINST it.

GIVES me a MUCH RICHER PICTURE of your WAY of thinking.

WE NEED to TEACH STUDENTS to do BOTH in desirable WAYS.

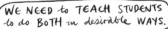

TEACHERS are MUCH more THAN facilitators.

THEIR ROLE is to ACTIVATE the LEARNING of PRECIOUS KNOWLEDGE

AND LEARN RESPECT for SELF and OTHERS.

Steen: I would advocate strong roles of real teachers. Even though you state that we have been all too much preoccupied with the role of the teacher, and not about learning.

John: No. I didn't say that. I said 'teaching'.

Steen: Okay, teaching. My idea is that we should invest more in the role of the teacher with a very good teaching capacity.

John: I agree with that.

Steen: We do also now and then have to criticize the mandatory learning ideology, seeing learning as the main focus of education and the solution to more or less everything (Larsen 2014a).

John: Of course, I've got to be careful when I use simplistic notions like "I care more about learning than teaching." But I ask you, if I went to Denmark, and I took a summary of all the professional learning offers in schools, I would bet that the majority it is about how to teach. It's about best practice. It's about listening to a teacher talk about how they teach. Instead, I want to emphasize the impact of that teaching.

Steen: But you also seem to be positive towards some of Gert Biesta's ways of writing and arguing. And he has this ongoing critique of the 'learnification' of education that we have touched upon many times already in our 'chat'. Do you find his critique relevant, maybe even convincing?

John: Yes, I very much enjoyed Gert Biesta's book *The Beautiful Risk of Education* (Biesta 2013), and his writings against 'learnification'. Let me outline what I see in his argument, and I would be interested in your reaction to this summary.

       He is strong that we should deplore the decline of the concept of education and the rise of its replacement, 'learning'. Note, he says the new language of learning: teaching facilitates learning, adult learning, lifelong learning, students construct knowledge, creating learning opportunities, developing the learning environment, the learning age, referring to students as learners, and the postmodern claim that we have reached the end of education, what else can be left but learning! His critique is that this misses the point of education, which is *not* that students learn but it is that students learn something, that they learn it for a reason, and that they learn it from someone. It undermines the role of the teachers who should be expected to bring something new to the educational situation, something that was not already there.

His main beef is that 'learnification' is turning education into a transaction in which the learner is the consumer, the teacher is the provider to meet the needs of the consumer, and education becomes a commodity. This presumes the consumer knows its needs, what they want to know, and this is highly questionable. Indeed, as I noted, Michael Young argues we should send children to school precisely to get that which they would not get if they did not go to school (Young & Muller 2013); and I would add, to appreciate why we teach and learn this rather than that. Schools are not merely technicist, effectiveness, and efficient, and should not sell themselves as easy, attractive, and exciting. Instead, Biesta argues, important educational questions about content and purpose should be seen as social and interpersonal questions, and not simply as questions of individual preference. He notes that education involves asking students difficult questions, can lead to disturbing challenges, involves taking risks and thus needing to build trust, to expose students to otherness and differences, and the bringing students into "presence of unique individual beings."

I certainly agree, and have implored that 'Know Thy Impact' begs these moral purpose questions, asks deeply about the choice and value of the content, and have continually argued for having a wide sense of purpose (including respect for self and others). Biesta is careful to say that learning is an okay concept, but overplayed. I would agree if it is the lip service we play to 'learning', but I want to go deeper and question the multiple meanings of learning, be clearer about the various (effective and ineffective) strategies of learning, and to ensure that learning is always placed relative to that which is to be learned.

I certainly admire Biesta's writings: they are crisp, clear, and confronting, and this is why he remains among the most influential scholars at the moment.

Steen: But if 'learnification' of education is a serious problem, how can you then promote learning opposed to teaching? In all your books and lectures you favor learning. I don't really understand you.

John: Gert's the kind of person who is miles ahead of the rest of us. Twenty years ago, he might have written about the overzealous attention to teaching. And he's right, that if we switch the pendulum to learning, we're going to have different problems. So, for me, it's getting that balance right. His new book overzealously reminds us of not making the pendulum swing too much, but I remind you that a focus of learning is for a reason — to enhance the experiences and outcomes for students. And perhaps, I have overstated the case towards the 'learnification'— using his word — notion, and hence want to try and get the balance right. But at the moment, in teacher education courses, in professional learning, we're so obsessed about how to teach. We use, instead, artefacts of students' work to demonstrate how teaching worked; to lead to debates about the impact of teaching, to better understand what the teaching meant for the students. We don't go to many professional learning sessions and learn about how teachers are thinking and making decisions as they teach or focus on students thinking and processing, and how they're understanding the material (or not). When we do analysis of lessons, we do content analysis. We don't do cognitive task analysis of lessons. We don't look at the nature of the thinking and processes that students need to successfully complete the work. We talk about how they should do it.

A current debate in Australia on progressions, we talk about how we can get a group of teachers to come together to decide on what the progressions our students should go through. Oh, my goodness! You're not going to find sufficient number of students who are going to fit their progressions. Instead, we need to map how students actually progress, and then allow for these multiple pathways to get to similar destinations.

How do you turn it around and say, "How do we understand how students progress?" Indeed, they progress, often depending on where they start, in so many different ways. Here's the analogy. If you're driving from Melbourne to Sydney, most people would go down Highway One. Some would go the coast road. Some would go the inland route. Some would start at a suburb in Melbourne: some at Williamstown, some at Moonee Ponds, and some in the Northern suburbs. There are multiple ways to progress to the same destination and any learning progression model must allow for this. But to inflict one set of learning progressions on every kid is criminal.

Steen: Okay. That's your point of view. But if teachers should, in a way, be more like learning facilitators, than strong teachers . . .

John: No. Facilitator is a terrible word.

Steen: You are right. It's definitely not a wonderful phrase. Here and there in your work, but even more during the chance we have had to exchange views and meet face to face, I have come to realize that you also have a kind of admiration for a classical teacher incarnating knowledge and loving the students.

John: Perhaps I – and we both – do think there is a romanticism in the notion of the teachers as an agent of improving the lives of students.

Steen: Maybe this teacher stands up as a kind of an ideal, or as someone you can look up to, having respect for her or his cunning and knowledge, piled up for more than 30 years, well read and a connoisseur of art and history, and also a professional when it comes to teaching. It seems to me that you, in your way of thinking, also accept a certain division of labor, and that means also to respect the teachers as professionals.

John: Absolutely.

Steen: And, therefore, when you start talking about a certain conflict between teaching and learning, I think that, in a way, you risk depriving the teachers of their primary skill of teaching, as teachers, and not only be there helping people how to learn from a servile 'learning agent'.

John: I hope not. It is the act of teaching that aims to lead to the learning – but the focus I want is more on the latter than the former. Of course, there is the act of teaching. We need to consider teachers as content specialists, as role models, as colleagues, as evaluators, and much more. Let me give you two cases. We looked at over 5,000 hours of transcripts of lessons. I was looking for examples to use in the article we're writing to illustrate when and how teachers taught students about *how* they thought, how they're thinking, how to get better at thinking. After 2,000 hours, we gave up. We couldn't find one.

Steen: But my idea is that if you have a very good philosophy teacher, for example, this philosophy teacher is not in himself that interesting, but his reading strategy, or his interpretation of a classical work, or his way to invite you into reading philosophy. . . . This teacher can tell you where Kant is making a mistake, or how he could be read in connection with his fellow men at that stage, what he is stating that Hume couldn't say or that Descartes was doing wrong. How did Kant lift up the concept of reason to a new sphere? A great teacher is pointing towards autonomous and daring interpretations, inviting you to open your horizon.

John: Yeah, but what about the student in the class that can't see and understand how you do that? I want the students to 'hear' how this philosophy teacher came to these decisions, how they reasoned, considered alternatives and critiques – the act of the learning. I can see you do it as you speak, I'm impressed. There are some noted people where you can hear them thinking aloud as they speak – what a luxury to be a student in their classes.

Steen: I guess that the good teachers, hidden from the eyes of the students, also see whether or not the subject needs a repetition or is crying out for an extra argument.

John: Sometimes experts are the worst teachers because they don't understand or they claim it is just 'common sense' and forget that because they are experts they have often overlearned many of the steps in their thinking.

Steen: You are right. It could be a problem. But if the teacher is just looking down at the book while she reads her manuscript from one end to the other, she might as well be replaced by a computer program. Real human beings deviate and are open to unforeseen exchanges and communication.

John: Absolutely correct. The science fiction writer Arthur C. Clarke once said, if a computer can replace a teacher, get rid of that teacher. Although I do note the amazing advances in robotics and AI in teaching. I watched a class being taught by a robot – and the students loved that there were few if any consequences if they got it wrong, they could ask the same question repeatedly without the eye rolls from other students, they could attempt and fail with no emotional response – often these relationship claims are what many argue is the essence of teaching, and it seems ironic that many students in this robot class liked the robot more than the teacher because there was no affect!

Also, this overlearning by experts is why some of our most successful teachers are not very good within teacher education.

Steen: You might be right. But it might also have to do with the selection procedures, mark differentiation, evaluation processes, and other power plays that the fleshy and living teaching is involved in and more or less voluntarily incarnate.

John: Too often the expert claims to tell what they think they did, and overlook the thinking processes that led to decisions to do this rather than that. They do not see the distinction between the knowledge and the comprehension of the knowledge, which is more often separate for novices but not so for experts, and they underestimate the deliberate practice they themselves had to become experts, expecting it quite quickly in new teachers. Further, they often can't see from a novice perspective. When you become a new teacher in your first year in training, I think the hardest struggle is to see the classroom through the eyes of a teacher and your students and not through the eyes of an ex-student. That's a skill, and that switch in identity is hardly ever taught. It's assumed.

Mary Kennedy wrote an article a few years ago that impressed me, where she said, a bit strongly, "You should never send a student out to a school in the first year of teacher education until you've taught them to see the class through the eyes of a teacher" (Kennedy 2005).

When you have teachers with the expertise to see the class thought the eyes of the students, it is impressive, it is a gift. We did a study – it was an accidental study – where 1,000+ adults (some parents, some not) were asked about who their best teacher was and why. It was interesting when we wrote up the article, as you're supposed to do a review of literature, right? The last study that we could find that asked about adults' perceptions of their best teacher was in 1941.

Steen: Okay!

John: Yeah, that was really surprising. And there are two things that dominated across those 1,000 adults. The best teacher was someone who turned you on to their passion, which is kind of the thing you're talking about, and/or a teacher who saw something in you that you didn't see in yourself (Clinton et al. 2018). Not one of those 1,000 adults talked about math, or history, or physical education. Not one of them. Now, that's not to say content's not important because you do those two things (passion and showing you see success in students) through content, through the passion. But that notion of having that skill to turn people on to your passion, to see something in you that you don't see in yourself, that to me is more of the essence of the teacher than the typical role model – of the content rich, behavior strong, imparter of knowledge.

Reading Gert Biesta on 'learnification' and teaching

Steen: Okay, let's now try to dig deeper into the newest Gert Biesta book: *The Rediscovery of Teaching* (Biesta 2017). We have already exchanged views on this important educational philosophical book that is definitely not a part of the empirical turn in education in which you seem – or seemed – to be embedded. His whole idea is that the teacher should leave the 'learnification' procedures and ideology behind and instead be engaged in producing possibilities for the pupil to become a real subject – that is, build an existential bridge to 'grown-up-ness' and a rich 'subjectiveness', as he labels his alternative.

John: Pity he has to denigrate the alternative with a horrible label. But I suppose that is why he invented 'learnification'.

Steen: Biesta's idea is that instead of having something that the students should live up to, certain standards, certain rules, certain regulations, like learning goals or competitive behavior, the challenge and mission of the educational institution is to liberate the pupil to become a human being, and also to allow the pupil or the student to interpret what's already there. So the individual existence is never living or being taught in isolation, but always as a subject stands in relation to other people, confirming your subjectivity, and to arguments, texts, and events, that the teacher has to open the pupil's and student's eyes towards.

John: So, what is his argument about why you do history rather than math?

Steen: I guess that Biesta would line up with Gadamer, and answer that you're 'always already' embedded in historical understandings and interpretations of what history is (Gadamer 1989/1960). That means that the society has already surrounded you in a contextualized way with certain narratives. You are brought up with narratives, for example, that Australia has a proud and rich history in which you stand, think, and 'breathe' . . .

John: Yes, but of course we need to question that history, and that is the aim of education.

Steen: But while we're already embedded in different narratives, we should not only have the fore-understanding and knowledge about them but also the power to question those narratives. And the teacher's role is to help to build up reinterpretation of standard values of normal interpretations so that pupils and students could also be liberated from them . . . meaning that they at the same time come to know about – that is, inherit – and transgress the tradition. That is the double idea and ambition of Gadamer and Biesta.

John: Go back a bit. You're saying that the role of schooling is to be liberating. That implies a future. Six-year-olds are six-year-olds. And I'm very Deweyian in the sense that a child's experience is now. I'm sure Biesta doesn't ignore that. The notion that I treasure is every six-year-old or a ten-year-old, they're living their life now. It is about them questioning now, not necessarily for their future. It is also about 'learning' how to experience, how to be curious, how to invest in more learning. This is why I have spent so much research time on 'learning' – far too much according to Biesta.

The notion is that there is a "Just Cause" as Simon Sinek (2020) has claimed. This is a specific vision about the future that does not yet exist, a future state so appealing that people are willing to make sacrifices in order to help advance toward that vision. My notion of the Just Cause for schooling is to create a learning environment where children want to come to learn, want to invest in learning, enjoy the mastery of learning, and where they are invited to reinvest in learning. We want schools to be places where children are taught precious knowledge, heritages of themselves and others, respect for self and others, and participate in the rule of law and fundamental premises of a democracy. Places where children want to explore, create, be curious, to relate and transfer ideas – as these are the very attributes we would want them to explore and exhibit when they are adults.

We do not create the future for children, they are creating their future now; they will critique, overturn current thinking, and create new futures. Our role is not to train people, equip students with skill sets, or in any way ask them to fit right into things as they are. We need moral outrage, compassion, and courage with the aim of collectively making goodness more reliable and sought after. The best way to do this is to create an environment in which information can flow freely, mistakes can be comfortably made, and teaching can be offered and received in such a way that all students feel safe. This notion of the Just Cause for schooling is rooted in our deep desire for children to enjoy childhood, as that is among the best predictors of learning how to enjoy being an adult and citizen.

Steen: I think that small students already know that they will become adults one day. So, you're always living in a now, directed to an unknown future. At the same time, this very now is influenced by the historical past. So the now (the 'contemporaneity') is actually a very complicated relation and full of tensions. The relation between history and the now is not a simple question of chronology, and one might say that the now has a relation to history that is not over yet and a future that is already beginning. And I think that, in the midst of the traditional chronological time logics in which we are living, it is possible to get inspiration and learn from thinkers like Kierkegaard and Gilles Deleuze. They both have the idea that instead of looking at your life as a series of chronological moments that always disappear behind you, the now (or the filled presence of deep moment, called *Kairos* in Greek) can be stretched, so it becomes a much broader perspective and a value in itself. This means that we possess another and much richer time concept than chronology, namely *Kairology*, as right-time philosophy, which has been conceptualized for thousands of years.

John: So how does that then work?

Steen: The idea is to establish and defend an alternative to the time concept that is too stressful and ever changing, giving most people the feeling that "We're always losing the moment" or "It's already too late." If you were given the right to reflect upon a future that's already beginning and a past that's not over yet, and we also acknowledged and felt time as a stretched out now, it would probably also change the role of teaching.

John: That makes good sense. But this is a great claim if I am 30 and have knowledge and experiences, and responsibility to see the future from greater heights. But if I'm 7, I probably have low levels of formal operational thinking, may be poor at imagining futures, and have lowly levels of moral judgments (at least if you follow Kohlberg and Gilligan; Kohlberg 1981; Gilligan 1982). How a 7-, 17-, and 30-year-old can process information about the world for their self and future is quite different. We need to be careful that these philosophers seem to assume a level of education and experience often beyond many school-age children. Hence, the importance, among other things, of teaching them how to optimally learn.

Steen: You are right, we must never forget that focus. One of my colleagues, Kristine Kousholt, made some observations in classes where the pupils go through the national testing, conducted by and contributing to the national test and thereby to the international PISA test system (Kousholt 2016). If you take second-year boarding school students, when they might be seven or eight years old, and they have to be tested, for example, in literature, mathematics, whatever, they start thinking that they could play with the things they should be tested in. They look to the side and want to discuss the questions and tasks in the tests with their classmates, or they start making other narratives instead of thinking that they should be time strategic and competitive. Maybe they only answer one out of ten questions, maybe because they think that nine of the questions are too stupid and all too obvious. These students start playing in and with the test situation because they don't have an instrumental behavior embedded in their bodies or an internalized test logic in their mind yet.

Instead of doing what the test tells them to do – that is to build up on a more adult way of rational behavior – the students start playing with language, start playing with mathematics, start playing with their friends. They misunderstand so to speak, 'the logic of the test' and never perform as the strategic time conscious and individual competitive subjects they we supposed to be. Therefore, the national testing system is falling apart and the figures of the tests seem too low or even useless for the test managers.

John: And as per Wittgenstein, she's saying students haven't yet worked out the language game of the testing movement.

Steen: Yes, they had *in medias res* invented a mutual language game but it was definitely not the same language game as the authorities had wanted them to play. And I think that that shows also a kind of conflict between this mastermind control logic that's imposed upon the school and the students' way of thinking and behaving.

John: No. Don't go there. That's absurd.

Steen: Why? Kousholt has conducted an interesting empirical field study and afterwards talked to the youngsters about their test experience and behavior.

John: No, you made a huge jump there. The question I'd ask in there is "What are those teachers doing to the students?" Some teachers would have taught the students the game, the right game from a PISA perspective. Many of them do (sometimes overly prescriptive). Many five- to-ten-year-old students are very compliant, and they want to play the testing or not-testing game. So, what I'd be observing in that classroom is the nature of how that teacher was interacting with the students and per-mitting them to play those games.

It's got nothing to do with jumping up and saying compliance. It's kind of like saying, "Here. The students are stressed when they do NAPLAN (the national tests)." Well, my gosh. How did the teacher allow that? The stakes are low for those students. The teachers have obviously over-communicated their anxieties. But, this is not true in the majority of classes. But, where it happens, I think it's more a reflection on the teacher than on any national compliance system.

Steen: I agree with you that you can learn how to come to master the test situation, also as a kid, and probably to 'install' a double logic, a kind of a dialectics, between the playfulness of being and also the more strategic behavior of being tested. But is it a good idea that the school enforces these self-governance procedures and expectations?

John: And also double logic in language games, like Bernstein's code-switching argued that often we need to switch from an elaborated to restrictive code of language (Bernstein 1971). In the elaborated code, we select from a relatively extensive range of alternatives, but in the restricted code the number of these alternatives is often severely limited. For many students they need to make this switch – for example, from home to school, from the playground to the classroom, when speaking with peers and speaking with teachers.

Steen: Yeah, you could 'install' a code-switching, even if you're very young. Because you're also code-switching in your everyday life – for example, you are your mother's son, your father's daughter, a sibling, etc. But the question is whether or not it is a good idea to force students at a young age to learn to switch roles in a strategic and competitive way.

John: Here's the thing that worries me. I and some of my students have looked at the code-switching, particularly from Aboriginal students going into regular schools. And some of these students can do it very well, but they don't succeed in our schooling system or in our society. It's like students at five who speak two or three languages. That's impressive. But some of them don't succeed. What on earth is going on?

I just admire anyone who can speak two languages – at age five or our age. I admire any five-year-old who can code-switch from home to school and back again. Our system doesn't necessarily succeed with these students.

Many years ago, I was very involved in Luria's work, a neuropsychologist from Russia (Luria 1976). One of his major notions was the difference between simultaneous, successive, and executive control.

Steen: Yeah, it is always a good idea to reawaken and re-consult old classics in pedagogy and education.

John: Our argument was that there are many different ways of thinking, and for young children there was an initial dominance of simultaneous thinking, and many of these Aboriginal students were adept at it. We liked this Luria notion of simultaneous thinking – which relates to seeing the whole and then parsing the details – and successive thinking – which relates to seeing the parts and building the whole. And one of the arguments we were saying is that, when children come to school and are taught to read, for many of them it is the first time they have to think from looking at the individual parts and building the whole. That is, moving from simultaneous to successive thinking.

Thus, many of the skills these young students have are not so valued in our schooling system. Which surely is a massive missed opportunity.

Now, the benefit of teaching reading is not only the skill of reading but also the skills of successive processing. But if they do not learn either skill (reading or successive) they have a double whammy against them as the schooling moves from learning to read to reading to learn. Maybe we should delay the teaching of reading and first teach the skills of successive processing (although there must be a context for such learning). When you go to some of the Scandinavian countries, including yours, Steen, where students start to learn to read later than in the English world, there are far fewer reading problems because students have developed that extra skill of successive processing from other school-related tasks.

Our Western society particularly values successive processing, particularly since the printing press and the dominance of reading, and if you do not have these processing skills you may struggle to success (particularly in our schooling system, which is dominated by reading, writing, and numeracy). Learning phonic skills is a successive task, whereas whole language is more based on simultaneous skills (knowing the story and then decoding the meaning). I would argue that students who could read can do whole language. Students who cannot read don't learn to read through whole language. They need to be taught the specific skills of successive thinking (phonics, phonemes, and so on – which my friend Marie Clay called learning the listening skills or reading; Clay 2005).

Scribner and Cole did a really fascinating study in Liberia (where I spent some time many years ago), working with the Vai people, who don't value successive thinking. The Vai children went out of their society and learned to read (Scribner & Cole 1981). When they returned to the Vai society, they were not valued, because reading was not seen as worthwhile. The successive skills were of little use to survive and succeed in the Vai society.

I know, from doing all the tests we developed, that I am an extreme successive thinker. I'm not very good at simultaneous. I'm reasonably good at playing the piano with music. Same with cooking. Same with map reading.

Many years ago, particularly in my mountain climbing and my bush walking days, I parodied people who read maps because I was reluctant to use maps, claiming a sixth sense about distance, topography, and direction. I could look at a mountain and see lines of access, ascent, and descent, and I could explain this in a very successive manner. And then one time, two of us got lost for four days in the bush. Absolutely, desperately lost. On the second day, we could see there was a bushfire coming in our direction and we knew we were in trouble. And I learned that, oh, my gosh, I better learn a map. In fact, it was quite an irony as we had a map. We couldn't work out where we were or where we were going. After a while we agreed that we were on this creek called Windy Creek, and indeed there was much wind funneling up the valley. But it twisted and turned, went back on itself, and confused the heck out our sense of direction. It was only at the end that we realized it was Windy Creek (of course, given how windy the riverbed twisted and turned), and that could have given us a good cue to what else was happening. Not the wind but the twists could have helped.

The net effect of this adventure was that I overlearned how to read a map. Survival could depend on it. Today I can read a map, but I know how I do it: very successively. Some people could look at a map and see the big picture, and then work out the details. I do the opposite. I can study the contour lines and build the picture. Yes, it would be great if I could process successively and simultaneously together, and certainly this is probably an attribute of the great pianists, the great painters, the great explorers.

Steen: Your very personal and rich examples from the field make me think that the combination between cognitive and social skills, unconscious embodiment, embodied thought and mapping of the world give me a much richer picture of your way of thinking than reading your *Visible Learning* books – and not the least a will and a possibility to criticize how, for example, Danish politicians, educational planners, and school leaders, have misunderstood your 'message'. The very primitive and instrumental ideas of creating an evidence-based, state-controlled school system (Larsen 2015d, 2017a) were said to rely explicitly on your scientific work (see, for example, the Danish school researcher Keld Skovmand's clarifying and critical analyses; Skovmand 2016, 2019a, 2019b).

John: Yes, sometimes I too struggle when systems pick out bits from my work, or choose a particular influence and miss the claims about the overlap of the various influences, and then get the system wrong. I recall one of your ministers announcing reduction in the time teachers had to work together and used my research to claim this was an 'evidence-based decision'. I had to then get up and say, to the contrary, the work very much depends on resourcing time for teachers to work together to develop collective efficacy fed with the evidence of impact. Also, some of your colleagues made claims about my wish for more surface level learning, whereas this is contrary to the claims in the book. So many critics stop and start with the data and completely miss my interpretation of these data. It means I still have work to do to ensure that the messages about the evidence are more privileged and critiqued, rather than just the data.

Given my penchant for successive thinking, this is why I like the Arthur Koestler notion I cited previously, that creativity and deep thinking is bringing together two or more seemingly unrelated ideas (Koestler 1964). This is the nexus of successive and simultaneous thinking. I also find it fascinating that rarely has anyone investigated when the right time is to teach students to move from more accumulation of ideas (which we call the surface knowing) to the relating of these ideas (the deeper knowing).

I am working with a PhD student on this problem, and he is using the aha moment to create this time of relating ideas. He is using a 1960s creativity test format to induce the moment and then videoing the reactions, recoding the emotional response, and interviewing the students. The task is to find the word that connects three ideas, such as Fly, Clip, and Wall. It is fascinating, as when they work out the answer (paper) you can see the aha moment, their emotions are so visible – mouth opening, eyebrows rise, eyes widen, cheek rise, and the jaw drops – markedly.

It seems strange we have never asked about the optimal moment to stop learning more ideas and start relating the ideas we have in meaningful ways. I am sure there is not an exact 'right' moment, but there needs to be more research on the right proportions of surface and deep thinking.

Learning to overcome obstacles

Steen: Let's touch upon the theme 'reflections'. If it is fair to say that you promote this idea that we have to have the teacher reflect more upon the teacher's own impact. I think that the teacher can learn from something else than reflections. You can also learn from actual obstacles that you are hitting upon. Like, for example, you think this mountain is an 'easy' mountain and then it is a 'tough' one, and a text can be hard to grasp and decipher. You can also learn from your fellow men – even from your pupils and your students and study how they overcome obstacles.

So, I would like to warn you – maybe even to criticize the whole *Visible Learning* logic – that this tends to be too mentalistic and backward projecting. The *Visible Learning* paradigm seems primarily to take place in the mind, in the inner being, and thereby fosters a kind of a circularity. I figure you could prosper from at least two other ways of thinking. One deals with the capacity of how to overcome obstacles – physically and intellectually – and benefit from these. Another point is that you learn in interaction with the social setting in which you are all placed. This does not only count for the pupil or student but also for the teacher as the 'pivotal' chairperson. And that means that you also have to focus on the communication among the pupils, actually on the communication patterns in the whole social situation – for example, examine the pupils' reaction towards what you present them for and ask them to do.

John: I agree. Indeed, I write a lot about learning from challenge, from overcoming obstacles, and the importance of the social setting.

Steen: And it is also important for the research(er) to look at how you as a teacher also possess and have access to cunning knowledge and several types of didactical skills you can use. You could give a lecture. And you can make a group work. And you can have a student to present today's lecture. Then you can have them go to do a fieldwork investigation outside the school building. Then you can have them to go interview other people than yourself and each other. Then you can inspire them to read a classic. That means there are so many didactical ways that you can use to practice your teaching role.

John: I absolutely agree.

Steen: And they are actually much more complicated than mental reflection on behalf of your own things.

John: But, remember, the two key notions of *Visible Learning*: when you see your teaching through the eyes of students, and when you teach students to become their own teacher. I play a lot of precedence on understanding, and thinking, and interacting with and among the students. In fact, Graham Nuthall (who we talked about earlier) was an interesting and very deep-thinking man. He spent quite a bit of time in the 1970s and 1980s going into classrooms. Every morning he put microphones on every kid, and every afternoon he went home and physically hand transcribed it and analyzed the discussions among the students. He didn't publish a lot, and his book was published after he passed away, *The Hidden Lives of Learners* (Nuthall 2007).

Graham's work really showed me that if you look at classrooms through the eyes of teachers, you see a very narrow perspective. Students have dramatically strong and powerful views of what it means to be a kid in the classroom. Indeed one of his maxims is that about 80% of what happens in classrooms teachers do not see or hear – and as you know I find utmost important and have emphasized several times in our conversation – there is a major and critical hidden life of students when they are talking among themselves in classes – often nothing to do with the lesson. We need to spend much more time understanding the language of students as they process what we teachers ask them to do. Perhaps more attention to student voice, but I mean more teaching students to talk about their learning, what they do and particularly what they do not know. How to seek help, how to evaluate the credibility of arguments and – particularly in today's world – fake news, wrong information, and spurious claims. Hence the attention to obstacles, to privileging error and not knowing, and to hearing how students are processing information from our teaching.

Steen: In the universities in Denmark we have more and more online evaluation programs. If you follow a series of lectures, given by a professor, then later on you are asked to give from 0 to 5 points as answers to questions whether or not you learned something, and if the lectures honored the course description and the learning goals. I think it's a very wrong and very narrow way to use evaluation.

John: I agree with you. Especially if the requests are about the teaching. We ask students what it means to be a good learner in this class, not what do you think of the teacher. If you look at so many of the student evaluations, especially at the university level, it is of the teacher and the teaching, and too rarely is it about the quality of learning or the impact of the teaching on the learning.

Steen: It's a little bit like if you are satisfied with a product and you like your computer and something. We tend to reduce complex questions of teaching, education, and *Bildung* to consumer satisfaction (Larsen 2016c).

John: The IKEA effect. We like it because we built it.

Steen: A good point. This idea is – utmost primitive – that you could give points between 0 and 5, and then the good teacher would love to have 4.5 for a year – then it's a success.

John: I certainly agree that too often student evaluations of university lecturers are biased to a particular way of teaching – favoring structured classes, focused on imparting and testing knowledge claims, lack of ill structured and deeper thinking, overly clear outlines and cookbook claims of ordering knowledge. Students want to know what they need to know, so they can tell it back to you. Such narrow demands by so many students are a major worry, and too many evaluating forms privilege this way of teaching.

   But here's a question for you on that. Let's say the evaluation form is on a 5-point scale. What if you found out that you have a lecturer across 500 students who only gets an average rating of 1?

Steen: Of course, this low figure will bring the lecturer into trouble.

John: I would agree that above a certain point, like above a 3 or a 4, most student evaluations do not tell you much. It kind of tells you that you turned up, you presented. A few years ago I was intrigued with a cohort of academics who got 1 and 2. I couldn't understand it. How could you get a 1? So I followed up. They don't turn up, they're rude, they do not return assignments in time, they're obnoxious, they don't have interesting or up-to-date content, they do not give feedback, and they exist. . . . Not many of them, fortunately.

Steen: But my idea is that, if you were building more upon reliable and a positive interaction with students and the school management relied more on teachers' professional autonomous judgments then the world would look quite different compared to the present rating and measurement society.

John: I'm with you, absolutely.

Steen: . . . then you could learn more from them, pupils as well as teachers.

John: Totally, that's the whole point of the first part of *Visible Learning*.

The important role of the teacher

Steen: In my country, when we read your work, we tend to think that you have answers to very many questions, maybe even too many. But now, I came to understand during our conversation that your primary perspective, your primary view on things, is to help the teachers know their impact on students. And hereby, knowing how to look upon the educational situation, the teaching and learning situation through the eyes of the pupils, and at all levels to reflect and try to improve attempts to become fully autonomous human beings. Those are, of course, honorable ideas that we share, but when it comes to educational philosophy and political a societal engagement, it seems to me that there is a much wider range of questions to deal with. For example, how do we get a more just society? How do we change the imbalance and all the different contradictions in society, and how do we deal with big data and algorithmic connected technology? How do we deal with culture, and how do we deal with different clashes between cultures? Could you please reflect upon some of these open questions? How is it, for example, possible to generalize something from the reflexive teacher's position, the self-critical and data-informed teacher, to all these other roles and themes dealing with educational philosophy in the broadest sense?

John: Certainly when you consider that the impact rather begs that question as to what each educator (and parent and student) means by the notion of impact. Whilst I prefer not to answer this question but to elicit it from those at the front of class and school as to what they mean by impact. I do have views about what I would do to answer it, and it is about students being students now. Schools are the most civilizing places in our society, and learning respect for self and respect for others is a really critical part of the experience of schooling. Particularly when it's so obvious that we go to school in a group, then that respect is very critical.

This goes to the heart of your question about culture – we create culture, even when we are immersed in culture; teachers create cultures in their class, some students accept, some rebel against this culture, and we need to teach students to do both in desirable ways. Here is where teachers need to collect evidence, data, triangulate that with their impressions and judgments – of course it is rarely hard data, but being aware of how students are adapting, enhancing the culture, and their levels and skills in working with others and respecting their own views of the world and themselves.

If you go out and ask students what the attribute of classrooms is they most want, it's fairness. They'll put up with inequities as long as it's fair. And surely we want that, too. But we need a lot more than fairness because you could be very fair about who you kill. We need to develop a just fairness, and certainly children have often strong views about justice (and many researchers have debated the various phases of justice that are related to development). So there's a lot more than that. But that sense of students, they do have conceptions of justice (see, e.g., Arendt 1958; Rawls 1971; Habermas 1989, 1991). There are at least two requirements that derive from the *Visible Learning* themes about knowing your impact through the eyes of students and that students being their own teachers – and that is that educators require remarkable skills in listening, much more important than talking, and they need to develop a high trust, a fair and just sense within the classroom.

Steen: But what I think is that if you are a teacher, then you are part of a giant division of labor in society. You have a certain privilege here. You are the cunning, knowing factor of upbringing, socializing students in an institutional framing. Okay, that's a kind of a privilege, but it is also more or less your obligation to tell people – maybe not a five-year-old, but tell pupils and students how this whole institution is organized, and what role the teacher plays in the school institution. So you have to put forward some major critical reflection upon your role as a teacher, the role of division of labor, the role of societal upbringing, the role of differentiation between what's in the control of the parents and control of the state, control of the individual teacher, how the historical development has been, etc. Do you think that that's also a part of it, to widen the perspective, not only to see the actual impact but also to see how the structural, historical development has been on the institution of teaching and the institution of the role you have yourself in the division of labor logic? Or is that too advanced?

John: I supervised a thesis a couple of years ago where the student was looking at the role of critical literacy. Now, here in the Victoria curriculum, this notion is banned and there is more attention to the qualities of literature. In Queensland, teaching critical literacy is legal. And the irony is there's more teaching of critical literacy in Victoria and virtually none in Queensland. And so when you ask that question, I'm thinking that the more you make it mandatory, the more the banned could be taught – and maybe needs to be exposed to students (within limits, of course, about porn, racism, violence, etc.).

Steen: Okay, so would I be careful about bans. Now, I will come up with a critique or at least a worry that your major line of arguing, and your basic backbone in your work is essentially a two-prong relationship. A relationship exists between teacher and student. But I think there are two things more to come to that logic in order to irritate it a little bit, or to make some structural adjustments of it, or maybe add some extra things to think about. And one is that it's never ever a pure dual relationship between a teacher and a pupil. There'll always be a matter, or maybe whole subjects – between the two protagonists.

John: And power.

Steen: Yes, there'll be structural power around and embedded in it – like, for example, Marx and Foucault have 'taught' us to be aware of (Marx 1976/1867; Foucault 1980) and we have already talked about earlier, when you uttered your vivid **pleonasm**. So that means that when I think about a teacher role, this role is at least addressing all three of them. There is, of course, the learning subject of the pupil. We have to think about what's going on here and to address people the right way, listen to them, and be patient and everything. But you have to know that the meeting you have with this specific student on a subject matter is very important. It's about a substantial 'things' like mathematics, lyrics, botanic, historical events. . . . And then, it's always taking place within a structure of power, and the relations between structure, power, and knowledge, and maybe even structure's 'telling' you beforehand that you should now make a selection, that'll normally see 80% pass the exam and 20% not passing. There's a kind of structural logic here in selecting, and judging, and evaluating pupils. And they know themselves that they are controlled within a frame that's much bigger than your personal teacher judgment. That's due to laws and regulations and normal censorship procedures. The historical heritage of the subject was described and maybe even sustained for ages. And so I would like to ask, how do you, then, address all the three aspects with your thinking logic,

I mean both the substantial, factual, and actual matter, the meaning of the subjects, and then, this structural power horizon, political legislation, the division of labor, technology, capitalism, etc.? All these giant 'things' also interfere in and with the classroom – not to forget the widespread and ever present *Four-Dimensional Education* program from OECD (Fadel et al. 2015), the PISA system, and the powerful policy documents. They influence and interfere more and more in the class-rooms. So there's no – what can I say – pure, cleansed meeting between a pupil and a teacher anymore. There's always a third strong agenda out there – and therefore in here.

John: Yes, it is messy and certainly society does 'interfere' in the classroom – as it should in a democracy (and without question in a dictatorship). This is why the debates about what is taught, what is valued, and the success of the teaching is so critical to be debated – and if we have added to this debate, all the better.

The teacher as the critical and decisive 'factor'

John: When the *Visible Learning* book came out, New Zealand came out in, I think, November 2008, and the press in New Zealand got hold of it (Hattie 2009). In early January 2009, it is mid-summer, school holidays, and parents are thinking about sending their children back to school. Also, the newspapers had nothing much to write about in New Zealand, but still wanted attractive headlines. So, I was the front headlines of the Sunday paper, interviewed, and in one case the reporter was helicoptered to my beach house for an interview. Then the (brand new) minister was asked for her comment, and she said, "We need to listen to what he's saying." And you're going to imagine that so many had a field day. I was accused of blaming the teacher, being anti-unions, overly influencing the government, and one blogger even had me having an affair with the minister.

But you're right. I was very careful to say the biggest in-school factor is the teacher. But that was missed. I don't resile from the fact that teachers are critical, but the variance among students is even more critical. But when you drill down to the factors behind this teacher effect it very much comes back to their expertise – it is not who they are or what they do as much as how they think and evaluate. This is why I'm now more involved with the political scene here in Australia to privilege teacher's expertise.

Steen: In his book *The Rediscovery of Teaching* – that we both have read and beyond any doubt are fond of discussing – Gert Biesta states that just mentioning the word 'factor' is an insult against the teacher (Biesta 2017). But I guess that you used 'factor' in a statistician's vocabulary, not necessarily implying that you can move around the factors like it's a warehouse or something. But would you say that you should be careful to use statistical concepts in a political education debate because they are misunderstood and misinterpreted as such?

John: Yes, this is a pure misinterpretation. I use 'factor' in the sense of an influence, not a mathematical variable to be moved around. But perhaps he was clouded by the use of effect-sizes as a means to identify the influence of the teacher.

Here's the problem. Politicians aren't great fans of qualitative research and arguments for all kinds of good and bad reasons. Too often, qualitative research does not stand on the shoulders of other qualitative studies (although see the recent advance of qualitative meta-analysis), and they too rarely have much power to generalize (but good ones indeed can and do). But, if an educational economics professor gave an article to our minister based on econometrics, they're more likely to believe it because it's black and white and not qualitative. The conclusions are more likely to be simple and direct, with fewer conditions and devoid of context. This is unfortunate.

Steen: Yep, and they're actually talking about productive factors.

John: So my good friends, higher education economics, and I love them dearly but . . .

Steen: They have an easy task.

John: No, they don't have an easy task but they have a more responsible task to get their interpretation and their language right because they're more likely to be listened to.

My worry in education is that teachers actually have incredible power but they don't use it. I know in the minister's office, they have whole teams of people that read his letters and analyze them and report back to him. And he listens to that. He gets so few letters from the teaching profession, and I think there's an obligation for teachers and principals to inform the minister.

Yes, I have a background in statistics, as you know. Yes, I learned that language. Yes, I'm reasonably good at measurement. I like to think and use measurement language (see Knudsen 2017). I wrote five versions of *Visible Learning*, and the first version was over 500 pages, resplendently cloaked in numbers, figures, interaction patterns. I finished this version, and Janet looked at it and said, "Oh my goodness. Who are the two people in the world you're writing for?", and that's why I threw that version away. The second was better, and so on through versions. But I think this is normal to write many versions before you are happy to release it. Ten years later, I hope I'm getting better at being clearer and maybe not misleading the reader as to my big picture story. Again, I think many critics have failed to see the 29 books I have now written or co-authored on the topic of explaining, implementing, and enhancing the original model.

Steen: Okay. Next question on the understanding of the effect question that we also touched upon in the beginning of our conversation.

John: All right. Gert Biesta says, "Effective for what?", and I think we've dealt with that. And he also says, "For whom?", and I agree this is a fundamental question when you ask, "'Know Thy Impact' – about and for what? For whom? To what degree of success?"

Foremost, for so many they quickly jump from the teacher to the teaching, often using the buzzword 'pedagogy'. I rarely use this term.

Steen: I know. That's very normal to use pedagogy in Denmark. Why don't you do that?

John: Because I think it's code word for too many interpretations.

Steen: You might be right but it is also a very useful word.

John: Pedagogy, in my narrow interpretation of the word, is the work of teachers. But so often it is merely a replacement for 'teaching'. But that's how it's interpreted, and I just think it's a code word for so many things, and it's not clear enough. It also means 'to lead the child', to have theories about how to teach children, that teaching should be contested and questioned, and in your country a pedagogue is a practitioner of pedagogy but with the wider notion of teaching children life-preparing knowledge such as social skills and cultural norms. Thus, I prefer to just use 'teaching'.

Steen: But here is, of course, a difference because in German and Danish universities, you can – until now – study pedagogy as a subject, and that would probably be called education here, down under, and in the English speaking world. But the major concept comes from German *Pädagogik*, and it implies also the normative question of the contested and utmost changing historical ideals and institutions for upbringing and processes of *Bildung*. But of course you are right. Pedagogy also deals with teaching, didactics, and different views on learning and socialization.

In old Greek, the *paidagogos* was a slave who leads students (young boys) from their home to school. *Agogos* means the guy leading and *pais*, kid or boy.

John: But coming back, if you use that word in Australia, it's pretentious. We exclude people who have major roles in teaching by hiding behind the jargon word 'pedagogue'.

Steen: We know every time we have to write articles in English, we have the problem of translation. Because we are not really allowed to use the

P-word, when you write in English, and then you end up talking of education, education, education more and more.

There is also another problem with the concept of education as I have stated earlier in our discussion. In Denmark, 40 to 50 years ago, when I was a kid, education was the thing you 'took' after you finished school. You became educated and trained as a professional blacksmith, carpenter, teacher, doctor, economist, etc. But the school was not a part of the education system. The educational window was maybe seven years, five years, or three years. Apprenticeship, being skilled, being a master of your subject, and then you worked the rest of your life once you were educated. That was also the case in the academic world.

And then suddenly the political rhetoric changed dramatically in Denmark and in many other countries, especially from the 1990s and onwards, and the educational continuum goes now from when you are born and it lasts until you die. Education and life-long learning from cradle to grave: 0 to 100 years. So now, the educational vocabulary semantics have taken over and colonized all the other ones (Larsen 2014a). Probably because the content of the word education seems to be more neutral, descriptive and open for planning, and not so loaded with ideas and ideals of *Bildung* and 'old-fashioned' pedagogy. We lose the German heritage and content and get swallowed and embraced by the dominant globalized Anglo-Saxon logic. This landscape is actually very interesting – and somewhat depressing – to study and to discuss.

John: It is indeed interesting. The history of teaching also has changed in my country. It has moved from a major focus on the three r's (reading, writing, arithmetic) to a more whole development of the child; it has moved from a rigid top down to a more open local interpretation; it has moved to give schools more authority to make local conditions. But then we have talked about Larry Cuban's stunning history of how the teacher has barely changed over the past 150 years (Cuban 1984). If someone woke up from 200 years of slumber, he or she could walk in a classroom and say, "Yep, that is a teacher teaching a student; yep there are the text books or worksheets; yep there are the naughty and the docile students; yep this teacher has good discipline," and so on. He or she would of course have trouble knowing how a phone, computer, or bathroom worked, but not teaching.

But you state in your writing that I forget to talk with dignity and curiosity about teachers. I disagree, I do continually. And you state that my work does not contribute to a renewal of the pedagogical vocabulary. I would disagree intensely on that. If nothing else, I have tried to create a different narrative about the expertise of educators – wow what an acknowledgment of their skills and professionalism.

Steen: Okay, but the concept of pedagogy in my view contains normative questions for upbringing, analyses of the present educational system, *Bildung* reflections, and educational philosophy in a broader scope. And there I wouldn't say that you were really contributing. Of course, during our communicative exchanges, I have come to know and understand you more, and I kind of respect your argument, that what you are especially hitting at is telling and teaching the teacher how to know about their effect upon – oh, not really effect, but their impact on what they're doing. So this critical self-examination, self-critique of the teacher's perspective, must be seen as your major contribution to education and maybe also pedagogy, as I can see. But you do not, for example, seem to have anything to say about basic questions in pedagogy, like the new-classic German educationalist Wolfgang **Klafki's concept of the double opening**, stressing that pedagogy deals with how to open the schoolkid to the world, and the world to the schoolkid (Klafki 2000).

John: Yes, I can see that his double sense is most worthwhile. Yes, it is the teacher's role to open up the various categories of realities to the student while at the same time via these realities the students need to open up to the realities. It is two way. This requires the student to develop self-determination, a critical stance, be involved in problem-solving, but this is a huge ask for all students. Particularly when he adds that the curriculum must address core problems of the modern world such as peace, environmental issues, socially created inequalities, effects of new technologies/intercultural education. These are huge asks, but in principle yes I see this as a major purpose of education, perhaps not agreeing with the topics, as this is daunting for many and requires prior skills to engage in these understandings, but it is a worthy outcome of 15 years of schooling.

This relates to sentence you write in your critical article of my work. In "Blind Spots . . ." you write, "Hattie does not see and does not want to know that the life and thought of this very student cannot be generalized and transformed into a best practice adduced ideal time" (Larsen 2015a). While I never use the notion of 'best practice', I want you to tell me more about this criticism.

Steen: Okay, I think that there is also now this transitional problem here because we have all these best practice narratives in Denmark, also in fields other than education. So while you were, in a way, becoming the big hit at the scene of educational planners, they were at the very same moment going for the ideology of best practices. So they combined the two – educational evidence logic and your impact studies were combined to an implementation of so-called best practice logic, so the related faults, flaws, and mistakes are of course not yours.

Is teaching an intervention and the teacher a resource?

Steen: Do you see teaching as an intervention, trying to enhance the input/output logic of schooling? Is learning an outcome or a production? Do you use these concepts from warfare, business, or economy?

John: Learning is a mechanism or means to an end, although there are skills in this process of learning. Is teaching an intervention? No, it's a lot more than an intervention. In one sense, it is a deliberate attempt to change a course of action, so in that sense it is an intervention. But the moral purpose part of teaching comes about the worthwhileness, the choice and defense of the content and outcomes (and impact), and the ethics of the methods of intervening. Yes there are inputs (we use the notion of skill, will, and thrill), and there are outputs (the same) but the development of the 'whole child' is the aim. Although, I am cautious about this notion of 'whole child', as others are also invoked in developing the whole child, such as parents, family, and many others.

I do not have a great problem with the notions of input and output, as long as outputs are more than tests and achievement. The black box between is the core of the teaching and education questions.

Steen: So, basically, it could be an intervention but it doesn't have to be.

John: Yes, it's more than just an intervention.

Steen: How are we to depict and understand what a teacher is? Can the teacher be grasped as a resource, a factor? Or is this type of language and thinking, this way of paraphrasing, insulting the teacher, and misunderstanding the role of the teacher?

John: Well, you're right, it could be insulting. There is a tension as one of the core features of the work is the expertise of the teacher – and it would be oh so easy to see this as blaming the teacher. Indeed, it needs to be the opposite, esteeming the impact of teachers (and school leaders) and this is core to my work.

I worry about our work here in Australia with recognizing and esteeming highly accomplished and lead teachers (HALTS). I do not want parents coming to schools and demanding their children to be in one of these HALT classes. We must ensure that all teachers are proficient, and that HALTS are seen as more supporters of fellow teachers, and be seen as the marvels of excellence, but never to undermine that if you are *not* a HALT you are somehow deficient. A tense tightrope. But the alternative to say all teachers are equal is just so not true that our credibility is shattered by such claims. We need to recognize excellence but welcome proficiency. I know that my airplane pilot may or may not be a HALT, but I beg that they be proficient – which is still a high standard. But I know some pilots are excellent and this also tells me that all can improve and grow to excellence.

Steen: But doesn't it mean that, based on your ideas of correlations, one is forced to treat the teacher as one factor among others in statistics?

John: Yes, they are one factor, but wow what an important one, and so many of the factors are related to *how* teachers think!

Steen: But when it comes to the school class and you say that we can now compare the relations between, for example, a table, a computer, a teacher, and the economic support per pupil, and whether or not there are two teachers, and also the size of the class, etc. – then it seems to place everything and everyone at the same level . . .

John: Technically, they're at the same in the league table of influences, but that misses the point. As I have written throughout, it is the overlap and *how* teachers think, their evaluative thinking, their capacity to seek evidence and question their impact, particularly with others, that is more the core – and explains the placement of so many of the factors.

Steen: That's probably one of the reasons why I talk about – and have written the aforementioned article called "Blind Spots in John Hattie's Evidence Credo" – because this correlation logic can give some kind of explanation of certain things and open it for an interpretation (Larsen 2015a).

John: Oh yes. But then I'd come back to you and say it may be a blind spot on my credo if that's all you think it is. But it is a blind spot if you start and stop with the league table.

Steen: Yeah, you should probably have done it a little bit different there and then with the league table. Because your readers came to understand them as separate and autonomous factors and your whole clue is that they are not.

John: Only for those who are not readers – but just glance at the league table alone.

Steen: It's also reminding me of the way we reflect in the market place. For example, we seem to rate the different features of a customized bicycle one by one as separate parts, but this way of looking at the world cannot be, without serious problems or even traps, transferred directly to education.

John: Yes, that's right. I recall from my undergraduate days learning the word 'polymorphous'. When a person comes to our work and says, "I want to see the university." But there is not a place we go to meet this place, person, or thing. It is a composite, an amalgam of ideas. In the same way when my colleague says to me, "But the university does not want me to do x or y," my reaction is, "But we are the university who says this." Ditto regarding the influence of the teacher – it is a composite. Like your bicycle, and we can see the parts, but it is also the ratio of how the parts are assembled to make the whole work that is the marvel, although starting with great parts helps.

Is the teacher a facilitator of learning or a gift?

Steen: Okay, is it then correct to say, and to claim, that teacher is a facilitator of learning?

John: I don't like that phrase. Facilitator has a very low level of cause and effect. In most learning situations, you cannot and should not be a guide on the side or a facilitator. Learning requires more active, deliberate involvement, although there is a time to shut up, stand back, let loose, but this is deliberate on the part of the teacher. We must not abrogate our role impacting on students, but please do not confuse this with didacticism, talking too much, being in front directing. We need to not be facilitators but activators of learning.

Steen: To facilitate is just to let things happen or to provide services. Is that what you think?

John: The major meaning of facilitate in the dictionary is to 'make easier'. If only learning was easy, but it is hard, it is a struggle, it is staccato, it is error and mistake ridden. Our role is to make learning easier, but to make learning appropriately challenging.

Steen: More than facilitating?

John: Much more than facilitating. When I see successful teachers, I see people who may look like they're facilitators in their presentation, but they are quite deliberate.

Steen: So you'll not use that vocabulary?

John: No, in fact, I write against both the concept of facilitating and 'guide on the side' because I think they demean the excellence that many teachers have.

Steen: And a completely other vocabulary will see teaching as a gift.

John: No, now you switched language. I make a very big distinction between teacher and teaching. I am much more interested in how teachers think, how they make the adaptations and moment-by-moment decisions, how they think evaluatively. Yes, I am interested in the methods of teaching but much more about why and how individuals make the decisions about the choice of these methods.

Steen: Yes, of course.

John: Tell me more about this notion of teaching as a gift.

Steen: Teaching is more than a gift. That would be too much to say, to expect, and to ask for. He or she is not a Christmas present, if you ask me. But teaching could be seen as a gift, a task, an obligation, and a necessity. I'm maybe going more for this Biesta logic where he states that teaching – you can see that in school, culture, and maybe in overall in human interaction – might best be understood as a gift. In the French philosopher Paul Ricouer's latest book that he wrote in 2003 when he was 90 years old, he depicted the **gift as a clue to mankind**'s profound and constitutive, interactive exchanges (see, e.g., an early version in Ricoeur 1995b). We give each other like presents and get something (each other) back in reciprocity. So he might have gone so far as he had seen the teacher – and not just the teacher's role – as a gift.

John: In that sense, yes, I could see that.

Steen: So you give the pupils a gift in presenting them mathematical puzzles or introducing them to historical events?

John: I think when a student has a teacher where they have an impact on that kid's life in a positive way – that is a gift.

Steen: Okay, and then, you can be gifted in your language?

John: In that sense, yes.

Steen: Yeah, but it's also a task, isn't it?

John: It's an obligation. A set of duties.

Steen: Or a necessity?

John: Yes, teaching's all those things.

Steen: But you will not rank them, will you? Or will actually you rank them?

John: It does not make sense to me to rank obligations, necessities, etc. Ranking is among the most simplest (its attraction) but not necessarily deepest forms of understanding.

Steen: Oh yeah, and you have probably also seen a societal logic: we wouldn't have had a society, the strong bonding, intersubjective communication and obligations, and mankind's interactions, without schools. Then schools and school teaching must also be necessities for the existence of a society, a *conditio sine qua non*.

John: Yes, but careful, as you have already said in Denmark, it is progression in learning, not necessarily being physically in a school, that matters. But yes, schools can be critical to the existence of societies. I note when dictators want to change societies fast, they start by shooting the teachers; they work hard to deny sections of the population having access to schools.

Steen: Okay, and Biesta goes on with a very interesting question. And I think it has a little bit to do with the same as the art world, the museums, opera, theater, music, and so on offer. He states, "The role of a teacher could be to give the pupils, students that what they don't want, or didn't know that they could want or would want," which means that the teacher is more a trickster than a learning goal facilitator (Biesta 2017: 27, 92, 94).

In addition, I always find giant and warm inspiration in the German word for guide, *Fremdenführer* (literally: leading strangers), and Thomas Ziehe's clarifying analyses of the 'call' of **the educational Fremdenführer** (Ziehe 2004). A good teacher manages to lead strangers (people he or she does not know yet . . .) to see and reflect upon strange things (they don't know yet . . .) – and by the way also to cope with and overcome obstacles. And thereby they all (both the teachers and the pupils) become somehow strangers to themselves (going through unforeseen formation processes of their characters). To conclude, the *Fremdenführer* is a good friend of *Bildung*. In sharp contrast, the guide just shows you what's already there and tells the audience the same stories over and over again.

John: I like this idea of leading strangers – it has a mystery, an openness, and a safe entry into a new way of thinking and being.

Steen: Great.

John: I so often hear claims that these experiences should be real world, practical, and useful or one of my not-so-liked words, 'authentic'. There are many activities and skills we need that would not meet these criteria. There are many that are not necessarily authentic, or real, or have long-term implications to do with jobs or whatever. There are certain skills, however, that they need: like learning scales in music, like drills in many sports, like overlearning the times tables. I do think that we should not allow students to choose for themselves completely what they want to do or don't want to do – if they did there might a lot of video gaming and chatting with friends. We cannot afford to deny students the opportunity to doing things that they wouldn't have known about. I think a major role in a democracy is that the voters, hence the parents amongst other people, should be the ones that make the decisions about the curriculum. Parents in the sense that the curriculum developers need to hear their critique, and I know this often ends up with debates about the edges, like how much sex in sex education courses, the place of teaching emotional and social aspects. For right or wrong, I do think there is an obligation there. I think it's, obviously, the professionals and the educators should have a major sway on that presentation. The good news is that many times the curriculum is ignored, or interpreted differentially at a local level. Yes, some are overly prescriptive (the Australian curriculum is about 2,500 pages long) and some not (the New Zealand curriculum is 39 pages).

Are the teachers too talkative?

John: One of my main themes is for teachers to stop talking as much and listen to how students are processing information, listen to what they currently know and can do, and listen to the goals and expectations that students have for their learning.

Related to this, we noted the upswing of teacher observation – people sitting in the back of the room with tick boxes, making videos and then spending hours coding them. I struggle to find much research that shows this kind of observation helps teachers improve their understanding of what is happening in their classes or improves the impact on students.

So, about five years ago I said to the team, "What can we do that can help teachers better see their impact (the 80% they do not see or hear, as we have talked about earlier), and also can scale up so it has an impact on students?"

And now, Janet Clinton leads this team here at University of Melbourne. Using the app we developed (https://education.unimelb.edu.au/research/projects/visible-classroom), a teacher can teach a class, and as they are teaching the class, on the students' iPads or on the whiteboard, everything that the teacher said comes up within three seconds of the teacher saying it (and reported with at least 99% accuracy). Some argued this was distracting but teachers soon found the opposite – students become more aware of tasks, listening to the teacher, and knowing what was expected of them.

Or you can use the app to record your lesson, upload, and you get diagnostics back immediately. Yes, it is not perfect, as it does not record the students. We had troubles with ethics committees, the costs were too high, and just the teacher voice was sufficient to lead to major improvements.

In the fully functioning live version, if the coding is not 99.5% accurate, we don't pay the people who do the speech coding. At the end of the lesson, the teacher can get a transcript of everything they say. Plus, if they want, they can get the students to rate the learning and the lesson.

It also automatically coded for 16 attributes like many of the codes in the Danielson and Marzano observation rating scales (Danielson 2012; Marzano 2018).

One of the aims is to get rid of the person sitting in the back of the class. Too often, they mainly focus on the teacher not the impact of the teacher, the issues of reliability of coding are notoriously problematic, and their presence can disrupt the lesson. This is not too surprising as they are viewing the class through their lens, their biases, and often in terms of a comparison with how they would have taught the class. No wonder the reliability is low, and the consequential interpretation poor. We know that it takes five observations over the five lessons to get any minimum quality of reliability. And that's totally inefficient. And so we've developed this app to do the 'observation' and it's getting there. Right now, we have a randomized control trial in England of schools that are using the app and schools that are not.

We know from all the efficacy trials that 70% of teachers improve by using the app about two hours a week for five weeks. Just getting the transcript and the diagnostics is enough.

"Oh dear, do I talk that much!" . . . "Oh, did I say this?" . . . "Oh, my god, look how . . ."

Oh, the verbosity of teachers. . . . They know they talk a lot, but many are surprised by just how much they do talk. I found the study in Germany where they asked teachers what percentage of time they talk and an average teacher thinks they talk 40%. They don't, they talk 89%.

Steen: I see and acknowledge the problem. But too talkative teachers may not – in my perspective – be the only or the major problem in schools.

What is the role of the teacher?

Why does the educational thinker Gert Biesta think 'learnification' is a problem?

Is it possible to imagine a society without teachers and teaching?

Are most teachers too talkative? Should teachers learn to 'shut up' more?

VII. WHAT IS THE RELATION between EDUCATIONAL research and EDUCATIONAL politics?

BE self-critical. REFLECT.

THE POLICY NARRATIVE needs TO BE ABOUT the EXPERTISE of THOSE who have THE GREATEST IMPACT on each CHILD.

FALL through THE MIRROR to the OTHER SIDE to SEE HOW OTHERS SEE YOU and YOUR BLIND SPOTS.

You have to ADJUST WHAT you could think OF AS PEDAGOGY and DIDACTICS to the 'LOGIC' of the SITUATION and STUDENT.

AN EVALUATIVE mindset INVOLVES:

- REASONING & CRITICAL THINKING.
- BEING OPEN to UNINTENDED OUTCOMES.
- ALLOWING for ADAPTATIONS to MAXIMIZE OUTCOMES.
- CHECKING ONE'S BIASES THAT MAY LEAD to FALSE CONCLUSIONS.
- SEEKING and UNDERSTANDING other's POINTS of VIEW.

THE NOTION of 'EVIDENCE' needs to be CONTESTED.

#1 THE gold STANDARD is NOT RANDOM CONTROL studies but 'BEYOND REASONABLE DOUBT.'

TEACHERS need TO BE MORE EVALUATORS than RESEARCHERS

ASKING about the ...

MERIT

WORTH

SIGNIFICANCE

of THEIR IMPACT

Steen: When you look upon it from the role of the learning subject, from the pupils or the students themselves, what you love is that they have a variety of different ways of thinking, and understanding, and working with problems. For example, if it doesn't work in that way, then don't use the same method. So what you dream about is that actually the people have a variety of strategies in order to learn and maybe even urge them to become a little wiser.

John: Yes very much.

Steen: But then it is paradoxically that your way of arguing is used or may be abused by political forces.

John: Yes, that is always a problem. I work in this policy space here in Australia and see that it is very much about the opportunity to create a narrative. So often the narrative about schools is about inputs (money, structures, curriculum) or outputs (accountability, tests, employment) which in one sense is reasonable – but rarely is it about the 'middle' (the expertise, the impact of teaching on each child). So, my aim in the policy space is to privilege this expertise and try and convince the educators to take more ownership of the quality control around this expertise.

Steen: Yes, we should not blindfold ourselves to accept so-called necessities. Because in 50 years or maybe in just 10 years of time you will look backwards to this period and say, "Well, that was too limited, what we did in those days." Because what educational scientists and people dealing with pedagogy in theory and practice are really good at is to maintain status quo or to forget the complexity of the past.

John: Of course.

Steen: From having been narrow minded or being encapsulated in the black school (as we often label the old authoritarian school prior to the 1960s) to reformed pedagogy school or the emancipatory school. And then you go: "This emancipation was not emancipation at all. It was blah, blah, blah." Then comes the quest for post-emancipatory and traditional schools. And you do also have schools celebrating enlightenment, post-enlightenment, and even post-post-enlightenment. Or you have modern school, pre-modern or postmodern school. We are really specialized in either idealizing or criticizing the past.

John: Maybe we should be post-futurists. I have invented a new word.

Steen: Yeah, but I wonder what this position implies? Maybe it is not enough to coin a neologism.

Well-being measurement and happiness indexes

Steen: I suggest we now talk a little bit about the prevailing well-being 'industry' that also claims it relies on and promotes true research data on humans. What do you think about this whole idea about collecting and quantifying qualitative for very fragile data – for example, happiness or well-being? My view is as follows: if we are happy, that is kind of a subjective feeling. And that's very hard to classify or to fixate within a frame of an institutional setting.

John: Look, I have no problems 'measuring' or collecting data on these attributes. Indeed, there is an industry of such measures – my concern is the same as with achievement data – but what about the interpretations? How can we interpret such data to better inform us to more positively impact on students? Too often, schools and systems collect data, but they rarely collect interpretations. Too often, schools and systems give tests, but they rarely use them for better prediction. Let's ask first for a debate about the reasons for collecting and quantifying such fragile data.

Steen: Right now, the different governmental logic systems, for example, in Denmark, they have this idea that we can force every school to make well-being tests every year. One out of three paradigms from the recent Danish school reform of 2013–2014 is that you should become as good as you can become at learning the subjects (do your things, get higher marks). Then the next one is that you should be given the best opportunity to make a social jump away from a less favorable class background. And the third is that the well-being (figures) should be higher every year, both for the individual and for the school class as a whole. So, in a way, what the political level tells institutions to do is that every year they have to produce happiness and well-being data.

John: Yes, there is a lot of discussion about well-being here in Australia, too.

Steen: For example, in Danish school systems right now, there is a whole collection of questions where you can have 5 points if you write or say something and 0 points if you say something else. And one is "Have you had conflict with your parents in the last fortnight?" And if you are a 16- to 17-year-old kid, it must be pretty natural that you have had conflicts. "I want to go drinking with my pals," or "I want to go to bed with that boy." And then there could be conflicts with their parents. It probably has to do with adolescence and being a free human being going away from home. But, actually, that's a low or negative score in the

149

well-being index. So, if people go through normal existential transitions, tensions, and crises and state, "Well, of course, I had conflicts," then the institutional machine gets alarmed or ashamed – while the figures are not nice or worth presenting for a critical or powerful third part.

John: But most of that's poor measurement.

Steen: Nobody's fond of a negative score in a well-being index.

John: But that's poor measurement.

Steen: Yeah, my idea is that we have enforced positive psychology in the school system. And it has become now a compulsory branding of the institution to produce happiness figures in order to show the parents, or maybe the local community, that we are the happiest school, the most well-being producing school, etc. (Larsen 2019b; Meyer 2016).

John: No, but what you are raising is more a measurement problem. I have no trouble with the notion of well-being. I can see that supporting well-being can enhance and relate to improved learning. For example, if it means things like, "I am happy to struggle in learning," "I feel like I'm invited into this class," "In this class, things are fair" – these are kind of well-being conditions.

My view of positive psychology is that it was invented to solve a problem. And it was more of a political problem. The whole movement of psychology – particularly in America – was moving to clinical psychology with a focus on what some argued was individual deficits. Yes, 99% of people who go to psychologists go because they have a problem. They don't go to get well. They go because they want to remediate something. And that's needed. So positive psychology has come along and said, "We're going to take all that over. And we're going to have this new language." Now, who doesn't want to be happy? Who doesn't want to have high well-being? And why shouldn't students have a sense of well-being?

But it's well-being about what? And identifying the 'what' is often missing, with programs that try to generically give students the language of well-being but not teaching them when to invoke the well-being strategies, and to be cognizant about the 'what' of well-being, which can have different notions of happiness, flourishing depending on what the focus is.

There are so many measures already related to well-being. I'm a sinner, as I too have created a well-being measure. There are thousands of them out there. They don't predict much. They're rarely based on a defensible model (ours was based on Adlerian notions of well-being;

Hattie et al. 2004), they tend to ask generically about a person's happiness. They rarely distinguish between the state and trait notions of well-being.

I use the word 'passion' rather than well-being. I want all (teachers, students) to enjoy the passion of learning. I want them to enjoy the fact that they can be wrong, and they can learn. I want them to experience the aha moment. I don't think that's measured by most well-being measures. I worry the positive psychology and well-being notions are yet another add-on. Another program to advertise to parents – do not worry we here in schools also care for the general well-being of your child.

And working in the team at the University of Melbourne, I don't see a lot of evidence we can do it very well. I am involved in various evaluations of these programs, and there is not a lot of evidence they make much difference. Yes, the well-being can be increased via these programs, but when students go back into their regular classes, there is no effect of these programs. One great program at St. Peters in Adelaide is starting with enhancing the well-being of the teachers, aiming to then ensure the classes were welcoming to these notions, and they could be included in the whole school approach to well-being. The impact was minimal, although this group of researchers and schools are most likely to work out how to best build in these programs.

Steen: Do you want to contribute to this well-being 'industry'? When the politicians and the leader of the state have declared that the well-being index would be progressing every year, then people who want to have educational institutional success, in the eyes of the politicians, they must back up with qualitative data what they have stated until now with quantitative data.

John: I have no trouble with well-being. I just worry that it's become so generic. I think it's becoming too much of a branding exercise.

Steen: I agree. It's always also a branding exercise.

John: When you look at the schools in Australia that are most into well-being, they are the rich, affluent schools. Why should students in the lower socioeconomic schools not have well-being? But we so often deny it to them, and I don't think, yet again, another add-on program is going to make much difference.

Steen: You can also see that the wealthiest states, they tend to be the most happy. For example, Denmark, Switzerland, Sweden . . .

John: Bhutan?

Steen: ... and Norway. Bhutan is the exception because they score high even though they have a low BNP per capita.

John: Yeah, but in the Bhutan case you're talking about a different concept of well-being.

Steen: Yes, while the happiness scores follow pretty much the social economic competitive logic of the nation – but also the level of trust, security, welfare, and individual freedom rights.

John: But just to be clear, from my point of view, I'm arguing that the *Visible Learning* work looked at achievement. Things like well-being are very connected to the culture of the school, which indeed can have major effects on learning (although of course enhanced well-being is a worthwhile outcome in itself). Take the claim that the number of years of schooling is more important than achievement, which is why we should be doing regular reviews in every schools on this basic question: "Is your school an inviting place for students to come to?"

Mandatory learning goals – the failure of upscaling politics

Steen: Your *Visible Learning* paradigm has been used as one of the prime sources of inspiration to give the government, and the leading educational politicians, the needed and wanted scientific legitimation to design and implement the national school reform in Denmark 2013–2014. In my view, your paradigm was not only used but also abused, as it became inscribed into approximately 3,000 mandatory learning goals, which the different school subjects at different age levels had to live up to all around the country. Thereby, *Visible Learning* program was radically transformed and it was instrumentalized from above.

John: I agree. This is a gross misinterpretation of learning intentions and success criteria, and goes back to the earlier years of behavioral objectives and the dulling of the curriculum and learning.

Steen: And how could that happen? How do you think it could happen?

John: But this is where we need to switch the discussion to how policy works. Too often policy works by creating a deficit or crisis to justify the preferred solution, which all too often is then mandated for all. I take the opposite view, we should have better diagnosis of the issues, better needs analyses, and most importantly we should scale up the success we have, not mandate a process for all – which sometimes disturbs the success many are already having. Because if you mandate a process like demanding everybody use learning goals and everybody then does it this way, then you ignore the essence of the profession, which is how the teachers interpret that and make those decisions moment by moment to make a difference to students' learning. If a teacher is having great impact on all students without using learning intentions, why would you change this teaching? Yes, using learning intentions may improve this teacher, but mandating without asking the impact question seems not good policy.

Steen: It is indeed very interesting to hear you reflect openly and critically upon the fact that the political interpretation of your work in Denmark led to a curriculum based on over 3,000 learning goals.

John: This is fascinating when so many other countries are moving the other way from specific goals, to a more whole rounded notion of what it means to learn and be educated (e.g., Alberta has a curriculum based on conceptual understanding). I know I am often 'blamed' for your adoption of these goals, but I have never argued for such an atomized curriculum, a narrowing of powerful knowing into thousands of goals, and would prefer to see more constructive alignment between the content of the curricula, the tasks and assessments, and the teaching methods. Getting the balance between the surface and deep is critical, turning students on to the joy of learning and knowing and understanding, often does not start from lessons focused around such specific learning goals. Learning is a (powerful) means to an end, and only one end is the skill and thrill of learning.

Steen: In 2017, the Danish political parties behind the school reform 2013–2014 and the present Danish Minister of Education, Merete Riisager, actually declared – after years of critique from politicians, researchers, and teachers and exchanges of views in *res publica* – that the approximately 3,000 goals do not have to be read as mandatory but only as "guiding" claims. The political power level seems to have become a little wiser, even though the whole apparatus of data-harvested claims and documentary teacher reports still exist (Skovmand 2019a, 2019b).

But, let us try to change gears and discuss what it means and implies – and how you can come to 'Know Thy Impact' as you write. Do you think that the Kantian notion of reflexive judgment is the right one to think about, concerning the learning impact? If we use Kant's notion of the autonomous reflection we honor a kind of a self-critical heritage from the enlightenment that you have to reflect upon your use of your reason without being prejudiced or perhaps being under pressure from another person's point of view, political and administrative power structures, and economic interests.

Or is it more likely that Luhmann's approach, which really wants to examine different logics of observation, can help you (Luhmann 1998)? The first-order observation could be to see what goes on between the teacher and the school students – that is, how they experience school life. The second-order observation could be how the teachers back up their practice with theory. The third-order observation could be how political and economic 'logics' interfere and intervene in schools. And the fourth-order observation could be to try to depict the blind spots being 'active' in the first three forms of observation and simultaneously attempt to strengthen your critique of the whole picture without losing contact with the first-order phenomenology of the active school subjects setting the take-off of your four-fold research.

How do you – in this preliminarily introduced Kant and Luhmann realm – build up your impact argument?

John: I think it's more of a Luhmannian approach as you've introduced it to me.

But I have a problem with how reflection is often used in education. Recently I was reading *Alice Through the Looking Glass* to my granddaughter, and this story helps with my problem (Carroll 1865). Alice did not stand in front of the mirror, and see and comment on her reflection. No, she touched the mirror and fell through, and saw how others from the other side saw her. Too often in education teachers reflect on what they think they see, and too often this leads to remarkably high levels of confirmation bias. They find five students who really got the ideas in the lesson and generalize from these five to all students. They find students who do not understand the lesson and find explanations why they could not get the ideas and rarely is it a function of their teaching and actions; they see and hear about 20% of the classroom (see Nuthall 2007) and generalize from this to the 100% of what occurred in the class that session. They can be very selective, usually with a high degree of confirmation bias, ignoring contrary evidence, speaking in anecdotes and war stories, generating from the few to all, and making claims about privilege (I was there you were not). Too often, this form of reflection reinforces prior beliefs about their teaching and impact.

I want them to be more deductive or abductive – to ask "What evidence would convince me I have not taught all the students such that make the progress I expected?" And also question whether their expectations of progress were good enough, whether *all* means *all*, and consider alternative approaches that may have been more efficient and effective. Often, this entails others critiquing and questioning, seeking the input from the students about their learning experience, triangulating with evidence from sources other than their own judgments, and using artefacts from all students from the lesson.

Ken Zeichner noted that there is too much advocacy for reflective teaching in general, and teachers' actions are not necessarily better just because they are more deliberate, intentional, or reflective (Zeichner 1992). John Dewey had it right when he claimed that reflection needs to relate to active problem-solving through identifying a problem, contemplating a solution, acting upon it, analyzing the problem-solving process, and if the problem is not resolved moving into a second course of action (Dewey 1933). This is the idea of seeking alternative solutions, adapting to the evidence of maximal impact on students.

I make the strong claim that the reflection needs to be focused on the impact on the students and not merely on the adequacy of the method of teaching. This problem is endemic particularly in teacher observation schedules. Both the Danielson and Marzano schedules focus more on the attributes of how one teacher and less than one-fifth of their scales are about the impact of teaching (Danielson 2011; Marzano 2018). The same mistaken focus on the teaching and the act of teaching is present in many video studies and lesson reviews.

In our work, we emphasize having an evaluative mindset – and indeed writing a book claiming that such thinking is the essence of the teaching profession. The mindsets related to reasoning and critical thinking in valuing evidence of impact, being open to unintended outcomes and allowing for adaptations to maximize the value of the outcomes, seeking one's potential biases and confounds that may lead to false conclusions, and seeking and understanding others' points of view leading to judgments of value or worth. These too are the fundamental skills of powerful reflection on one's impact.

Steen: Thanks for your clarification, John. In Denmark, these years, there is a tense debate between two different views on pedagogy. The critics call the standard one-size-fits-all educational thinking a 'pure' pedagogy while they favor a so-called 'impure' pedagogy (see Rømer et al. [eds.] 2011, 2014, 2017). The basic idea from those critics is that pedagogy is always 'impure' because you can never go with the same kind of ideas into any subject because you don't have an a priori general clue about how to teach and evaluate, and how to design and implement the goals of any learning system in advance. The idea that there exists a unified pedagogy for all subjects, for all pupils, at all levels the critics call 'pure' pedagogy.

And the 'impure' pedagogy movement in Denmark – in many books and public lectures – states that – instead of thinking that a one-size pedagogy fits all – you could say that, due to every context, every class, and every subject, you have to adjust what you could think of as pedagogy, and didactics, and learning goals, and whatever, due to the concrete 'logic' of the situation. The advocates of 'impure' pedagogy are of course – which will not surprise you – 'pure' anti-deductivists. So from the teacher's side you ought to base your pedagogy and your 'intervention' on the actual factual knowledge of what should be going on in this specific class on this specific day.

So, you can never have a set of strict instruments in your box or in your basket, independent of the class context, the history of the situation, the subject matter, and so on. And the critique was now from the 'impure' pedagogy people that, for example, your way of thinking, this evidence-based logic, this learning goal logic, this whole examination and testing logic, was in a way a too 'pure' pedagogy because they, more or less, have as the main argument that these 'pure' people, in believing in 'pure' pedagogy, would think that they could offer and implement a standard solution for all situations, cases, and classes.

So, in this sense, it seems to me that also you have to take into consideration what the 'impure' pedagogy argument claims that we – as teachers and researchers – also have to pay respect to different content (subjects, themes), obtain and integrate knowledge of different situations, and have an open and welcoming eye for different subjects, for different problems, for different groups, for different classes, different ages, etc.

John: But you've polarized it. There are skills of adaptation and most teachers are excellent at adapting – sometimes adapting interventions to fit their a priori ways of teaching, but many times to enhance the impact of their teaching on the students or adapt the innovation out of interventions. But there are probabilities about effective methods. I struggle to be put on one end or the other. I recognize that the moment-by-moment decisions that teachers make are the core of the success – hence the dependence of how teachers think (the mind frames), the notion of evaluation thinking, and the essence of expertise relating to how high-impact teachers think.

I am not a fan of overprescribing and note that too often systems overprescribe curricula and thence this becomes dominant; as we have noted earlier it is as much the skills of knowing, the curiosity of discovery, and the desire for our students to want to invest in more learning that is what we ask of our teachers. I'm a fan, no surprise, of the New Zealand curriculum which, for every subject, for every year, is only 39 pages, as I have already noted. It correctly puts a tremendous responsibility on the school to make decisions about the content. And that, to me, esteems the profession in a way that very few countries do. The polar extreme is when someone sits in the backroom and decides: "This is what you're going to do at 2 o'clock on Thursday afternoon." Obviously, some countries still do that. So your bipolar claims are excessive; although I see the importance of esteeming expertise – to reflect from the outside, to evaluate one's impact, to make moral purpose decisions about what to teach to what depth, and to develop the core evaluative thinking skills.

Steen: Sweden, for example, is well-known as having a strong national curriculum.

John: I have noted Michael Young's argument that we send students to school to get that which they wouldn't get if they didn't go to school (Young & Muller 2013). And that then begs the question of what that content is they 'wouldn't get'. It's kind of like you were saying before – our heritage is part of that. But there's a whole dispute on what our heritage is. Of course, this too is a core content that they would be less likely to be exposed to if they did not go to school.

Steen: I like Young's argument.

John: But that's where teachers need to be involved in the debate about curricula. I take the strong argument here in Australia that the health of a high school system is very much a function of the health of the subject specialist associations where they have these debates. We should be codifying great themes, ways of thinking as much as the content, because when the content is privileged, then surface level learning is clearly mandated. I have never met a group of educators on a curriculum committee who want to take dollops of content out of the curriculum. Every time a curriculum is updated it seems to get expanded. The Australian curriculum is over 2,500 pages!

The relation between research and politics

Steen: But the delicate relation between research and politics seems to imply that you have a double agenda all the time, John. Your *Visible Learning* approach primarily wants the teachers to be more professional and to communicate with them through books, courses, and speeches to make them reflect better about their impact, about their roles as teachers in society, and about what's actually going on in classes. And also be able to listen to what other teachers can tell them, and what experiences in other classes could inform them about. But at the very same time you want to influence politics.

John: I do.

Steen: But when you enter those two different fields you need to know and to reflect upon the fact that they do not have or obey the same code logic to draw upon Luhmann's vocabulary. The first one deals with questions like being better to teach or being bad to teach, and do the students learn something or do they learn nothing. That's the code of education.

The other is how you get power over decision making in politics, which is a completely other code logic. So, do you think that demands a split in your personality? Among the researchers you use one language (concerning knowledge and truth) and among the politicians another (concerning power and influence)? Now and then ethical concerns might 'sneak in' the science sphere and in politics but you can't be sure that it happens.

John: I know the two different vocabularies.

Steen: And when you go to teachers' union meetings or talk to teachers in school in the suburbs or in the faraway countryside in Australia then you are more in line with the standard educational code and you don't question what people are doing in a political- and a power-related perspective, I guess. So, do you then have two different languages?

John: Oh, totally.

Steen: Or do you have a unison language – or even a meta-reflective language of your own . . .?

John: Well, I have to live with myself. I can't have a split personality. The core notion is being true to how I interpret the evidence, even if it conflicts with the political imperative of the moment.

Steen: You seem to have 'grown' a bifurcated tongue.

John: Oh, I do. I acknowledge that I have to use a different language when speaking with fellow academics than when speaking to policy and political people. We each have our jargon. I know in my writing I am quite adept at writing in the academic language, but it carries little when talking to politicians. Also it is often not the best language to talk to teachers, and hopeless when talking to parents. That is why I surround myself with people who have those skills, so we can do it together. Does that make me, therefore, schizoid?

Steen: No, not necessarily.

John: Similarly with politics, I have had long training, starting back in my West Australia days (1980–1990s), of learning how to speak with politicians. Too often we personify politicians as a category, but they are unique people. That's the first step you have to learn when you deal with them as individual people, understand their thinking, their motivations, their visions, their agenda.

It is a bit like how we academics write for and talk to teachers, and too often the assumption is that teachers do not have strong theories of teaching, too often we have determined views about what works for them and not, and we have much evidence from their practice that informs them of their next steps. To ignore this is to certainly turn them off, but just as important is that they are rarely then turned on to what we might have to say. Ditto with politicians.

My fascination is that most politicians usually have the best of motives to make a difference. So why do they do such silly things (Hattie 2015)? And there's hardly a politician I've met who is not decent, has an imperative to improve the system, but too often they latch on to the cosmetics of schooling and rarely deal with the central issue of esteeming and enhancing expertise.

For example, last night, I had a minister from overseas ring me (actually close to Denmark), and he was a brand new minister seeking views. He wanted to know more about my work, wanted me to visit his country, and asked about the most important things he should do first. Now, I am nervous about proscribing anything, particularly when I know so little of the history – both longer- and short-term history – of schooling in that country. I learned many years ago, when I went to Liberia in my 20s, that you never make pronouncements about countries without knowing the history about it and their background. Yes, expertise in the country is necessary, so I am able to speak about my research, but they must do the translation to their context.

The other thing I've learned working with politicians is you listen to them. They have needs and motives. If you walk into a politician's office and give them the answer, you'll walk out and then nothing would happen. There is a code and a language of politics and it is necessary to learn their language to then be able to influence them. For politicians, the most critical audience is their voters (not the academics). They so often interpret advice in terms of how it will appeal to their voters – and this is not being cynical, as this is how it works. They want the best advice but have a lens of how to make it succeed with their audience. When you work with them you need to help them translate educational ideas into language for the voters – and more and more voters no longer have a child or grandchild in schools – so it is not just the parents but the voters.

Too often, as educators, we talk to them without understanding their logic, their contingencies, their languages. I have seen so many politicians wait and hear the incoming demands, requests for funding, and too often educationalists have no idea how it fits with the mandate, current policies, and with the minister's view of what best to fund. So often educationalists have the same mantra: Minister, my school is excellent, I have excellent teachers, you must come and visit us, but we need money for a new science block, a new toilet. Minister, my school has xx ethnicities and xx languages, we are unique (most schools across Australia have these attributes) and so on. But this is now the norm. In the many years I have sat on the minister's side of the table I have rarely heard an educator asking for more resources to develop expertise – it is nearly always for things, buildings, and for more autonomy. Despite Australian principals having had probably more autonomy in the western world, too rarely work with other schools to develop combined expertise, the mantra seems to be 'give us more money and leave us alone'.

The same for others in the school sector, for example, vice-chancellors or presidents of universities. As many ministers have said, if you get a group of vice-chancellors in the room, and they start to tell you things you do not want to hear, all you need to do is throw $10 on the floor, and they have a fight over it. They want the money and they want the autonomy. They rarely want to help the minister do his or her job, which is to make an impact across the country to show that you're changing the nation, that you're helping the students, and enhancing the economy, the future, and the voters.

I would have a rule to never ask a minister for a one-off solution (for *a* school or for *a* university). Unless the solution applies across 1,000s of schools it is unlikely to impact policy. We probably need for education from political lobbyists how to argue in the policy circles, and nearly every principal has told me – yes, I know this, but he can make this exception for me. We have over 50 groups claiming to speak for school leaders across Australia and I struggle to know what any of them stand for – other than providing professional learning for their members. They continue to speak to the politicians but with such divided voices that this gives the minister the option to pick and choose his own ideas. I cannot imagine the minister of health would develop a policy without asking, "I wonder what the medical professional body would think about this policy." But I know the minister of education does not have any second thoughts about what the education policy groups think. Wait, look enough, and he can find advocates.

The greater problem I have with the political scene is that, when you ask many of the parents about what they wanted to invest in schools, sometimes it's not in the best interest of students. For example, the ABC here in Australia asked over 1,000 voters to rate from a list of influences from *Visible Learning* what they would invest in, and their results were negatively correlated with the evidence. What the parents wanted most was not in the best interests of the students.

In my quasi-political role here in Australia I have now worked with over 30 ministers and directors-general from every branch of political persuasions. I am adamant that my only advice is my professional education research advice and I never advise on politics. I am prepared to say it as I see it on the basis of what I know, and have informed ministers when I disagree, and I am very clear not to advise when it is out of my expertise. One of them rang me recently and asked me about something. I said, "With respect, Minister, that's not my area of expertise." They value that.

Further, if you break a confidence, they will drop you like a hotcake.

If I have any success in this political arena, I want to be known as the person who re-introduced the notion of expertise back into schooling. As the research from *Visible Learning* shows, and from my work in measurement of teacher effectiveness, we have the majority of teachers and schools doing a stunning job enabling their students to gain more than a year's growth for a year's input. Our role is to esteem the expertise that enables this and most importantly to scale up this expertise.

I worry, as too often happens when expertise is not valued, that resources are asked for and then the amateur solutions abound. I note the massive increase in wages now devoted to teacher aides, to minimally educated teachers, and to bringing in substitutes to excellence. Yes, it costs more to create time for educators to work, plan, and evaluate their impact together, to develop and improve the expertise already there, and to induct new people into our profession.

Steen: Thanks for this enlightening description of the delicate relation between educational politics and science.

I have this idea, while I'm reading your newest book, *10 Mindframes for Visible Learning* (Hattie & Zierer 2018), that you have come to realize that you need a stronger narrative in a philosophical way or in a kind of utopian hopeful way, like Martin Luther King's *I have a dream* and all that stuff.

John: It's always been there, Steen.

Steen: Yeah, it's probably always been there but now you feel an urge and a need to write and proclaim it out loud.

John: Yes, you are right. The critics have convinced me that more than what I wrote in that book is needed. Because people, as you've said many times, have misinterpreted *Visible Learning*, which was a research book about meta-analysis, as being the answer to everything, and it's not. I tried, but clearly was not convincing enough, to say that there is more to schooling than achievement, that students do not leave poverty at the school gate, and that the social and moral purpose questions about the reasons for education need to be included.

Steen: And, in those days, when you were writing those books, you were more, I would say, statistician or technician?

John: I was. Of course, I was very focused. I am a measurement person, not a sociologist and I did bring a lens of more of an educational psychologist to this literature. But if there is another interpretation of the data from other perspectives I will be the first to welcome and honor it.

Steen: But now you feel . . .

John: That book was never written for the general public. It was never written for teachers. My goodness, it's full of numbers and data. It was my tenth book and I never imagined the spread of readers it would attract.

Steen: . . . the need and the urge to give an extra narrative.

John: Well, I think it's an opportunity that I have now been blessed with. What luxury do we have as academics . . . most of us as academics, me included, we could've spent our whole life teaching in academia, and no one would've cared. People actually care about some of the things I say. So I have an opportunity to say some of these things, which is why I'm talking to you. Why I have now written another 20 books, I speak widely, I support the implementation of the ideas – what a sense of wonder this is.

Steen: Another thing is that, if you go think in line with Luhmann, our inspiring theoretical assessor, he would say, "Well, a university is not the human being there. It's not the person and does not possess a psychic and mental sub-system. You cannot comb the hair of a university nor look it into its eyes." The university is a communicative sub-system.

John: Oh, it is. And yet there's more to a university than people. The concept of a university is a polymorphous notion – it is a collection of individuals, and we as the individuals within a university are responsible for the collective impact of our home.

Steen: And if you read the German sociologist Georg Simmel's 1908 text *Wie ist Gesellschaft möglich?* (*How Is Society Possible?*), one of the founding fathers of sociology, like Auguste Comte, Émile Durkheim, Max Weber, and Gabriel Tarde, then you would probably be inspired to say that even though we are a part of the more or less compulsory social order and subjected to powerful structures there is also an existence of an extra social behavior. Meaning that we are not with our full personality embedded in social communication structures (Simmel 1910/1908).

John: But we build systems. And as you have continually reminded me, we need to be the critics and conscience of not only our society but also our own institution.

Steen: We 'have' social communication systems, but we also 'have' persons and human beings and they are not exactly the same. They cannot be completely identified as social communicative roles. So they will always be kind of a non-identity between the human beings (in an existential perspective) and the sources of communication (in a social perspective).

John: All right. In the same way that Mercedes-Benz is more than a group of people.

Steen: Yeah, you might say so, but my view that we – as researchers and also as political creatures – are changing the role of communication with research, politics, and actions of all kind. And that's also interesting to acknowledge that we are constantly engaged in changing the whole societal communication about things, not the least through research.

John: Exactly, and I've said this a hundred times. All I did was create a story. Did I create a single piece of new data? No. Because I reflected on what others have done. My contribution was the story.

Enforced strategic self-doubling

Steen: My worry is that the more you invest in this ever-ongoing and mandatory strategic self-doubling of learning logics, meaning that you should learn about your own learning effect as a teacher and your own learning outcome as a pupil, while you're respectively teaching and learning, the more you do that, the more time and attention you take away from subjects and substance, from deep reading, immense studying, and free-thinking (Larsen 2016a).

John: Well, you may be right. But one core impact question relates to the choice of subjects and substance, so they are very much present.

Steen: My idea is now that if you've become too preoccupied and pre-obsessed with this learning logic, then suddenly the students will be more and more interested . . .

John: No, no, no, no.

Steen: . . . in learning strategies and learning goals than literature, math, and history . . .

John: Come on. As our meta-synthesis on learning strategies show, there are few strategies that are devoid of an application or a content. We scotch the myth that developing generic learning strategies is worthwhile. Yes, students can get better using some of the strategies, but they are rarely transferable. Take developing working memory – we can enhance it generically, but the transfer to other topics is close to zero. By playing working memory games you get better at working memory games, and that is it.

Steen: Okay, it might be a good idea that the teachers, students, and pupils can go back and listen to tape recordings. Very often when I give super-vision for master works in process, the students activate their mobile phone tape recorder because they want to hear what I say at their own tempo after the meeting.

John: Well, we're providing that for them. But that is the least of the value. We want to influence the interpretative lens teachers have when they review their impact. We do not want them only to be selective and choose the parts they recall, that impacted on them, we want them to see who they did not impact on, about what, and have more considera-tion about all the students.

Steen: And probably it's a very dense communication. And maybe I have ten dif-ferent ideas, and they only write down three of them, and forget the rest.

John: Yes, and among the seven forgotten and 'deleted' ideas there may be more information. And there is the context in which you're thinking.

Steen: Yes, the context of utmost importance. Very often, I also write com-ments and questions into their written assessment and thesis papers in process because one thing is what you talk about, another thing is that if you actually write "Strengthen your argumentation here," "I suggest that you read another book of theory for inspiration," "This is a reverse logic compared to your statement above," etc. So, a very good thing is to give written feedback, and at the same time, oral feedback. I try to make it possible to come to see and acknowledge if they manage to improve their argumentation and style of writing . . . next time we'll meet.

John: We're at the moment in a randomized control study. Two hundred schools using the *Visible Classroom* technology, 200 not. We kind of know that the bottom 10% to 15% of teachers, in terms of impact, have least impact with this methodology and dislike using it. They say, "Why should I listen to my disciplining the students, hearing their voices, what would a nine-year-old know about learning." But if we don't deal with the 10% to 15%, we're not solving the problem of scalability.

The majority of teachers love it. They do have a fear of it being misused for all of the kind of reasons you're talking about (such as misusing it in high-stakes accountability), and we share that fear. But my point is, and the big point coming back to what we were talking about before, I do think there is an obligation of the system to provide resources for teachers to see their impact.

I do think, for instance, as we know in some of our early studies, in the efficacy studies in England on this, that we went into some schools and used this technology, some who barely looked at what they said now wanted to know how they were being heard by the students.

Now, this is one of the other criticisms that you haven't made, but many people have made, of my work: "He blames the teachers. The teachers have to fix themselves. You are going for the cheapest intervention by asking the teachers themselves to 'fix thyself'. My argument is that what I'm arguing for is the most expensive intervention of the lot. You have to create time, resources, and employ experts to work with teachers to accomplish the instructional part of the *Visible Learning* model. It's not an add-on. As can be seen in my books on implementation, it is often tough to develop evaluative mindsets, to engage in developing collective efficacy, to have a focus on enhancing learning as well as the content, to give and hear how your feedback is received, and wow there is a deep level of trust needed for teachers to have these discussions.

Steen: And that's why you criticize the Danish minister of education, Christine Antorini, for her deeds in 2013 when the new school law was enforced against the will of the teachers and without even inviting them to take part in the former political negotiations.

John: Yes, totally. She missed the point completely. Your system whereby teachers had time during each week was a powerful resource to enable *Visible Learning* to work.

Steen: But she and the government, the majority of the political parties, and do not to forget the semi-god-like minister of finance, and the leading school bureaucrats wanted to diminish the hours of preparation the teachers used to use and not the least to implement the learning goals as the new and mandatory gold standard in Danish schools.

John: Now, I want to take the hours of preparation away in the sense that I don't think that the only task teachers should do when they're not in the classroom is prepare and mark. They should also critique their impact, and they can't do it as well by themselves as they need professional learning communities run by people who know how to privilege this narrative of impact, who know how to build trust, and who can avoid any whiff of accountability.

Steen: I know that these learning communities, professional team spirit initiatives, and so on were also a part of a critique against what you call 'the private practicing teacher' or whatever it's called in standard literature. But it is my worry that we tend to forget and even repress that probably all of us (the adults) during our school time met and were inspired by important and outstanding teachers, and I guess that they might have happened to be 'private', experienced, and self-grown – but of course also educated and professional – teachers.

John: Yes, I have written about the teachers we recall we had, and they were too random an occurrence.

Steen: And those days are probably never coming back. Now you're part of a bigger team.

John: I'm not prepared to let even the best teachers go back into their room, close their doors, and do their work. They've got to be part of the solution. It is their thinking we most want to listen to.

Steen: Okay, I will think about another question for you. Why do you, favoring and honoring very strong data-grounded narratives, also place a big role in the idiosyncratic and personal – for example, that you had to escape New Zealand and your non-stimulating rural family background to become what you are now? Meaning, that even though you're a deductive guy and you want to gather quantitative things on behalf of which you can deduct, you also tend to be very idiosyncratic and maybe even inductive, at least when it comes to your own story?

John: Yes, if I had stayed in my town I think I would have gone mad. The horizons were closed, the ambitions trivial, and the opportunities few. And I have no problems with induction, and enjoy working with qualitative and inductive experts as they enable me to see the data, the class, and the evidence from different perspectives. This inductive method is just not my skill set.

Steen: That means that you also, in order to strengthen your narrative, become a 'private practicing researcher', addressing personal life context stories right in the midst of your work and talks.

John: Yes, it is wonderful to listen to these powerful stories, to have the luxury of reading others' experiences, and to delve deeply in the literature about our profession.

Steen: And my problem is that, if we go too much in the direction of teams, we would also have very boring teachers. It could be that each of them should have a standard theme, they should not be personal, they should not use life history because it cannot be generalized.

John: No, no, I'll take you to Skanderborg schools in Denmark or to schools here in Melbourne, and you tell me those teachers who embark on the *Visible Learning* journey are less personable, are boring, and are self-absorbed. They are the exact opposite.

Steen: Because . . .?

John: Because they do not engage in the typical war-story mentality of professional learning. "I did it this way. This is how I did it." Let me watch you so I pick from tricks and tips to add to my arsenal. Of course I respect that you teach differently than I (as long as you acknowledge that I too can be idiosyncratic and do not change me). But in my team delivering *Visible Learning* professional learning, one of our rules is that you cannot talk about your classroom because that legitimizes your war story and legitimizes the participants to see their world through their own war stories. And too much of our discussion in education is about seeing the world as we have seen it for so long. Here's the strong argument that underlies these war stories: When I talk about my war story, you can't possibly have a view because you weren't there. You don't know those students, and you don't know what happened. You can only see it through my eyes. That is not good enough.

Steen: That's true. But I think that my worry is combined to this whole logic of university course administration where what they more or less want you to do is to make a kind of a course description that is non-subjectified, non-contextualized, and not based on deep experiences. The practical hope and claim are that every other colleague could take over and run it their way because the ECTS-module course is made so anonymous and general, so it doesn't have any kind of subjective spirit, or historical, or even life historical, narrative of the man or woman who created the course.

John: No, no, no, let's be careful. I'm not sure it's a problem. Take direct instruction. Take a lot of the work I do. It's scripted. People practice the scripts. But when they get in front of the students, if it looks like a script, feels like a script, smells like a script, then it's a failure. There is a balance here. It isn't carte blanche. It isn't laissez-faire. It isn't do-it-as-you-like. It's not like saying to the airplane pilot, "Fly the plane as you please." There are rules. There are scripts. But it's the decision making that you make when things don't go according to the script that is the essence of good teaching. And so I think you overplay the argument that scripting is bad. I think scripting is kind of like building the mental maps, building the model that you can deviate from. Also it means that your resources can be then used to make the modifications, the adaptations, the evaluations to enhance the outcomes.

Take for example, a teacher (different from the one mentioned earlier) that I have been shadowing for eight years now. About five years ago he told me he did not want to get better as a teacher. Of course, I was shocked until he clarified – he wanted to not be better as a teacher in a typical classroom. He wanted to work closer with other teachers, to spend more of his resources with the students, so moved to open plan classes (3 teachers with 90+ students). After a couple of years he said, "Don't tell anyone, but I do so much less planning here than I did in the regular class; I have my weekends back." That is because in his school there are three semesters in a year and each teacher takes responsibility for planning one term – for two terms he has no planning. It does mean that the three teachers have to bond, have trust, and to know each other's preferences and dislikes about planning and teaching. Now he spends so much time working with the students, as he trusts the script.

Evidence management

John: There is so much debate about 'evidence' and rarely is this notion queried. Here in Australia, at the moment, there's a big debate about building an evidence institute for teaching. My fear is that we'll become like What Works Clearinghouse, and people will be employed to take academic research and translate it into easy language for teachers. This has not been a huge success.

Steen: That's also what it's used for in Denmark, and it also functions as a major politics of knowledge institution stating what counts as research and what does not count (Larsen 2015d).

John: It's not a very powerful way of doing it. When you look at the evidence – and the UK Education Endowment Fund (https://educationendowment

foundation.org.uk) did this – it doesn't make a difference to the quality of what happens in classrooms. One of their first randomized control trials was giving teachers books and resources (including summaries of *Visible Learning*) and of course little changed. Sometimes we underestimate the importance and value of the 'evidence' from teachers' viewpoint – evidence from their years of experience. It too can be valid, critiqued, wrong, and we can learn from it. It is harder to harness, too often comes as n = 1 stories, but it is still a legitimate form of evidence.

Steen: We should probably ask the students then, I think (Batchelor 2008).

John: They should be involved, and they certainly have legitimate forms and stories of evidence. Absolutely. And that's my argument about building an evidence-based institute: there are multiple forms of evidence. The most important form of evidence is to allow teachers to contest their view of evidence in the same way they want to contest my academic view of evidence, as we should contest students' form of evidence. But so often, and you did this just then, teachers won't allow them to be contested because they say, "You weren't there. You didn't know. My students said."

More important, in many ways the days of evidence are diminishing; the days of implementing evidence are with us – and this is much harder. The focus needs to be on disseminating and mobilization.

Much more than evaluations

Steen: But what about evaluative thinking, I know you have a very positive view of evaluation and professionalizing evaluation. So these e-words and procedures seem to have become a part of what you will think of as enlightenment, self-critique, and know your impact and all that.

John: It is going further than that because the notion of evaluation is about merit, worth, and significance. It's not just how big the effect and the nature and magnitude of the impact. It's also about the value of that impact. To me, it's trying to bring together the notion of judgment, critical thinking, and values. It is not merely, "You get this impact; therefore, you've done a good job." It might be the wrong stuff that is the focus of this impact. Evaluative thinking involves reasoning related to the teachers' critical reasoning, the decisions they make about 'where to next', checking for unintended consequences, being more aware of potential biases, having skills in knowing one's impact, debating this notion of impact, and seeking other points of view. Your main argument is that it is very much *how* the teachers are thinking that matters, and the same can be applied to how the students are thinking about their learning, progress, and achievement.

Steen: But what I am thinking is the danger that the evaluation rituals are drowning the teachers in this neverending meta–meta–meta–reflection about learning and describing the goals of the school, blah, blah, and that contributes to an alienated language and ends up being very time and energy consuming. If you lose contact with what actually was the burning fuel of becoming a teacher, the dream of becoming a teacher risks vanishing while you are being swallowed by the unstoppable evaluation machines (Larsen 2004).

John: So what is the burning fuel of becoming a teacher?

Steen: That was maybe, also, to live in the midst of equations and figures, and the wonderful, exact, but also now and then enigmatic world of mathematics, and all kind of substantial stuff, but also to give and share a sense of that wondrous, wondering feeling to other ones, students and youngsters.

John: Exactly, to have an impact on others.

Steen: Or maybe if you're a physics teacher and begin to open the students' eyes to a giant physical approach, expanding the universe through the history of different cosmologies, introducing the pupils to Big Bang theories, the first traces of life on Earth, and you start debating how we are placed in the midst of all these planets, stars, and galaxies . . .

John: You have the passion.

Steen: . . . Well, mankind was only here for a short while compared to the history of nearly 14 billion years since the Big Bang. So mankind – 'the we' we are – has probably been 'around' here just for one second (approximately 200,000 years in the most recent Homo-form, reminding us of modern man . . .) out of the whole day if we take that to be 24 hours since the Big Bang. Now, what happened the first 23 hours, 59 minutes, 59 seconds? That's worth discussing. And now you are the geologist, biologist, big ape (hominids) investigator, whatever. So I think that many of these teachers, they have these dreams that we come back to these subjects and questions, and not to waste their time with learning goal agendas and evaluation reports.

John: Sure. They want to share their passion.

Steen: So there's kind of . . . with the best intentions, you have a lot of impact to discuss how we can arrange learning goals and learning processes the best we can do. It's more or less looking like a very abstract management kind of language, and that's the danger of this – for example, that the false risks to sneak into a word like 'impact'.

John: Yeah, I can see that.

Steen: That it ends up being planning for planning's own sake.

John: I agree. But this is why I want to move to the evaluative thinking because I want to stress that notion of value. You can have impact about the wrong stuff. So there has to be an evaluative component about why you're doing this rather than that.

Steen: Value-additive thinking, it must be another concept of value because normally, if you had value, you would have it in the economic sense. It's a question about maintaining or accumulating. But I think that a very positive value, in another sense of the meaning value, could be that you overturn your prejudice and maybe dare to change your life trajectory, and that you do not stick to or pedestalize petrified cultural conservative or religious values, the other big tradition of using the value semantics beside the economic field.

John: But this is why the merit, worth, and significant notion are the core of evaluation. And that forces you to have to defend such things as, "My job is to have students know this stuff" – the indoctrination notion – or, "My students are to know this stuff, so they can question it. They can get passionate about it. They can overturn it."

Steen: I think that we can envisage two counter-poles, depicting two extreme positions. Either to indoctrinate and decide everything top-down or not to be there at all and just to let the students do whatever they like.

John: That's right.

Steen: Position number two will, for example, honor soft power imperatives, like "Come up with something you are interested in."

John: That's right, but interest also need to be developed – some have very narrow or unproductive interests, and as I noted earlier, often we become 'interested' after we have some success in learning.

Steen: "I don't care about mathematics. Just invent it yourself." Of course, both positions are more or less ridiculous.

John: Yes, wouldn't it be great if we could choose either/or, when the answer need not be at either extreme?

Steen: So somewhere in the middle, where you have your cunning, knowing teachers, at the same time, the value of a good, unforeseen, until that very moment unheard interpretation coming from a kid, a pupil from the last row in the classroom, could be fantastic.

Data-driven teaching without interpretation?

Steen: Let's move back into your field. It has been said in educational politics that teaching can be data driven. Is this a misunderstanding, while you are in favor of a view of teaching as an interpretation of the collected and available data?

John: No, even that's not right, absolutely not. You've heard me say 1,000 times that it is not the data but the interpretation of the data. Of course, the interpretation is more robust and defensible when it based on valid and information rich data, but it is the argument and claims based on this evidence that matters. That is why I am fascinated and interested in the moment-by-moment decisions that teachers are making during a lesson – how come they make this interpretation rather than that from the data/evidence in front of them; and how they check on the impact of their interpretations. Part of it comes from the data, part of it comes from past experiences when confronted with similar data, part of it comes from previous knowledge, a lot is pattern recognition and match-ing with similar encounters, and all is based on the models of teaching and learning that they have entering the class.

Steen: So, basically, this language about data-driven teaching is not your vocabulary.

John: Never.

Steen: Yeah, that's it. Congenially, Biesta claims that teachers and pupils, or stu-dents, always take part in what he called: *The Beautiful Risk of Education* (Biesta 2013).

John: Yeah, as you know I find this title wonderful.

Steen: Meaning that there can be no security for their interaction, neither for the result in advance. So he always talks about the risk of education. Is that a vocabulary that you find promising and useful?

John: Risks are not necessarily what it is about. I am as interested in the mitigation strategies for risks, but it is not as nice: "The beautiful mitigation of risks in education." As a former head of school in four universities, I saw my role more in terms of risk mitigation, otherwise you reduce or eliminate risks – and where's the fun, growth, and excitement in this?

  We can't lead students into danger. We can't indoctrinate them. We can't do certain things to them. But most learning is a risk – what I know could be wrong, I may need to revisit some of my assumptions, I may need to invest to learn more, I may need to seek evidence about where and how I am wrong. Even in the models I have developed in education there are risks built in. The notion that a model should say more than it explains automatically introduces risks, and that risk is the fundamental essence of learning.

Steen: D'accord. How is it that we have come to live in a competitive society, which actually changes all the time, as do the rules we live by, and this very society has fallen in love with security or demands for security and does therefore not invite to radical experiments? It cannot stand risks and, at the same time, it's a very risky, competitive society. It is obsessed with control but flirts recently with disruption ideology. It demands security that it cannot provide.

John: I agree with you.

Which code differences characterize educational research and educational politics?
How can educational science be used to legitimize educational politics?
Is the *Visible Learning* program primarily written for teachers or politicians?
Which consequences will it have for future educational politics that will be far more data-driven than today?

VIII. IS IT POSSIBLE TO REVITALIZE THE GERMAN concept of BILDUNG ie THE FORMATION of CHARACTER and the HIGHER IDEAS and IDEALS of EDUCATION?

BILDUNG relates TO THE FORMATION of:

the CITIZEN

THINKING

CHARACTER

Bildung

SCHOOL SHOULD PRESENT the BEST of WHAT has BEEN
THOUGHT CREATED WRITTEN

YOU SHOULD be PRESENTING also the WORST THING that MANKIND HAS EVER DONE.

HAS the CONCEPT of CHARACTER changed?

YES.

RICHARD RORTY

WE NEED to BRING CURIOSITY to THE fore at ALL AGES

MORE OPPORTUNISTIC.

and now

SELF-CONTROLLED and STRATEGIC,

WE NEED to TEACH STUDENTS to BE OPEN TO OTHER interpretations and OTHER EXPERIENCES.

to

WE HAVE moved from POLITE and DISCIPLINED,

3 YEAR OLDS ask WHY?

8 YEAR OLDS ask WHAT?

FOUR!   THREE!

15 YEAR OLDS ask WHY NOT?

WE NEED to KNOW that WHAT we HAVE learned MAY be SHOWN to be WRONG TOMORROW.

THE PURPOSE of education IS to DISRUPT OUR COMMON UNDERSTANDINGS.

Steen: There is a very big subject that we haven't touched upon but has my major interest. And this is about the untranslatability – but even more about the unrealized positive implications – of the powerful and rich educational historical word *Bildung*.

John: *Bildung*, yes.

Steen: In an American, Australian, or English version, it will probably be translated to education, formation, or edification. Somebody would even say culture.

John: Character.

Steen: Formation of character, okay, that's one attempt to make a proper translation.

Let me give a little presentation of the theme. When we go to German language, we have *Ausbildung* for education and therefore the suffix *Bildung* as a part of that word. In Denmark, we have exactly the same. Education is *uddannelse* and *Bildung* in Danish is *dannelse*. So, in these two languages, in these two European languages, we have the *Bildung* aspect inscribed in the word for education as a memorable and important part. We don't have that in the English, American, and Australian languages and contexts.

So, let's go back to this history of the concept *Bildung* in the German tradition, at least. It's a mixture of, I guess, two or three narratives. One has its roots in Christianity, where you have the Bible stating in Genesis 1:22 that man was created in God's image (*imago dei* in Latin). In this way man is created by power much bigger than him- or herself but also with the capacity to try to live up to that ideal image even though man can't and should never try to become God (*anti superbia*, anti-arrogance). But we are created in this logic of being bigger than ourselves. That's the first narrative.

On the other hand, the leading bourgeois class of Germany, the liberal bourgeois class and the enlightenment – and some of the romantic – philosophers started to secularize the *Bildung* concept and combine it to practical way of thinking and acting in the world. Some of them stated the ambition that the task was to 'realize' mankind in your own person, to give your character the right form and lift it to the highest spiritual heights. Or you could aspire and strive towards big, leading figures in societies. It could be big authors, big thinkers, and you could mirror yourself in what they have achieved. So you could look up to something: the high culture, the high knowledge, high autonomy, and self-determination. All these kinds of principles were now embedded in the picture, in the mirroring of who you should become. That's the second narrative.

And then, the third narrative comes out of the struggle of whether or not to maintain that *Bildung* concept. For example, the leftist 1968 movement – in Europe and the US – that were harshly against it, furiously to kill it because they said it belongs to the ruling bourgeois class, their values of behaving well, and having all these kind of normalization logics attached to the *Bildung* concept. So they, in a way, try to get rid of the *Bildung* concept and to leave the established traditions and different taste and style regimes behind.

Today, there are forces out there, at least in Denmark and Germany, to revitalize the *Bildung* concept. Not that we should become God, neither should we 'realize' mankind in one person, neither should we now think that we should impose cultural values from the upper class towards the lower classes or anything of that kind, or white man's superior dominance to black people, or whatever. But we could maybe start thinking about revitalizing the *Bildung* concept, maybe also to qualify a substantial critique of the present ideology of 'learnification' – which is not exactly Biesta's nor my cup of tea.

So, let me now try to present three interpretations of this multifaceted and highly contested *Bildung* concept in an attempt to revitalize it. One could be to say that it has to do with our knowledge, meaning the capacity to think and to know something about something. Meaning that *Bildung* has a component here of knowing and thinking, which you could call the formation of thinking, the formation of knowledge making, knowledge achievement, knowledge scaling. Another perspective could be that every time you have to deal with a school, a university, or a gymnasium (high school), you have to deal with formation of the citizen. The pupils and the students have to take part in the public debates and be active political citizens. So that's formation of the political skills or the citizenship skills, also how you behave in a civil society and also in a cosmopolitan world sphere, all attached to this *Bildung* of the citizen logic. And the third dimension could be the formation of character. How do you become a subject with a personality and will of your own? How do you become an open-minded and curious identity? How do you become a subject worthy in itself with dignity, with aspiration, hope, power, strength, humility, etc. Here we are focusing on everything 'attached' to a person, his or her formation of character.

So, this triangular revitalization logic of the concept *Bildung*, how do you view and interpret that? And how do you comprehend the more or less untranslatable concept *Bildung* in educational research, and how have you dealt with that? I guess you know some of this heritage from and discussions in the maelstrom of the German thinkers from Herder, Humboldt, Kant, Hegel, and many others. You know, they were the *Bildung* fathers, and in 1809 Wilhelm von Humboldt established Humboldt University in Berlin, which was built upon this *Bildung* logic.

Humboldt's slogan was "*Bildung durch Wissenschaft*" (*Bildung* through or via science). So, how do you view all this?

John: Let me ask you a couple of questions first. What does that *Bildung* logic, particularly as your portrayal into those three different kinds of dimensions of *Bildung*, how does that help understand or answer the question about content?

Steen: My way of thinking is that every teacher who has a kind of a right, and privilege, and maybe also the obligation to present a concept — mathematics, or literature, or interpreting biological systems of life or whatever — they have in a way a *Bildung* task. So, the first part of my revitalized *Bildung* logic would be that they're presenting both 'old' and new knowledge of their subject. They're inviting people to reflect upon that knowledge, to have access to that knowledge, to study the field, and to know how the field has changed. So, if it's like, for example, physics, you have to know Newtonian physics, and to learn some quantum physics, and what Niels Bohr and Einstein had to say, meaning that you have to know the history of physics as well. If you're studying economy, you also have to know the history of economic science from Malthus, Smith, Ricardo, Marx, and onwards. So, the idea is now that the teacher plays an important role when it comes to knowing and thinking.

John: If you are teaching, do you have to understand the history of being a teacher? Do you have to understand the history of your country, of being an educator? Because many don't.

Steen: I think that, at least, to know a part of the history of the subject that you are presenting is helpful . . . and if you have two subjects you have to come to know more . . . I don't know how it is in Australia, but in Denmark you are . . . normally, in the old days, now it's maybe falling a little bit apart, but you had maybe one or two major subjects in which you could teach in a school. And you had broader disciplinary knowledge of everything else, but you have at least two main subjects — for example, maybe you are the literature and math teacher, or maybe you 'perform' three subjects such as physics, chemistry, and biology, or the English, German, and Danish language.

John: In the jargon, there's a canon.

Steen: Yeah, in a way, but it is not fixated, once and for all, and definitely not only a national one. If you as a teacher try to get hired in a Danish school, the principal will probably ask you, "Are you primarily a literary teacher, or a math teacher, or a German teacher, or an English language teacher?" You will probably get classes in the higher grades due to your main subjects that you know of. I guess it is the same case here. So, my idea is that, when it comes to the *Bildung* question, the teacher's role is, of course, at all three levels, to invite different processes to happen to the subject matter. If we deal with, like, biology, this subject does also have to do with *Bildung* processes pointing towards the political sphere and to the formation of our lives as citizens. Of course, it also has to do with what is actually the respect for nature, and how we handle resources, and how we ought not to anthropomorphize nature, and how we deal with the pressure from the economic growth paradigm . . .

John: It takes me back to when I was a 14-year-old doing science at school. I don't need to know about mitosis and osmosis and all those things to do that.

Steen: No, but in a whole life perspective of maybe ten years in school, you'll come to know about osmosis and you'll come to know about ecosystems.

John: But you're not helping me here because what I'm hearing you saying now is that there is a canon.

Steen: Not a national cultural conservative canon.

John: And I don't need to know osmosis to have character and to do the other three attributes of *Bildung*. I need enough to know to respect nature and society and values. I'm struggling here.

Steen: Yeah, my view is now that schools are also inviting you into the field of what is at stake in research.

John: Yes, but schools usually demand you do it. "You must do math. You must do biology." Defend that.

Steen: But, at the same time, you say that, of course, it's demanding something, but it's also inviting you. So, my thing here is, can we invite people to become whole human beings? Not everybody should be intellectuals or academics from the time they are a five-year-old or an eight-year-old, but at least a school has here the heritage that it could present . . . maybe not a canon, but more in line with the American philosopher Richard Rorty's view: "School should present the best of what has been thought, created and written."

John: Oh, that's an interesting debate. And who decides what is the best?

Steen: And he also said, "You should be presenting also the worst thing that mankind had ever done," like big wars, cruelty, slavery, genocide, exploitation, inequalities . . . (Rorty 1989, 1999).

John: Like the Holocaust.

Steen: Yes, crimes against mankind, bombing of civilians, the Holocaust, Nagasaki, Gulag, state terrorism, totalitarianism, terror attacks, radical economic inequalities, and so on.

John: Let me ask you a different question here, then. It may probably be true with you too. When I was brought up in a country town in New Zealand, there was no television, we had no car, hardly left the town, and there was no sense there was a world . . . I knew there was a world outside New Zealand, but it was invented and barely real. I remember studying Belgium at school. I was an expert on Belgium. But it was a country on a piece of paper. It was a thing. It had no reality to me other than what I read in books. Today, that can't happen because of the social media in the world. To what degree has that opening up of the world altered the Danish and maybe also German view of *Bildung*?

Steen: It has changed dramatically.

John: Tell me more.

Steen: And the whole thing is that this *Bildung* logic has come into crisis because it's harder than ever to maintain and legitimize some kind of a canon and to dare to substantialize what *Bildung* is and could be.

John: Oh, and the three concepts you've got?

Steen: Yes, it is maybe harder than ever. . . . I just gave you my interpretation of three-level concept. It's also harder than ever to maintain there is substance of a matter which is the discipline of the knowledge of math or of biology or of literature.

John: But has the concept of character changed?

Steen: The concept of character has changed you could say from socio-psychological background or from sociological studies that the way we are 'formatted' as characters, the way we are trained, the kind of personality with success and so on, they are changing. Maybe, before we were supposed to be more polite and disciplined, and now we are destined and doomed to be self-controlled and strategic subjects, but we can also

180

break the rules, disrupt reality. Many of us have to embrace and favor creative and innovative thinking and thereby challenge or even break the routines and rules. At least, that is how the propaganda gets voiced and how ideas and ideals of forming new personalities spread all around the globe due to the new type of cognitive capitalism, and new types of societal and competitive logics. We have to 'realize' our human potentials in the marketplace to get attention and success.

In 2011, the Danish political scientist Ove Kaj Pedersen wrote a book called **The Competition State**, and ever since, he has been a very well-known public figure in my home country (Pedersen 2011). He depicts the predominant opportunistic personality of today. Decades ago, the citizen was disciplined and obeyed authorities, and other scientists state that in the first part of the 20th century the neurotic and self-controlled personality blamed her- or himself for having sexual feelings and desires. In 1998, the French sociologist Alain Ehrenberg wrote *The Fatigue of Being Oneself – Depression and Society*, stating the modern subject tends to become more depressive than neurotic due the pressure of having to be a transparent person and an ever lustful and sexually active character (Ehrenberg 1998). So of course, the last century has witnessed very different views on the formation of the ideal character and how we are 'formatted' in modern societies.

John: I know that the concept of *Bildung* is very dear to your society. But, as you explain it, those notions of character building, openness to experience, are also dear to this society, but they're not as core as they are in your society. I don't want to overgeneralize, those attributes are here, but they still beg the moral purpose questions about what is that character about, what is that formation, what is the 'best' and 'worst' we need to pass on? What is it we're trying to do? And I think we would agree that schools shouldn't be the sole, maybe necessarily, the prime arbiters and decision makers about answering or even being responsible for these decisions.

Steen: You're partly right, and our colleagues back home also proclaim, while they study what they call informal learning, that learning and contemporary *Bildung* is going on everywhere, in social media, playground activities, in youth culture groups, neo-tribes, etc.

John: Yes, I am asking who now has more responsibility to ensuring that *Bildung* as having an impact on that child?

Steen: That's a good question, and a possible answer does also imply that you thoroughly deal with the pivotal question of this book we are in the midst of making of right now: *What is the purpose of education?* Because

181

education, as soon as you listen to that word in German or in Danish, also contains the question and irresistible heritage of *Bildung*.

John: Agreed, but help me here. Distinguish between what is education and what is schooling? They're not synonymous.

Steen: No, they are not.

John: I know this is too mechanistic, but what proportion of responsibility for *Bildung* is the school as opposed to the home as opposed to other parts of a child's life? And I have a hunch that, in your society, your schools are much more responsible for *Bildung* than in our society.

Steen: At least as a part of the self-appraising narrative, but I don't think in the real world that it's that different. But it is important to remember that words and concepts are not exchangeable. They also bring or carry a history with them. So, my idea is now that, as long as we still talk about *Bildung* every time we talk about education, because it's in the word in German and in Danish, then you're also talking about a responsibility of the state and of the teacher and of the institution and so on. And it's probably not that present in Australia, the US, or England . . . because you might want to favor references to culture or value, also coming from and voicing other parts of society. For example, honoring religion and the church, respecting nature and sustainability, praising mankind and human diversity, etc.

John: In many ways, whilst it's not true, schools shouldn't make those decisions.

Steen: No, when it comes to religion or the right not to believe, this question is in principle a personal one and not a school or a state affair. But when it comes to 'higher' principles, it is a task, for example, for a university not only to 'produce' students with good marks and good skills and whatever but also to 'produce' a kind of a respectful revitalization of the concept *Bildung*. And the substance of that is highly debatable and a contested theme. Some people from the government have begun to talk about *Bildung* again the last two years or so after having oversteered the educational sphere with harsh New Public Management logics for years. Is the system slowly waking up again after a long, devastating hangover? Both Søren Pind, who used to be minister of research, and the present minister of education, Merete Riisager, two very different conservative liberals – an oxymoron that gives meaning in Denmark – both of them promote *Bildung*.

    Instead of trying to get rid of it, which former governments have done, they have promoted it as a state task. Actually, and that has been highly conflictual, because in the 'older' days, five or ten years ago, it was primarily two minorities, critical people from the leftist side who wanted to have a kind of a substantial and critical agenda, and then on the other side utmost conservative people maintaining traditional national, historical, and religious values, who were talking about *Bildung*.

Passion and the non-neutrality of *Bildung*

John: Let me come back to passion, because I think I want to make a connection back to *Bildung*. If you have passion – and I would argue that it's communicative – you can see it and know it is present. And one of the values of teachers with this passion to impact onto students is that it is also a connection back to character formation and how you can, as an educator, turn students on to the love, the joy of the struggle of learning?

Steen: Yes, but it's not easy to know beforehand.

John: But it happens. There are great teachers that exhibit this passion. And they can exhibit it in every subject. And this is part of what I'm trying to argue in the *Visible Learning*. One of the major issues confronting us relates to the skills of implementation, particularly when you talk about the implementation of passion. I'm a great fan of Michael Barber's work, which may not surprise you, and his work in England where he looked at the implementation of policy and he has this model called *Deliverology* (Barber 2010). It's an interesting work (but perhaps an unfortunate title). Now one of his criticisms is that his model can implement bad things as well as good things (which is kind of a great problem to have). One of my worries about *Visible Learning* is that if you have wrong content, whatever that means, then the model will allow you to implement it. So getting the implementation process is paramount.

Steen: I agree. A totalitarian regime abuses its power and controls people.
          But they also have schools in the US fighting enlightenment and stating that you shouldn't hear about Darwin, evolutionary biology, the Big Bang, etc. – due to a strict reading of the Holy Bible, the history of mankind is not more than approximately 6,000 years.

John: My students were brought up in North Carolina. They learned about the War of Northern Aggression. They're learned about this 'Dishonest Abe'. This is in their curriculum and in their books. They had Confederate soldiers coming to the school to re-enact 'southern victories'.

Steen: It sounds stupid. It must have been an exotic and tough experience for your students and a thought-provoking experience for all of you.

John: But then I come back to another notion. And I have a hunch it's related to *Bildung:* openness to experience. When you look at the research on the influence of openness to experience as a teacher, it's slightly positive but very close to zero. That worries me. Because I think being open to experiences is a really critical and important notion, and I want students to be taught to be open to alternative views and interpretations.

Steen: Of course, but please be aware that there is another translation problem popping up here in the midst of our conversation, because in Danish and German, you have two words for 'experience'. One is immediate experience, like I experience a movie, or I experience a bird flying by (which is *Erlebnis* in German and *oplevelse* in Danish). And the other version of the word contains the deep notion, the elaborated and thoroughly reflected interpretation of the experience (which is *Erfahrung* in German and the congenial word in Danish: *erfaring*) and thereby not the immediate, instant, or 'automatic' experience.

John: Tell me more.

Steen: Built into that double wordplay that we have in German and Danish we can, for example, talk about a critical pedagogy of experience in the deep sense (*Erfahrungspädagogik, erfaringspædagogik*), as many longhaired Marxists, leftists, social liberals, and people who have read John Dewey did in the 1960 and 1970s. Students are of course also building up their experiences in a reflective manner, in- and outside schools. If you have a really deep experience (*Erfahrung, erfaring*), you have the knowledge about how to relate to different experiences (*Erlebnisse, oplevelser*), and how to navigate among them, and how to reflect upon their validity, and embed them with a certain status and weight in your life. When experience number one is lifted up to experience number two it can be said to be inscribed in your life and be a part of your character. So *Bildung* – seen as the formation of character – does also contain strong and irreplaceable experiences in the deep and reflective sense.

John: But go the next step. Should we teach students to be open to other interpretations, other experiences, and to an openness that even goes beyond that?

Steen: Yeah, that's very important. It has also to do with what I do love – as I have repetitively 'confessed' during this talk of ours – the Popperian principle of falsification and the German philosopher and sociologist Jürgen Habermas' claim that every utterance, every communicative expression, every speech-act in principle could be wrong – that is, it could be fallible. This position is called **fallibilism** (Habermas 1991,

1989). And I think this fallibilistic approach is very important also for a teacher's standpoint. For example, it could be that what we know of right now of Big Bang theory, the history of mankind, and the Missing Link, and whatever, is only knowledge that we have now, and it could be dramatically changed tomorrow. Besides, you often get the option to encounter and interpret new knowledge, if you dare and/or are allowed to open your ears and eyes. Now we know, for example, that we have approximately 4% Neanderthals' genes in the human species, which we didn't know 40 or 50 years ago.

John: Yes, this is the openness to experience, that I see as so critical to the purposes of schooling. We have to be ready to unlearn what we were told was backed by evidence. We can be wrong.

Steen: Yeah, but it is also important to stress that not everything you have learned in school is questionable and should be unlearned. You also have to qualify what you know and try to back it up with arguments and life experiences (*Erfahrungen* in German, *erfaringer* in Danish). You have to learn to combine deconstruction, construction, and reconstruction and at the same time be open to unforeseen events and 'the new'.

John: The narrative is more like saying, "Now your job is to question and improve and enhance or replace we think we know." Now, that's a very hard-ask for a ten-year-old.

Steen: You are right. But people are also examining and testing what's possible and what is claimed to be the established truth when they're students. Every time they make a little play or do things with or talk to their friends they are testing whether or not this tower will work, or these stalls have the right relation to one another.

John: If you take the E.D. Hirsch argument, we shouldn't be doing that (Hirsch 2010). He has listed what he considers is the core knowledge, the essential knowledge that all students should learn. He argues there is a canon of precious knowledge, and perhaps we should not be teaching students to question this canon. Just learn it!

Steen: That has been a part of this American way. First, you have to 'lift' the students into things, in a very solid, traditional and disciplined way. And then you can come to learn to question it afterwards. I think it may be possible to do both at the same time.

John: I think it's fascinating. When you ask a three-year-old . . . what's the most common question a three-year-old asks? "Why?"

185

Steen: Yeah, it's "why?", and very often young students pose profound questions about and between cosmos and their own existence. They want to know and understand . . . everything.

John: What's the most common question an eight-year-old asks? "What?" Something's gone wrong between the *why* (the essence of making sense, of building a theory of mind) and the *what* (which privileges the facts, the canon, the knowledge). Where oh where did the curiosity go?
When you're a teenager, it's "Why not?"

Steen: And then when you are, like, 25 it is: "How do we get money and how do we get success . . .?"

Is knowledge still an emancipator?

John: When students start to learn in school, somehow the dominant language about success from the students' view is "Bright students know lots." Being smart is knowing lots, learning quickly, listening to the teacher, finishing on time, and making sure the work is neat (and long). I have no trouble with knowing lots, but I worry about how much we have to know and what it is you have to know. But there's a tension there: "I need to know lots, and I need to relate ideas and thus understand, comprehend, and want then to relate new ideas to this new world view on the topic." And there is the irony in this world is that despite everything that we've talked about, those people who end up with lots of knowledge are more likely to do what we're talking about than those who have less knowledge. Those who learn best to play the 'knowing lots' do better on our exams (which privilege knowing lots), in getting higher paid jobs, and being esteemed by peers. Despite all the capabilities, the 21st-Century Skills, the *Bildung*, the desire for understanding, curiosity, building new ideas, the development of character, knowledge is still seen as the great emancipator.

Steen: My argument is that the more knowledge you have 'digested' and 'loaded' in a self-critical way, the higher probability there is that you to come to know – or at least come to respect – what you do not know. That's Socrates' logic, and it's actually true. That the more you can see the fragility of knowledge, the more autonomy and openness you have gained.

John: Okay. So help me get through this. This is a huge task.

Steen: . . . and at the very same time, we come to touch upon the negative dialectics of schooling. Because, the ideology of schooling is proclaiming that we are primarily piling up knowledge to get personal security and success in life.

John: Yes, building the bank.

Steen: Yeah, it looks like a bank. But the whole clue is now that if you are a real lover of knowledge, you will know that it's only there for a while and that all people get richer when they share what they know (Gorz 2010; Hardt & Negri 2009; Larsen 2012). The money world is honoring a different logic. Giving a dollar away, you lose it.

John: Okay, so let me then push you on this one. Let's assume, because this is contested, that there is a distribution, normal or whatever, of students in terms of their achievement in schools. Well, those students that are below the average are, if we define achievement more in terms of knowing lots, going to struggle to have the knowledge, struggle to have the comprehension, struggle to see the character things that you're developing, struggle to make the kind of **fallibilism** we're talking about. Aren't we leaving them out?

Steen: I agree with you that there is a problem, because what is hard is when you come to know things that can question your background. An example, if you are a Muslim girl and you start listening to other people telling you about – or even open an access to – sexual freedom or how you can arrange the world without religion or whatever, and you read texts from the time of the enlightenment questioning everything that your family stands for. Or if you start reading all kind of interesting text about Marxism and a critique of exploitation and what I know, and your father is a worker and he loves the company. Or if you come from a rural background and you read all these urban intellectuals making jokes about countryside backwardness or whatever. Every time a pupil or a student comes to know such things, it can be really painful, because now they have to go back to their parents or to their old mates and dare to tell them, "Well, I think, that everything you believe is false." Or maybe a little more diplomatically, "This could be seen and done in another way." It might sound harsh, but quite often it seems to be the case – and definitely not only for schoolkids and students – to react to new frightening knowledge by 'inventing' an unwillingness to lose their former naivety.

John: Yes, I can see that. I also note then among 'educated' people that the distinction between knowledge and understanding, between knowledge and skills, between 'knowing lots' and C21st Skills is more a blur – and too often they see schooling as needing to privilege 'knowing lots' as that is how they believe that they came to be 'educated'. And then when we add character, ethics, and culture to this equation we have a real dilemma.

Steen: Of course, there exist people like that. But there are also people living in this mixed power logic structure, in a tension between the school 'system' (based on knowledge, arguments) and the family 'system' (based on 'eternal' traditions and given authorities).

John: Yes, of course.

Steen: And it might have the consequence that such pupils or students become defensive in learning new stuff because they have to protect what they came from. Because it takes too much of them to make all that conflict and fuzz when they come home, and therefore, they block off, and they say, "Well, I don't want to listen to that. I don't want to know that. I don't want to change . . ."

John: And they decide that, not the educator.

Steen: You might say that it's too dangerous and challenging for them to lose their 'roots'. But of course, you are right, we also have to face this other problem that it could be far too advanced to have three, four, six different language games going on at the same time for an eight-year-old coming from a not-privileged class background.

John: Those students deserve what we were talking about as much as anyone else.

Steen: Of course, they do.

John: How . . .?

Steen: I highly respect the teachers out there, who do their best to 'lift' people from so-called underprivileged background into highly advanced fields where people are learning about physics, or about mathematics, or literature, or history, in a way that they will benefit from forever. Because what is important dwelling upon the ontology of man, our being in the world, is, that we are always already in a process in becoming and that is an open and neverending possibility and right for everyone. We all have the task to study enigmas – and maybe also dare to become enigmatic to ourselves, as Kierkegaard wrote in *Either-Or* (Kierkegaard 1959/1843).

John: But imagine if I come from a family where my family doesn't care about those ideas. They've survived very well. They're second-generation unemployed. They comment, "We're surviving okay. We get our beer, we get our excitements, have our debates, we have our fun, and we watch our football. . . . We don't see the value in schooling." I know, for example, that out here in some country areas those parents are right, as there are no jobs, so what's the point in going to school? Moreover, if they want their students to go to high school, then they have to leave the community, and this increases the chances of them not returning to the community – so why value this form of education? So imagine I'm coming from a family with that kind of viewpoint.

On top of that, I'm not the sharpest knife in the drawer. I don't have a lot of those intellectual abilities. I see my chances at success at this game called school as minimal. What's the responsibility of education and schooling in these cases – where educators can have quite different aims and purposes from the parents, the culture, and the community. I'm implying that some of those students won't have the acumen to have the kind of reflectivity and potential to success, but the barriers can be outside their control. What's the purpose of education for them?

Steen: But, John, my double or even triple triangular logic of *Bildung* can also be helpful here, because a lot of the social protest that was there forever in society also came from people from underprivileged groups. To be able to take part in the political and societal life, *Bildung* is indispensable, and it implies that you see yourself as becoming an active and critical thinking citizen. You might also interpret the history of the unions and their right to petition and negotiate, and to form society as *Bildung* in a mutual and collective perspective.

John: I'm not talking about underprivileged, but you're absolutely right.

We also need to be careful as lower socioeconomic status can be a mere proxy for prior achievement – and this can create a vicious cycle – students from low socioeconomic resourced homes (SES) are seen as lesser achievers, but when you statistically partial out the prior effects of achievement from SES, the SES component is nowhere near as powerful as many claim.

Steen: Right now, there is a vivid protest movement in Mexico called the Zapatists, fighting for political autonomy and revolution. They live in the mountains and rural areas far away from the big towns, and they're organizing their own villages.

John: Similarly there is a great book by Scribner and Cole about students from the Vai culture in Liberia leaving the area to go to school and learn to read and write – when they return they add little if any value to the culture and have minimal chances of success as these skills are not valued (Scribner & Cole 1981).

We need to be so careful about privileging a particular form of 'knowing', as it could not be valued, it could downgrade in our future society, and so many students from lower SES have gone on to transform our society.

The dialectics between extension and incarnation

John: I use this model that says you go from having an idea, to having many ideas to relating the ideas, and extending the ideas. This is based on Biggs and Collis' SOLO model (Biggs & Collis 1982).

I know most will know Bloom's model, but we reviewed this and found about 20 studies ever asking about the validity of Bloom and all found it wanting. As I noted earlier, in 2000 they came out with the second edition that added cognitive complexity as another critical dimension, but most users of Bloom seem to ignore this addition, preferring the model even though the authors changed the model quite a lot almost 20 years ago. The SOLO model privileges the cognitive complexity, is easy to understand and use, and helps a lot with cognitive task analysis when preparing lessons, making judgments about progress, and knowing where to best move next.

And, also, by having that kind of model, I'm privileging precious knowledge. Because my argument is that you can't relate and extend unless you have knowledge and ideas. Learning is always about something. But there are strategies of learning. There is a bit of a twofold blow here as more often students above average have multiple strategies of learning and know that when one strategy doesn't work they know how to use another. Students below average often don't have multiple strategies. So when it doesn't work, they keep using the same failed strategy. Now, what I'm reading Biesta saying is that language of learning can be destructive and negative, whereas I'm saying, "We need deeper understanding about the processes of learning, and when you use the SOLO model it highlights the learning of knowledge and ideas as well as comprehending, critiquing, extending, and relating valuable ideas."

Steen: As an alternative both to your view and to Biesta's, my credo and philosophical approach is that every time you learn something, you come to incarnate it in your bodily-being-in-the world . . . to use a combination of Heidegger's existential ontological hyphen-concepts (like, for example, being-in-the-world and being-in-language) and Merleau-Ponty's anti-dualist concepts (like, for example, our bodily perception of the world and our bodily being anchors us in and gives us the world).

John: Oh, exactly. But whoops, there is a problem called forgetting, and I think the process of forgetting is much more fascinating at times than learning.

Steen: . . . and not only in your 'inner' mental cognitive structure. Every time you incarnate something that's worth incarnating, you extend your bodily and mental synthesis. That means you are now grasping more of the world and gaining a wider range and freedom. Grasping more of what life can give you. So, a double movement between incarnation and extension exists and it is of utmost . . .

John: But why would you call that learning?

Steen: . . . importance, and I would call that, embodied, embedded, and enacted knowledge . . .

John: It's the consequence of learning. Kind of like Einstein's claim that education is what remains after one has forgotten everything learned in school?

Steen: . . . and an incarnation–extension–dialectics, due to heavy inspiration from the German body-phenomenologist, philosopher, and psychiatrist, Thomas **Fuchs** and his book *Ecology of the Brain* (2017), and his fruitful co-work with the German philosopher of mind and cognitive scientist, Hanne de Jaegher, *Enactive Intersubjectivity: Participatory Sense-Making and Mutual Incorporation* (2009). And if you like you might call that my attempt to rescue and renew the widely abused, very unclear, and semantically nearly emptied concept 'learning'. But of course you also have to reflect upon the complicated relation between remembering (memory) and forgetting (oblivion) but I propose that we postpone this debate to another time, another place.

John: But isn't their role, a fundamental role of teachers, to be concerned about how you go about doing that, which is what I call learning?

Steen: I understand your argument, but when I read Biesta, I have the idea that he wants to put our critical attention to the fact that we, for many years, have blamed the teachers for being teachers, and having wanted them to be learning facilitators instead. The societal consensus has – so to speak – deprived them of their world opening and igniting 'call'.

John: Oh, I agree. Facilitator is not my favorite notion at all. We do indeed need to go back to the claims about teachers igniting the flame; turning students on to the excitement of learning, knowledge, and understanding;

and enticing them to be motivated to want to return and continue the pursuit of precious knowledge.

Steen: The teachers were supposed to be supervisors, guides, or coaches – or maybe just to come by now and then to check the ongoing learning processes.

John: I know you're not Biesta, but I would like to ask him this question: When a teacher is successful in teaching you something, would you credit him or her?

Steen: Great teachers are able to open a new world for you, for example via texts. Some of these texts might be very hard to grasp. The teacher's job is to present an interesting and enlightening perspective on them . . .

John: But would you credit the teacher for being able to teach it?

Steen: . . . and invite you to dwell amidst the beauty of their language, style, and rich argumentation. For example, if you read Adorno, or you read Ernst Bloch, or you read . . .

John: Oh, exactly.

Steen: . . . Roland Barthes, Gilles Deleuze, James Joyce, Samuel Beckett . . .

John: But would you credit the teacher? Say that was a great way of teaching you to do it.

Steen: The teacher cannot be treated as a solo cause of a successful opening to the words and the world. A triangular process takes place: the teacher's effort, the content of the text, and the way the pupils and the students understand and interpret the teacher's words and the text.

John: But my point is this, we struggle to credit teachers and often they too do not take the credit for the change they enact with students (in the things you have just cited, for example). I want to credit the teacher because I think, in general, they deserve the credit for their success. Biesta starts from the half glass empty that people want to blame them. Now, I want to credit them for their success in enacting the changes, for having clear views about the defense of the changes they are enacting, and for their passion and skill to do this.

Steen: I think that Biesta, as I, both of us, we come from this continental European side of the world, and here we have experienced how all these learning hymns and ideology have become an important part of the apparatus of control.

John: Oh, sure. I understand that.

Steen: And that might be very different 'down' here and experienced and observed from your chair.

John: But that's not how he writes. He writes about 'learnification'. He talks about this. He's an important person. People read him. He's convincing and a beautiful writer. And they're going to read it and say, as he says, "This move to the focus on learning is kind of evil and nasty." I think his a very unfortunate misuse of the word 'learning'. I've no troubles with learning goals – but they should be particular to the lesson and certainly not, as some in your country seem wont to do, on a national level. I want more. I value teaching learning strategies. And so on. Ironically, I still do claim that among the ultimate aims of this process is to teach students to become their own teachers – so they know what to do when they do not know what to do, they can have the debates about what is worthwhile and precious knowing, and can access the resources and people to enhance their learning and comprehending.

Steen: I could maybe understand learning goals in parts in primary school in a local setting (for example, plans for achieving math and reading skills at certain age and class levels), but when it comes to the university, you should have the free choice to study subjects . . .

John: Sure, to a degree . . .

Steen: . . . and follow your own road to wisdom, knowledge, and *Bildung*.

John: . . . learning is about something.

Steen: Biesta thinks that we shouldn't leave the students with a right to build up their own critical judgment. And that's what I'm criticizing him for now, because in my mind, based on the enlightenment heritage, this is envisaging a double movement (Larsen 2017a). You should, at the very same time, respect superior knowledge that you don't have and those people possessing that knowledge. Look up to them, honor them, learn from them, of course. At the very same time, you should train, practice, and learn to apply your reflexive judgment and your reason (*reflexive Urteilskraft* and *Vernunft*, according to Immanuel Kant), and qualify your interpretative skills (due to thinkers like Friedrich Nietzsche, Hans-Georg Gadamer, and Paul Ricoeur). The evergreen message of the enlightenment is this: Get out of your self-indulged and self-imposed lack of using your reason, and incarnate all these precious capacities in your own person.

John: Yes, that's right. This is *Bildung*.

Can we ever 'get rid of' the concept *Bildung*?

Steen: In contrast to Biesta, I find that both these ways are of high importance. At first, you have in a way to obey a higher order, and to strive for higher knowledge. Then, you are slowly and silently transformed to become superior, even megalomaniac in your own interpretation attempts. I think that the dialectics between the two is indispensable for a life alternating between honoring and producing. And now I'm looking forward to Biesta's answers to the critique I just mailed him, because it's kind of disturbing to me that he is not having an idea of *Bildung* in his work. He apparently doesn't need it, and he seems to say, "*Bildung* is a worn out concept of the old bourgeoisie class of Germany. We cannot use that concept any longer. We can only use the concept 'teaching'." No *Bildung*, no learning, only the teacher's role is here to stay, according to Biesta.

I think this position might risk leading to a traditionalization, but his idea is not that the teacher possesses knowledge of solid substance of what is to be infused in humans or in pupils, but that that the teacher can open for the exteriority. There comes in this kind of semi-religious, Emmanuel Levinas' logic. Levinas was a Lithuanian Jew, living and writing as a philosopher in Paris. Most of his family didn't survive the Second World War. Levinas basically states, "When a Nazi wants to kill or torture you in a concentration camp, he could do all the worst to you that you could ever imagine, but your eyes will protest. Humans can never be forced to complete silence and be deprived of their sense of moral and justice." So, all ethics start from the silent talk of the eyes.

And, therefore, this kind of idea that there is an extra transcendental logic to ethics and to the exteriority now becomes built into Biesta's view on education. And he thinks that if the teacher has and plays a leading role in education, it opens for a free – what can we say – meeting with exterior. So we get the chance to get in touch with transcendental power of, and maybe also outside, the world we know.

John: The transcendental, yeah. Freire tries to build on it, too (Freire 1970/1968).

Steen: And that's semi-religious. It's profanized religion, in a way.

John: So tell me more about this peculiar notion of 'studenting', and what was the word he also used, the . . .?

Steen: . . . 'pupilling' (Biesta 2017: 23).

John: 'Pupilling'?

Steen: But these words and neologisms – that 'ing' the 'things' to make nouns become living verbal nouns – are actually not his own inventions. He quotes other thinkers. Instead of learning, where it says that you are a learner among other learners, you should stick to your role as a student or a pupil. So in order to kind of build up another alternative approach to learning, one could stress the dynamic being-as-becoming and there-fore loudly proclaim, "I'm pupilling, I'm studenting."

John: One of his criticisms, and I agree with this, is that if learning is just the cognitive, and it doesn't include the emotional, social, the physical, the motivations, and so on, it's too narrow. And, of course, it is. But to invent a new word, like 'studenting', or 'pupilling', it's a surrogate for a more holistic notion of learning. So all he's doing is inventing 'learning' using another word.

Steen: Maybe, but my worry about the concept 'learning', for example, in Denmark, is that it has been going far away from what you stressed, that learning is always about learning something, more into learning for the sake of learning.

John: I agree. And all this 21st-Century Skill stuff, I'm not a fan of that (Grif-fin & Care 2014). I worry as some countries are inventing C21st as a new subject in the curriculum. Yes, there is evidence that learning how to problem solve, to be critical thinkers, learning study skills can be improved by going to classes on these topics – but the transfer into the domains of knowing are close to zero. We need to build these into subjects – and that involves great teaching. Too much of the learning for learning is vacuous, but it can be fun and engaging.

Steen: And which are absolutely without substance. And it's reflecting, also, this ever unstable capitalism, where you have to be flexible. And in order to be more flexible, you have to be more preliminary (Larsen 2014b). I guess I demand more.

John: No, it avoids the debate about *what*, and so does Biesta . . .

Steen: And what about the *why*?

John: ... because he talks about the transcendental notions. It's all about something, and you talk about looking through the eyes. I can teach you to look through your eyes differently.

Steen: I agree with you that Biesta has a problem with the *what* and the *why* questions. Because he doesn't want to 'mess' with the concept *Bildung*. And he seems to think that the *Bildung* fathers, and a few mothers, they were primarily there to uphold an elitist concept of a bourgeois class's privileges.

John: But, historically, it was, wasn't it?

Steen: Of course, it was. But my hope is that *Bildung* can be rescued, revitalized, and transformed to become a critical concept (Larsen 2016a).

John: But what's wrong with having a set of moral philosophies that are intrinsic to your notion of teaching? Then the debate is "Are they the right moral philosophies?" Like if they are the Nazi philosophies, they were very successful in their education system, but they're not defensible. If they're more like Dewey, they're very defensible, and they're very democratic.

How are we to translate the German concept *Bildung* into English?

Will it be possible to revitalize *Bildung* in today's educational institutions?

Is *Bildung* for everyone or just for the already privileged?

How can *Bildung* be understood as a way to incarnate and extend our being-in-the-world?

IX. HOW to DIFFERENTIATE
BETWEEN the HOW, WHAT, and WHY of EDUCATION

Steen: In your latest book – touched slightly upon earlier in our conversation – written together with the German educational researcher Klaus Zierer, *10 Mindframes for Visible Learning: Teaching for Success*, you're talking about the *why*, and the *what*, and the *how* – that is, the *how-ness* – of education (Hattie & Zierer 2018 and reviewed by Larsen 2018a). I find that really interesting and promising also in relation to a lack of such profound questions in your former books (of which I have reviewed three: Larsen 2013b, 2014c, 2016b). Besides, I have written a philosophical text called "What Is Education? – A Critical Essay" as a contribution to an international student edited anthology with the title *What Is Education?* (Larsen 2017c).

So, I welcome that debate and acknowledge that you now say that it is not just a question of *how* we do things – it is also a question of *what's* going on in education. And maybe even also *why* we need education? So, could you please reflect upon these three different and important little words: *how, what*, and *why*. I guess you think that it is much easier to make a *how* description than to present and defend a fundamental *what* or *why* answer.

John: Yes, it is.

Steen: You could describe what's going on, even though it may take a while – collecting statements, policy papers, data, empirical analysis, meta-analyses. But the 'whatness' is a more radical question. And the 'whyness' is a very, very, very harsh question, as Nietzsche wrote, "If you possess a *why* in and for your life you can cope with nearly any *how*" (Nietzsche 2009/1889).

John: And you see that in children.

Steen: Yes, but what is your answer to the questions: why education, what is education, and how is education? How are they three related? Are some of them practical questions, some of them empirical questions, some of them philosophical, some of them existential?

John: I'm not sure you can answer the why question empirically.

Steen: I agree completely.

John: I'm a learner. I'm in the luxurious position that I'm paid to read other people's work, and interpret, and make connections. One of the things that fascinated me when I was going through the thinking about *Visible Learning* is that you rediscover other authors who have already been there – for example, Paulo Freire, whom I have already mentioned several times during our talk. You know that I read his book, *Pedagogy of the Oppressed*, and in many senses, he could've written *Visible Learning*, without all the numbers and the statistics (Freire 1970/1968).

Madeline Hunter also could have written the book (Hunter 1982). When I read what she was writing, I'm saying, "This is the same thing, without all the numbers." But this may be the meaning of the word – we re-search, we search again.

There is the continual emphasis on developing critique, building of seeing oneself and society from the 'other side' or outside, esteeming the evaluative thinking. How can we then find content that can invoke these skills and judgments, where students are asked to make evaluative comments, and entice them back to the place of learning called school?

I'm a great fan of William **Purkey's invitational** school model (Purkey & Novak 1996). When I first met him many years ago when we had offices almost next to each other in North Carolina, he told me about his invitational learning. I thought, "Well, yeah, in schools like here in North Carolina, he's right, but not in schools I've worked with in Australia." I was so wrong. Purkey's claims are a massively different way of thinking about subject matter as he says, Steen, I want to invite you to learn about history, or mathematics, or becoming a barista. And so there's an obligation on me as the teacher to invite you. Schools must become the most inviting places for students to want to come back to.

I'm not a fan of saying, "This is valuable for the rest of your life." Because, I know that math teachers say that, and history teachers say that. But if I asked a math teacher to help me as a Year 10 kid with my history homework, they'd say, "I don't know that stuff." They've just violated that assumption that doing history or doing math is necessary for the rest of your life. Last week I gave the example about me thinking that the sun goes around the earth. The world does not stop because I have this wrong notion, nor do I need to know the correct claims for me to be a researcher in my own field. But too often we tell students that they need to know all this stuff for the future success. We overplay these claims and they fail to convince.

The notion of the purpose of education is about we educators inviting students to partake in our passions for content and understanding. I would want students, as they go to and leave school, to have a passion about learning something. Wouldn't it be nice if that something had value and was socially desirable? But the choice of content and tasks need not merely be justified because of immediate value or purpose. A lot of the stuff that we ask students to do they don't and won't see the value. Take, for example, me as a musician. I spent, and I still spend, hours and hours doing scales. There is not one concert I've ever been to where a pianist has played scales. It's a skill I need. It has no value in the end product. When I teach students cricket or other sports, we go through drills. There is no time in the game where those drills are seen but you need those drills to overlearn basic skills to then build other attributes (of music, or sport).

Steen: Yeah, but you still need basic knowledge of the discipline in order to liberate yourself from the discipline.

John: Correct.

Steen: In my view it is both important to learn something and to acknowledge *what* you are learning – that is, the substance of the 'learned' (the topic, the matter, the profound questions and arguments, the rich knowledge bank). Learning for its own sake – 'learn to learn' – deprived of a content is not enough. This autotelic dimension of getting in closer *what*-contact ought not be forgotten in the so-called learning society.

John: Definitely not.

Steen: There was a critique in Denmark, a debate going on, about whether or not your *Visible Learning* approach could end up being a kind of educational nihilism, because some of the people were translating your approach to this argument: It's better to 'learn to learn' than to come to learn and know something substantial.

John: Yes, the *Visible Learning* program is more about the *how*, but it begs the *why* and the *what* questions. I made this point at the start, but it was forgotten. And to be fair, I never imagined the book would be so read and critiqued – and too many critics want a different focus for the book, want their pet theories and beliefs acknowledged in the book, and of course want more about the why and what. Since this book I have tried to address these questions.

I see the criticism that the book was kind of content-neutral. But that doesn't mean to say that educators should be content-neutral.

Steen: That's a good and precise remark, John. It is important for teachers to invite the student or pupil to envisage a wider horizon and provoke and tear their passion to get deeper in contact with the actual matter at play. It demands that both the teacher and the student or pupil invest their interpretive, skillful, and playful approach to the 'things' at stake.

John: My kind of way out of this is that you, Steen, are the teacher, and you have views about what is invitational, and what you're going to do in the content. I have views and they're different. It's critical that we, as the adults in the room, critique each other, as students should not be limited by one's teacher idiosyncratic views about content.

Steen: Of course, we need more profound debates in education and pedagogy and attempts to enrich and qualify the public sphere. That is also something that's lacking now in the Danish school and university institutions.

John: Oh, I see.

Steen: You have, I call it 'Balkanization' of the academic work. There are so to speak little regimes of the 'Serbian' phenomenologists and besides them, you have the 'Croatian' positivists, and beside them, you have the 'Muslim' social constructivists, and then the 'UN' system theory champions, and they all have their own agenda and their own 'churches' including devoted communions of colleagues and students. The problem is that they're not talking to one another any longer or reading each other's book in their enclosed silos, and I find that really depressing.

John: Well, yes and no. Certainly, in my early career I taught measurement, statistics, research, and design. Most of my colleagues weren't involved, didn't care too much what I choose to teach but this does not mean I was Balkanized, as my constituency was my measurement and research colleagues, and I worried about them. I wanted to be up to date, I did not want to be critiqued by them that my content was old fashioned, incorrect, or not reflecting the current debates.
         Now, it seems anyone can teach research, design, and statistics. And I see it being taught, without attention to what the world of researchers in that area are saying because someone has sat down in the managerial university we're now in and said, "This is what the students need to know, and how they need to do it." It is more transactional than critiquing the essence of research design, measurement.

Steen: After the Second World War, Germany was rebuilt. The whole country had to be re-created after the 12 self-destructive Nazi regime years, 1933–1945. The university system also had to be reshaped.

John: Yes.

Steen: For example, at Technische Universität in Berlin where the engineers were being educated, the new university authorities were told, by the Americans and the English war winning powers, to establish a professorship in philosophy, especially dealing with morals and ethics. It was mandatory for the future German engineers to be able to think of themselves as being more than perfect masters of technical engineering, construction, mathematical measurement, and statistics. They always also had to have a profound view upon their ethical responsibility, the broader societal perspectives, and all that.

Because with logistics and transportation technology you can organize mass transportation of men, women, and children to Auschwitz, and how to make it the most effective. And in order to make it cost neutral the Nazis could confiscate their valuables, sell the gold in their teeth, their hair, and whatever. So to prevent the world from giving birth to more Adolf Eichmanns just being able to do calculations and enhanced transportation logics, the whole idea was that you had to bring fundamental ethical moral judgment into their education program to prevent any possible abuse of technics and instrumental reasoning.

John: Exactly. Education is an ethical business and it is the value and imperatives of how we apply our efficiencies, research design, and measurement to impact on educational problems.

Steen: The teacher of today is also an agent of responsibility as to what goes on here in the classroom, implying that the teacher must be concerned with much more than testing, effectivity, and best practice procedures.

John: Let me make an observation here. Let me go to ethics in the university system. And, you know, I'm sure it's true in Denmark as it is here and in many parts of the West, that we have to go through an ethics committee or institutional review process. It took me a long time to realize that that the university ethics process was not set up to protect the individual. It was set up to protect the university, and I think there's a lot of that that worries me.

My argument at the school level is that I want those moral purpose debates at the school level. The minute it becomes a debate at the system's level, the systems will protect themselves, and they'll not say, "Why do this rather than that," but "You do this rather than that." And your critique, Steen, is very much of that top-down system where you abrogate the responsibilities and opportunities of those at the school level, who make the day-to-day decisions, to have those debates about what we're talking about.

Not just *how* but also *why*

Steen: I guess that the debate on *Bildung* in the political sphere, which we have touched upon, might be seen as a reaction towards the 'meaningless' and empty metaphysics of neoliberal management in education. The politicians might have felt a certain accumulated lack. Maybe it's wrong, but I see a parallel here. You also seem to have felt the need to make a new narrative on top of all your statistics and all your books. Was it because you came to think that there was too little to say from John Hattie?

John: It wasn't too little to say. I said a lot.

Steen: But you did not use to talk or write much about *the purpose of education*.

John: No. I said a lot about the *how*. I didn't say much at all about the *why*.

Steen: So, you also want to say something about the *why* and the *what*?

John: Yeah.

Steen: So, I think the same is the question now for politicians who have been in power for so many years in Denmark stating that we primarily have to make a cost-benefit analysis of education and try to make the different parts of it more cost effective, and apply more governance to the field . . . but now the semantics of *Bildung* is returning. But we'd better watch out because the false could sneak in to the *Bildung* concept. That is what Ernst Bloch, a German philosopher, wisely said. The more we tend to forget the power of the words, more often we forget that the false could sneak into the positive words. And that can also happen to be the case now.

John: Sure, there is the criticism that you and your colleagues have made of my work, and the argument that *Visible Learning* should not be in Denmark because it doesn't attend to the issue of *Bildung*. My argument to that is, no, it doesn't make pronouncements about *Bildung* being present or not. I say quite often, the *Visible Learning* work is more about the how, and less about the why. But that doesn't deny that the why isn't critical. And, yes, implementing *Visible Learning* can work in a Danish system because indeed it has been implemented and worked in a Danish system. That is, there are numerous schools that have interpreted and implemented the model into their schools. And the concept of *Bildung* has not been ignored, trampled on, or damaged.

Steen: But how do you then address this *Bildung* question here? Is it on behalf of the responsibility of the teacher to maintain some kind of ongoing debate about maybe this triangular logic, which I mentioned earlier in your conversation of *Bildung*, meaning the respect for knowing something, becoming a citizen, and formation of an autonomous character?

203

John: Totally, and that's why I use 'Know Thy Impact', it begs that moral purpose question.

Steen: Do you actually see your 'Know Thy Impact' philosophy or your research field as a kind of a contribution to *Bildung* logic in the German and Danish sense or is it something different?

John: It begs the question in Somalia, in Southern California. It doesn't answer that question. The core notion is for schools, wherever they are, whatever the culture, to address the question for themselves as to what they mean by impact. It's kind of like saying you've got the mechanism, but you still have to ask what you want the mechanism to have an influence on. And going to your concept, I think this is where the profession of a teacher should have a more major say in answering this notion of what is meant by impact in a society. But, because we don't have a profession of the teachers in many places that do see this as their role, it defaults to the politicians to do it for them.

It is akin to modern universities allowing the senior managers to negotiate, speak on behalf of the university, whereas the senior professors should be the ones speaking for the future of the university. We have defaulted to allow the managers to do this, and they have adopted this role supposedly speaking for the professoriate. We need to take back our ownership of the character of the university. Same with schools, but we overburden the educators, we fail to give time and opportunity, and hence the managerial ownership seems to have taken over. I would hope it is not too late to have robust discussions about these core *Bildung* claims. The best we seem to get is when there are debates about curriculum changes. But this is too narrow.

Steen: I have this idea that, if you try to build up a strong position of a contemporary concept of *Bildung*, it also implies a social critique questioning society's overall development. For example, I will proclaim that if you want to 'foster' and 'fertilize' character *Bildung* – that is, the formation of character – then, standing on that ideal or hope, you have to criticize that now it's impossible for students at 'my' university, Aarhus University, to defend their own master work in an oral exam, and not the least that the students are forced to write the master theses in just four to five months. The system wants to 'save time' and cut expenses, but risks destroying the quality of the master theses and limiting the freedom of the students to think and work with patience and at their own tempo. So when I ask, "How do the possibilities and conditions for *Bildung* – that is, the formation of character in a rich way – look like?" The answer might be that within these restricted, harsh regulations, the system actually risks destroying and diminishing the very conditions and possibilities for *Bildung* processes at the university. So, that's also why I emphasize that it is important to defend a revitalized *Bildung* concept that can be fused to a kind of revitalized concept of critique. And critique actually descends from a Greek verb meaning the capacity to differentiate, *krinein*. The noun *krisis* in Greek also means the turning or tipping point. Like a fever can have a critical moment, either you die or you get rescued. So, interpreted in the vivid heritage from *krinein* and *krisis*, critique is both a capacity to differentiate and the knowledge about and the will to change things (Larsen 2014d, 2018b).

Through this double approach, you might get the possibility to defend schools and universities as societal and institutional invitations to pupils and students to become wise, active, and freethinking human beings (see Flexner 1939).

John: I have no trouble with what you're saying, but there still is that additional notion of how the concept of *Bildung* helps answer the question about the *what*. In the very crude sense, *Visible Learning* is the *how*, the *Bildung* is maybe the *why*, and we've still got the *what*. And that's too crude a distinction. But I do see your imperative to have healthy debates about all three – the *how*, the *why*, and the *what*. With society placing so much responsibility on educators to resolve all social ills, with so much pressure to be in the 'top five' PISA rankings, with so much pressure to speed up childhood, and with so much pressure to be worldly – these debates become more critical. I also note that educators have done a pretty good job at taking on these additional roles, usually with no increment in salary, no extra recognition of doing this by society, and there comes a point where this is going to unravel. Maybe it is a great time to ask more about the purposes of schooling.

I recall a debate about purposes in Australia in the 1980s and every school, every community, was invited to participate, and the overwhelming reaction was schools were civilizing institutions where parents wanted schools to build relationships – the respect for self and respect for others' claims. High achievement was mentioned, but was far from the top purposes. Similarly, in New Zealand in the 2000s there was a major debate about the purpose of schools, but it fizzled as it failed to capture the imagination of the core players with the legislative and political strings. Whatever the way, I believe it is a fundamental responsibility of the electorate to have this debate – although that worried me as it can turn to instrumentalism very quickly, can ignore that children need to experience childhood and sometimes be protected to have this enjoyment, and can turn into debates about future work (or why we cannot predict future work and thus an overplay for so-called C21st Skills). Bring on the debate about *Bildung*. We can learn a lot from you.

Ontology and epistemology of education

Steen: Thanks. In two texts – the already mentioned "What Is Education? – A Critical Essay" (in Anton Bech Jørgensen et al.[eds.]: *What is Education?*, 2017b) and "A Critical Essay on the Exercise of Critique. On the impossibility of Reconciling Ontology and Epistemology" (*Danish Yearbook of Philosophy* #51, 2018) – I have argued that not only is the ontology of education not the same as the epistemology of education but also that the ontology and the epistemology cannot and should never be reconciled.

Epistemology of education can be all kind of attempts to collect statistics, do meta-analyses, or to interview people and pile up empirical data of economy; and regulations and laws; and historical documents, all that, archive knowledge and factual knowledge. But the process of ontology of education is something different. That is the way we are already always being in a process in which we are changing ourselves, interacting with other people, and the world in which we are living. Therefore, of course, you're right. If we had a *Bildung* plan, a kind of set, fixated sentences, we are not begging the question any longer, we are 'just' answering it with a dogmatic approach. But that's not my position.

John: Yes, I can see your distinction between epistemology and the ontology of education and certainly see *Visible Learning* as more addressing the former than the latter.

Steen: My view is that we should open this field of the ontology of education and combine it to some kind of, of course, self-critical attempts to formulate or to utter something about *Bildung*, and critique and combine all these things together: ontology of education, critique, and the concept of *Bildung*. That might be able to give a better defense of schools and universities than just 'Know Thy Impact'. That's my idea and my argument.

John: I would be happy with that, even though I would argue that the impact question begs that question about ontological questions. So, if you were rewriting one of these articles, tell me about the notion of Procrustean solutions that you see that I've done (Larsen 2015a, 2017b).

Steen: Okay. The whole idea about Procrustes comes from the old Greek story of the highwayman who catches people and locks them in a bed. Long people's legs are chopped off and short people's bodies are stretched to fit the size of the bed. The Procrustes bed is embedding the logic in which the complex reality gets violated by force to fit into a given form (Adorno 2005/1951).

John: Yep, it's also a very big concept in factor analysis. Where we use factor reduction methods and rotation to find the best person to fit into the 'bed' – the optimal factor solution.

Steen: Your "best person to fit into the 'bed'" seems to be an average person. But my argument is that the ontology of education, in principle, does not have a Procrustes problem because it does not want to go to (this) bed. But, if we turn to the epistemology of education, it seems that it has to accept *to be hosted in the painful Procrustes bed*.

So, when I was criticizing your work, from the first moment I read it, my idea was that, if you go for this meta-analysis, and you say, "Well, I got 1.40," or as you once stated, 800 meta-analyses, "and I have 250 million data on pupils . . ." – I could see that you had taken away so many long legs and stretched out shorter legs in order to press the very diverse and qualitatively different data to fit into a big, quantitative, and powerful data logic (Larsen 2011).

John: No. But you could see now what I tried to do, and maybe I didn't write it as well, was to come up with a set of propositions to model. To use this analogy, I was trying to construct the most comfortable bed to fit the data. And I'm very old-fashioned. I think models should say more than just explain because that's how you more readily falsify them. And so I made claims about the visible learner, the passionate teacher, the 'Know Thy Impact', emphasizing articulating what success looks like, and talking about the strategies of learning. Sometimes I get emails from critics saying, "There's no meta-analysis on 'Know Thy Impact'." Well, there can't be. It's a meta-story of the meta-analysis. It's my interpretation about what discriminates between those influences above compared to those below the average effects. It is the story or model I propose such that I could be wrong. And you're saying, it's not only it could be wrong, but that I'm too limited. And I accept that.

My very first 1989 article on these ideas was rejected for very good reasons. The editor came back and said, "Look, we like the article, we like what you're doing, but you just got data on it. There's no story." And that was a very, very worthwhile thing to say. It certainly woke me up. In the same way that someone said to me, not many years later, "You put feedback up near the top, but you never describe what you mean by feedback." And that led to a 20-year venture to answer that question.

And so here's the thing that surprises me. In the 30+ years since I first wrote about the meta-synthesis, no one has critiqued the model. You and others have critiqued the method, and there's web pages out there correcting the details, and there's nothing wrong with that. Perfectly legitimate. But there has been no falsification of the model, no alternative models. And what you are talking about here today is, so far, not falsifying the model, but you're questioning the limitations.

Steen: Probably, you might be right.

But I'm also very curious to know whether or not your new approach going for the *what* and the *why* questions of education, will force you, in one way or another, to come closer to the *Bildung* discussion that has been going on for more than 200 years in the continental Europe?

John: Yes, it will force me to come closer but the answer to the *Bildung* question doesn't change or negate the *how* part of the model.

Steen: But do you, for example, in your way of thinking, have a kind of a mirror-reflective logic? We have witnessed major shifts and transformations in the ideal images of *Bildung* in which we mirror ourselves, since the concept was born around 250 years ago. Now, the *Bildung* (please remember that the prefix *Bild* in German equals 'image' in English) has often been fixated, forcing you to look up to ideals in which you should form yourself to perform the most competitive way. It could, for example, be to be a polite pupil, to know the curriculum by heart, and to respect and honor authorities, including your dad and mum. It could be to be a devoted believer in God or to go to war for your country. There were some very strict ideas and ideals in the mirror, in which you had to form yourself in the old days. Today, I envisage the risk . . . and I have used the picture many times in Denmark that instead of all the past fixations now the mirror has become a blank slate. A loss of substance and ideals, no big ideas, a loss of orientation. . . . And there you are looking into the mirror and primarily asking, "What's in it for me?" meaning that you are requested and forced to see a forward-going and strategic version of yourself, but no substance of subjects any longer. The mirror has become empty and you have to form and build up yourself to become flexible, competitive, and first and foremost self-leading and strategic (Larsen 2015c, 2016a).

John: I see much in the mirror but need to be careful not to inflict that image on others – but as you say help students see the mirror-reflective logic, build their own and come to understand its compatibility with the logic that their society asks of them. Critique it, rebuild it, and where possible change it to improve so others can partake in also building their logics.

Steen: And that's a danger.

John: Well, of course, it is.

Steen: If you have a whole educational system without history, without deep experience and value discussions, without ideas of *why* and *what* it's doing *what* it does – but only 'how-ness' and only instrumental things . . .

John: Yes, but because *Visible Learning* is more about the *how*, does not mean that the *what* is not important.

Steen: . . . then the mirror is only a blank slate, and if you are just gazing yourself and posing the question, "What's in it for me?" and you 'answer', "There is nothing in it for me, so why should I deal with it? Why bother, why care . . .?"

John: I agree with you. That is why respect for self and respect for others is core to me. If I wanted to influence my own sons in any way, it is that I wanted them to learn to give back.

Steen: And that could be a problem.

John: In many ways, that comes back to the criticism that you and others have made correctly about politicians using my work. They have a set of beliefs and assumptions particularly about *Bildung* and the content, but they use me to justify their belief systems.

Steen: So my idea is now that you seem to have begun to place or project ideas and things in this *Bildung* mirror, at least for the teacher. For example, 'Know Thy Impact' and see your teaching and what goes on in the classroom from the eyes of the pupils.

John: And I want us to teach students become their own teachers.

Steen: Yeah, and support autonomous thinking and fertilize critique. You seem to have inscribed a lot of things in the mirror: ideals and dreams – maybe even regulative ideas, as Kant would call them. And I can also catch a glimpse of a counterfactual principle of hope, and it's coming . . .

John: You're absolutely right. And I'm no philosopher. That's why I need you.

Steen: . . . pretty close to the *Bildung* slot.

John: Yes, it is.

Steen: And as I said, that is what we are reminded of every time we use the word 'education' in German (*Ausbildung*) or Danish (*uddannelse*) we come immediately to think about and to co-reflect the suffix: *Bildung* (*dannelse*).

John: Whereas, here, and you know the criticism in the West since the neo-liberal notion, education has become more mechanistic towards how we run our schools and preparing students for a future economy. And we're now less likely to have those *Bildung* discussions.

Steen: Yes, you are right. Besides, it's pretty boring, I think, when you read what comes from the majority of educational policy documents. One is that everyone and everything has to be cost-effective. The other thing is that it has become compulsory for education to be labor market directed. We should have the right match, as they call it, between, for example, university production and the needs of the labor market.

John: And I don't oppose that. But like you, I want much more. I oppose the narrow utilitarian view when it gets too strong. I have a secret though – the neo-liberalists won. There seems less point fighting them but much purpose to expand their horizons.

        What is fascinating despite the success of neo-liberalism is that they are pretty hopeless at forecasting. For example, we don't have a data-workforce policy for education in Australia. But AITSL (the organization I am chair of) is responsible for building one.

Steen: But do you think it's possible to anticipate and design the future? For example, my dad, he was a very successful naval engineer (constructing and building oil and container ships made of steel). But if the educational system has continued to build on this logic from the 1950s and 1960s then it would have been pretty stupid, for in 2018 there are nearly no jobs left for ship-building engineers in Denmark.

John: Yes, but this is not good forecasting – you can start from the present and ask how can we have more of the present; you have to be much adept and agile in anticipating changes. The example I gave earlier about the workplace requirement for interpreters, collaborators, and team players is a need right now, but the education system still does not seem to realize it. Let me give you another example. Last year, in one of our states, there were 350 students who graduated from teacher education as creative arts teachers. There were two jobs. We knew that there would be so few jobs in that sector, and even less for 'geography' teachers but we still pump them out – this is not fair to the students who invested four years of loans, funds, sweat, and anticipation when we already should have known this and told them up front.

Steen: In the macro-sphere, it has also to do with the logic of capitalism and the volatile state. Jobs are not created for the blue eyes of the people. If the workforce is not worth to exploiting, the jobs will not be offered to the workforce. You are forced to be or to become marketizable.

John: No, there's just no need for these kinds of teachers. There's many teachers out there already qualified and trained who want those jobs. My point is the state is investing an incredible amount into something where there's no return. Now, there's another argument that I've heard many times from many politicians. I would rather have students go through teacher education and not get jobs because they'll be better parents than if they went through law, or arts, or science. The belief is that training to become a teacher makes a better parent.

Steen: That's an argument?

John: Oh, yeah. Very common. To justify the overproduction. There is a serious question that we have to face in your country and my country about over-education relative to the job market. There's a serious problem in our universities. When you and I went through and you got a PhD, there was an expectation that you could get a job in a university. In fact, someone's invented an index for the number of applicants qualified for an academic job in different disciplines. For example, for every job we have in this university, there are probably 80 PhD students who could do that job.

Steen: Yeah, I know that. It's a harsh competition. But the state could also now and then try to invest in new jobs and promote new societal activities.

Do we over-educate?

John: But let me give you the other side of the statement. And this is the question I'm asking you, and it comes back to the *Bildung*. Can we over-educate?

Steen: Can we over-educate? When it goes back to my speculations on the ontology of education, I would say no, because you can never come to know too much about a 'thing' (a subject, a topic, a craft).

John: These potential creative arts students are investing five years of their life. For what?

Steen: Well, you can become a little wiser than 'your' fellow student or you can become a better thinker.

John: There's a conspiracy here. The message is that if they do this PhD, things will open up for them. That's the implied claim. There are more opportunities if you have more schooling.

Steen: That's a lie today, of course.

John: Thank you. So you can over-educate.

Steen: I don't think the problem is over-educating. The problem is that we have now made a PhD factory logic, in a way.

John: Over-education.

Steen: How could it be bad that people know more than they knew before?

John: I'm in a dilemma here. We now ask for degrees to do jobs that do not require the skills learned in these degrees; we now ask for qualifications and care somewhat less about what the courses are in that degree; and we encourage students to stay in schooling as an alternative to being unemployed. There is a case for claiming that many are in a state of being over-educated.

Steen: And it's not bad that they have gained more knowledge about science and maybe even done some research. Autonomous thinking and reflection, critique and the capacity to differentiate and validate, how can all this not be a good idea?

John: I know, but I come back to the question of the purpose of education and it's like my colleague Pat Alexander argues, that schooling, for example, is not responsible for developing excellence (Alexander 2004). Competence, able or sufficient are lower standards that schools can aim at. The question I'm asking is, is there not a limit of what we are expected to do in our schooling system? Of course, I can see the view that there's never an occasion when you can know too much, unless it's about undesirable things. There are many exemplars of over–education, and some are questioning the need for so much investment in schooling that then leads to over-education.

    Bryan Caplan has argued that gaining a degree is a form of signaling – and students are hungry for signals, as this is what the labor market pays for – credentials acquired not skills learned (Caplan 2018). His is an extreme argument, that most education beyond the mastery of basic literacy and arithmetic is a waste of time and money, and therefore governments should sharply cut back on subsidies for education and actively discourage its pursuit. Most schooling is for sorting the labor and dole queues, producing little valuable learning, and in particular, there is little need for the topics taught in most high schools or universities – students strive for the degree, not the content of the degree. He asks the question: Would you want the PhD (the credential) and not spend four years learning while you get it, or would you want the four years of learning but not get the degree? Most graduates want the former – as this is what the employers ask for – the degree is the signal; the nature of content is almost irrelevant.

We forget most of what we learn in high school or college within five years. More than 50% of adults fail 'intermediate' or 'proficient' mastery of basic quantitative questions (an example of a task of this level is calculating the total cost of ordering specific office supplies from a catalogue), a third of science graduates do not know that atoms are bigger than electrons, and so many students rejoice when the teacher cancels a class.

Steen: Of course, you can come to know how to kill people or come to know how to intoxicate them or whatever.

John: Yeah, as I mentioned, one of my other research areas is adolescents in prison. We've done a lot of work on that over the years, including researching the notion of solitude, loneliness, anomie, and asocial behaviors. It really highlights that young adolescents who become criminals engage in similar process of learning as music students and sports jocks, and gifted students. They want increasing challenges, and to have a reputation to enhance in front of their peers. Their focus, however, just happens to be socially undesirable. Most teenagers thrive on challenge. Like you noted, the focus of their challenges is what we may term desirable or not.

Steen: I also know of sociological studies showing that. Deviant behavior patterns are important to study.

John: The fascination is at age 17, the incidence of teenage crime declines dramatically. Most explanations don't account for that massive decline. Our model does account for this decline, mainly because attraction to the other sex becomes the focus of the new challenges. But that's another story.

I'm asking the question about what is the desired levels of education? Are we over-educating? But you are also asking about the nature of this education, and the case of teenage criminals highlights this social desirability of *what* this education is focused on. There are claims about socially acceptable or not topics and beliefs that are part of this focus.

Steen: But you can also pose this whole thing in a more maybe positive way. When my parents went to the gymnasium, the high school in 1948 to 1951, they were maybe among the only 1% to 5% of the whole population attending this higher form of schooling. Move to the mid-1970s when I went there, it was more like 25%, and now about 70% or 80% of all young Danes go to high school (the others attend a more technical and vocation-based school).

John: And ditto in Australia.

Steen: It's not bad.

John: I know. It's changed the nature of the universities.

Steen: Through the last 20 to 30 years or so, more people than ever before in history have had the chance to get a higher education. Society has made it possible – and mandatory – for people to get access to knowledge and science and to train their capability to think, write, and reflect.

John: Now, that's a good thing, and we need to be careful not to make claims of being over-educated for all young people.

Steen: That's a good thing, but of course it can be hard for first-generation university candidates without family background from the university to crack the code of studying. But I agree with you that it has also to do with this invitational logic that you were talking about before. Because when I have these students sitting there for supervision hours and they present their papers and we discuss their papers in order to make it explicit to them what is the demand of writing and composing a thesis in the right argumentative way – we also come to discuss their life ambition and future dreams. All of this transgresses the university curriculum and is not directed solely towards the job sector. I think that's what I really like about dealing with students, that you take part in their attempts to form their character and academic style.

They do not become your friends, but they become real human beings in front of you. And now and then they come or write back to you one, two, three, four years later, and say, "Well, what we debated those days was important to me ever since. Now I have written this. Read my new text, my new book." Or: "I now have a job, using these thoughts and skills I learned as a student in the university days." As a teacher, you also have the responsibility of forming the next generation's academics.

John: And particularly, as I mentioned earlier, when you go and ask adults about their best teacher, it is about those very things you're talking about. They wanted to turn you on to their passion, and/or they saw something in you that you may not have seen yourself.

Steen: Yeah, because if you are treating them as they are an object or a factor or whatever, then it's really below standard, obviously, and besides, it lacks mutual respect and ethics.

John: My little joke, in *Visible Learning*, which no one got: Isn't it fascinating that one of the common characteristics of excellent teachers is passion, but you can't measure it. My little joke is that you can't measure it using a standardized test, but, oh, my goodness, you can see it and you can feel it. The concept of passion, I think, is a very, very core notion.

What is the gain in differentiating between the *how*, the *what*, and the *why* of education?

Why did John Hattie recently begin to deal with the 'whatness' and 'whyness' of education?

Is it important to differentiate between the epistemology and the ontology of education?

Do we over-educate – and if we do, is it a problem?

X. IS THERE a PURPOSE of EDUCATION?

BY DEVELOPING a fair, INVITING and DEMOCRATIC CLASSROOM CONDITIONS you are IMMERSING STUDENTS into A WORLD we WOULD LIKE THEM to REPLICATE and BUILD. IT needs TO HAVE a SENSE of TENSION, DISEQUILIBRIUM and CRITICAL perspective.

SCHOOLS are THE BREEDING place for OUR DEMOCRACY, AND SURELY the MOST CIVILIZING institutions IN THE LAND.

AS THE earth BECOMES MORE flat, STUDENTS CONFRONT the WORLD of DIFFERENCE, BECOME world CITIZENS, and NEED to BREAK DOWN SIMPLISTIC nationalistic BOUNDARIES that WERE ASSUMED to be IMMUTABLE.

I WANT a SOCIETY WHERE you LEARN MANY ideas but ARE ALLOWED to be CRITICAL of THESE ideas AND ANY NOTION of THE ESTABLISHED NORM.

DEVELOP a PASSION

AND LEARN TO BE REFLECTIVE

TO COME BACK and LEARN MORE

TO GO DEEPER

CRITICAL and CREATIVE

WORK as if YOU LIVE in THE EARLY DAYS of a BETTER NATION

STUDENTS will CREATE the FUTURE

IF STUDENTS do not GET FOUNDATIONAL SKILLS by 8, it is HARD for THEM to EVER CATCH UP.

JOHN'S BIOGRAPHY would FEATURE...

- THE AMAZING RANDOMNESS of OPPORTUNITY
- THE NAIVETY of the WORLD he LIVED IN
- THE INSULATION benefits OF A SMALL TOWN

Steen: We have occasionally touched these coming themes already, but now I'd like to pose two giant – and for philosophy of education, inescapable – questions to both of us. Let's dwell on them for a while. The first is: *What is the purpose of education?* And the next one is: *Why does mankind need education?*

First of all, this profound question: What is the purpose of education? Do you see the purpose of education as end goal directed, meaning that education has a **telos**, a kind of necessary future directedness towards something out or in there, and if you do, does education then also function as a beginning, a foundation, a necessary condition? I'll just pose these questions, then we make a kind of a scene for them. Okay? Or is there an overreaching purpose of education, like the purpose, or a wide range of different purposes, in plural, for education? Is the purpose question a perspectivist question, and thereby different seen from perspectives of teachers, pupils, students, politicians, school leaders, administrators? Or is there a kind of a – what can we say – overall purpose that we all have to listen to or respect that's beyond perspectives? Calling out loud for universals, metaphysics, ontology . . .? So a lot of questions. At least three, four questions here. But the first is, you seem to think that education is not 'born' with a telos. Is it then a (first) beginning? Is it kind of something you stand upon, or even a purpose we stand in while we are asking these pivotal questions?

John: Now, I want to answer it slightly differently. I want to answer it in terms of the Deweyian notion of the kind of society that we want to esteem, develop, etc. And that then has multiple answers, as you know. I also believe that by developing a fair, inviting, and democratic classroom condition you are immersing students into a world we would like them to replicate and build. It needs to have a sense of tension, disequilibrium, and critical perspective, again the attributes we want them to cherish and build. They are the future, they will make the future, so we need to build respect for self and respect for other, and most important we need to develop the skills, competencies, and capabilities necessary for what we and they consider human existence in our and then in their world. This world is changing, of course, and quite different from the world I was expected to be part of when I was in school. Now the world is more flat, students live in this world of difference, yet struggle with the breaking down of the simplistic nationalistic boundaries that were assumed to be almost immutable to us. Trying to find foothold in the technological world (that many of us disparage and fail to understand their liking of this world) and in an over-information-rich world – one that we could only dream of (when I was a kid, one sign of affluence was the presence of an encyclopedia in the home!).

As well, and I realize it is a simplistic notion, is that I want a society that's – oh, dear, Gert Biesta would hate this – a learning society. A society where you learn many ideas but are allowed to be critical of these ideas and any notion of the established norm. And it comes back to some of the core parts of *Bildung* you talked about earlier in our conversation about developing respect for self and respect for others; developing a culture of self. This is very central in the concept of a learning society as I see it. One of the pleasures when visiting classrooms is to see 5-year-olds immersed in their learning society – and seeing a group of 15-year-old youngsters in their learning society. Asking them what it means to be a learner in this class, and hoping they will talk about the hard work of learning, a passion to come back and learn more. Like a willingness to go deeper beyond the facts and ideas of the class, and the skills to be reflective, critical, and creative about these ideas – and it does not matter too much if this is about civics, music, or math.

Steen: So your basic answer here again(!) is, as I listen to it, very sociological. It's based on how we interact, how we respect certain rules . . .

John: Yes, learning the rules of the game – particularly as to then be so well placed to advance, critique, and improve these rules of a civilized society.

Steen: . . . of interaction in a society. And it's not a historical answer, and neither is it a philosophical answer.

John: If it was historical – I don't want to reify what was. I want students to live as students as much as they can. It is not about preparing them for a future 10 to 15 years away. It is about the now. I think that our 5-year-olds need to be 5-year-olds today and learn what it means to be joyful, questioning, curious, and build the precious knowledge to be even more joyful, questioning, and curious. They are the future, especially as they invent the future.

Steen: And that also means, probably, your answer to the second question would be that education purposes have to be plural.

John: Yes, absolutely.

Steen: Does it mean that different interests and power structures in society have formed the changing historical purposes and narratives of education?

John: Yes, absolutely.

Steen: So in your eyes there is no overreaching visionary purpose of education or a kind of obligatory and stable logic of education?

John: No, but at the same time there is a core, and it comes back to that respect for self and respect for others. The Nazis didn't have that philosophy. They respected only certain others. I worry about where America's going in its designs of certain others. I find it fascinating in the world at the moment where we're talking about free trade and, well, we want free trade (well most of us do). But we're doing the opposite with people.

Steen: We don't have free rights for people to move wherever they'd like even though commodities, capital, money, pictures, and signs are allowed to do so (Safranski 2003). The global society is a vivid paradox.

John: And that's not the kind of society that I think is valuable. I'm not a nationalist. I won't stand for the flag, which is the symbol of too many closed societies. I am a person of the world (and yes, I have this luxury which is denied to so many). I think the whole notion of xenophobia is the antithesis of what we're talking about here.

Steen: So, in a way, the purpose could be to realize and 'foster' the world citizen?

John: Very much so. And we need to protect the world as much as we develop it. I never underestimate the ingenuity and creativity of the collective to reframe problems, to invent solutions that not only advance society but redirect it (for example, the car solved many of the urgent problems caused by horses and carts; the iPhone solved many of the problems of the old telephone system; and so on). The inventors of all these once went to school and learned about learning and developed precious knowledge – such that they could question, create, and go deeper into their content areas.

Steen: Clear-sighted Immanuel Kant was writing about the world citizen and the cosmopolitan state in his philosophical essay **Perpetual Peace** in 1795 (Kant 2007/1995). He depicted the cosmopolitan state as a "great political body" in which every member state receives its security and rights from a united power and from decisions in accordance with the laws of a united will. The task of this cosmopolitan state is to safeguard and implement every world citizens' security and rights. This vision of the cosmopolitan state lifting the unproductive tensions between competing and more or less unfriendly nation states up to a higher and more peaceful level is not realized yet even though Kant envisaged it years ago.

John: Correct.

Steen: And this cosmopolitan view, it could be understood as your purpose of education?

John: Yes, but purposes in plural.

Steen: But then, it seems to me that there is at least a little tension, or a twofold or bilingual logic here. Because one is then to state, what is the social laws of interaction in the now? Meaning, how do we interact with other persons right now in this situation? The other thing is this dream, or hope, or regulative vision of something that could happen. That we could become political human beings (citizens of the word, in German: *Weltbürgern*) . . .

John: Oh, but our students are already inventing new forms of social interaction, and will continue to live and grow in this world – a little uncomfortable and somewhat unfathomable to us, who like the world we created.

Steen: . . . much more than nationalists, which is a kind of a political vision or dream . . .

John: Yes, it is.

Steen: . . . not fulfilled yet, due to Ernst Bloch's unforgettable and powerful view on our vivid future hopes of realizing the potentials of the not-yet in the present now (Bloch 1986/1954–1959).

John: There is a wonderful quote on the wall of the Scottish Parliament building: "Work as if you live in the early days of a better nation." Yes, we have to enable children to have not only the skills to solve problems, not only the knowledge to help solve problems, but also the skills to create new problems.

Between societal diagnostics and future hopes

Steen: Much to my surprise – knowing that you are primarily trained as a statistician – you tend again to favor, honor, and apply a kind of a sociological take-off, maintaining that we have to cope with and handle this present social sphere with all its problems and tasks in which we are living. At the same time you don't seem to be preoccupied with longer historical lines in order to state whether or not we might have lost something in the past or we could gain something in re-consulting the past. My third observation is that you have a strong and passionate vision of what could become a better hope embedded in the now, but also leading to a better future. Is this a fair description of your credo?

John: Yes, change and improvement can start with an individual, with a small group, and in schools. Michael Fullan claims it mostly starts in the middle (Fullan 2015). I think you have individual skills that you should have to enable creating future hopes. There are many 'I' skills, such as a sense of confidence, seeing oneself as a change agent, being aware of one's proficiencies to have and gain, great conflict resolution skills, a desire to attain success collectively, and most of all skills in demonstrating social sensitivities. There are also many 'we' skills, such as a belief that the group one is in can organize and execute actions, a belief that the group can be successful, and a shared purpose to learn. Too often schools focus too much on the 'I' and ignore the critical 'we' skills – as they are the essence of living productively in society.

Steen: When it comes to radical political change of societies, we can take two different examples, and the first one could be Cuba. In 1959, 90 guerrilla people stole a motorboat – called Granma – and sailed it into Havana, and then they changed the world. Ninety dedicated guerrillas were enough to let the old regime fall. Or you have a very, very, small vanguard party in the Leninist revolution of Soviet Union in 1917. They stormed the Winter Palace, removed the Tsar and his power apparatus, and they changed their society. But now, it doesn't seem probable that the world can be changed these ways.

When it comes to radical societal changes, we could maybe say that Mark Zuckerberg and Steve Jobs are today's immaterial guerrilla people on the virtual Granma motorboat version 2.0. They are also vanguard Leninists and changing the world dramatically, but only to place themselves and their business empires on the top.

John: I'm sure that when the historians look back to this time, Mark Zuckerberg and Steve Jobs probably had more political influence in terms of uniting the world, for good or bad, than any particular individual in the political scene. If nothing else, the 'we' are not just people who look like us.

Steen: And does that also have to do with the purpose of education, that you kind of teach people – or you could say people have to learn – how to reflect upon these power structures of modern or globalized communication?

John: Yes, because these enhanced connections bring this power into the here and now – often far earlier for children that it did for me. If I wrote my biography, it would feature the amazing randomness of opportunity, the naivety of the world I lived in, and the insulation of the small town. Not anymore. Not only do we have the rule of law, we are now inventing the rule of living in a flat world.

I have spent many years coaching cricket, focusing on 17- to 20-year-olds. One of these boys became an airline engineer. I remarked that this would let him get to many places in the world. Oh no, he said, we sit in the basement at the airport and monitor every plane as it is flying. You would not believe what happens mid-flight, and it was his role to problem solve, diagnose, and fix the planes – my point is that today's young adults seriously build the plane as they are flying it.

Why does mankind need education?

Steen: Let's now move back to the second very big question that has been debated for thousands of years: Why does mankind need education? You can find different answers to this question, if you go back to Augustine's *De magistro* (*The teacher*), and even further, if you go way back to Plato and his dialogue *Cratylus* (Augustin 1876; Plato 1989). And in enlightenment philosophy and the new humanism, there were many people coming up with answers to the question. Kant wrote that man is the only creature in need of education (Kant 1971/1803).

Philosophical anthropologists have claimed that humans need education because we cannot rely on our natural instincts and therefore we have to move from first to second nature. Let nature be nurtured according to, for example, Hegel's conceptual and historical philosophical view of the spiritual development of man and society (Hegel 1979/1807).

How do you view and value these philosophical claims and take offs? Are we as educators and educational scientists in need of a philosophical anthropology? Is it worth it to try answer a question like: Why is mankind in need of education? Can you give answers to these questions, or are they simply too far out, too speculative for an empirical working and preoccupied scientist?

John: Well, with my usual codicil that I'm not a philosopher, I was very entranced with Rousseau's *Emile*, and the conflict about the purpose of education making a man or a citizen (recognizing that Emile was a male). He wanted Emile to be brought up surrounded by nature, and learning about sentiment in their teens (Rousseau 1979/1762). This seems pie in the sky in today's world, some kind of Summerhill. Although there are some great examples (John Marsden heads great schools here in Melbourne that are more aligned with this approach that the usual school – seehttp://www.candlebark.info/).

And I'm a great fan of Michael Young, who I read quite a lot of as a sociologist (Young & Muller 2013). He argues that we need education to learn that which we wouldn't learn if we didn't go to school. I think that's the best justification that I've heard for justifying some of the topics we teach in school – to make the person and the person in society. If there was no education or schooling then we would not know what we don't know.

I've just read a book of an American girl who was brought up in quite a racist place in North Dakota, where she didn't go to school, ever (Westover 2018). Her parents were gun people, and they were protecting against the wicked government, and so on. She ended up getting a PhD. And the story is how she did that. She got out, but there are too many students who are brought up in impoverished situations who do not know the options, the alternatives, and the opportunities. A major purpose of schooling is to provide these options and different perspectives of the world.

Steen: The most extreme example of an anti-modern tribe must be the Amish people. They are still riding horse carriages today.

John: Yeah, but even them, they are exposed to the world. They just have a view of living in it. And they actively reject many parts of this world. But some people don't expose their students even to the world. Like this case with this woman in North Dakota. Now, that's the extreme, but it makes the point that there is a major role for schools. And it's your argument about Richard Rorty before, to expose people to alternative ways of thinking, how people have thought differently.

I certainly don't think the role of school is to prepare you for life, because it denies the fact that you're living as a kid. Like with my own students, I wanted them to enjoy being a 6-year-old, and a 10-year-old, and a 15-year-old.

Steen: Yeah, you shouldn't sacrifice the now on the altar of the future.

John: No.

Steen: That's what you did in the old days. You'd say, "Well, this is hard, and it has no sense, but you'll get wiser."

John: Oh, you hear it in schools every day.

Steen: "You'll get pie in the sky when you die."

But, John, is there a profound philosophical anthropology behind your *Visible Learning* program?

John: Yes. I think there is a tremendous obligation on those of us who demand that students spend 15 years of their life in schools, which, by the way, is longer than we ask some people to stay in jail for murder. If we are asking them to stay in schools, there is an obligation that we do have a positive impact on them. Of course, we have to question what that impact is. And you shouldn't have a good teacher by chance; it should be by design. I do think there is a moral obligation to question the efficacy and the impact of teachers and schools, which is very much underlying the philosophy of what we're doing with our *Visible Learning* program in schools. It does beg the question, the ultimate question, of the value of that and the worth of doing it. Because I emphasize the notion of impact, it is forcing debates about the essence of what we value and wish to develop in the nature of children, and one of the most critical impact issues is developing children to live in the world.

Steen: But that's only touching upon the *how* question, stating how we – the teachers – can have bigger impact. How we can make better interpretations of the learning data. It is basically also a question about *what* and *why*, like we have already stressed and discussed.

Is the school born with a purpose?

John: I lose more sleep over the political job than I do over my day job because the stakes are so high. As an academic, I can write a book, I can get criticized. In fact, it's a luxury to be criticized. Because, as you know, 99% of articles are not even cited – not even by their own author. So the fact that I've got criticism, I've got to treat it as a luxury. But, in the political space, the stakes are high. You're really dealing with real people's lives. The agency, Australian Institute for Teachers and School Leaders, is owned by the federal government although most educators believe they own it – it generates a third of a million hits to its website a month, and is also responsible for implementing government policy. It is a delicate gift, balancing responsiveness to the needs of educators and working with nine states and territories and federal government.

Steen: Yeah, and much money is involved. Let's try to change gears now. Another thing is, if we call this – our mutual – book *The Purposes of Education*, the profound question is, if the role of the teacher primarily is to invite people to enter an institution that possesses an a priori purpose.

John: Yes, this is a part of it.

Steen: Do you think that the school is born with a purpose, that it has a kind of a will or logic of its own? Is the school system born with a purpose? Or is it open for ongoing and changing interpretations stemming from the pupils and the teachers?

John: Well, when you think of how our current school system was born in the 1800s, part of it was very economic, part of it was very much building the labor system. And that still is the case. It serves as a training ground for employers, but over the past 100 years we have so much more as purposes of schooling. Schools are the breeding place for our democracy, surely the most civilizing institutions in the land.

So often I hear that the schools of the future will look quite different from today's schools – with visions of students working at home, no longer school hours or even school as a place. But we have a society where both parents often work full-time roles, and someone has to be with the young children. Yes, this is not saying schools are babysitters, as they are more than that, but they do include this role also.

Steen: Then they are compensatory in a way. But of course, I also think that, from the very beginning, one argument was to produce a common workforce, a more skilled labor, being able to read, write, do math, and so on. It was also a national project. You should be a part of your nation, study and learn the myths of the nation, and learn to become a real citizen. And maybe be able to come from the countryside, learn the national language, and to have the possibility to move away from your regional sphere, physically and mentally.

John: But there was another assumption which I'm sure was not explicit at the time, but I think is an incredible pressure on us as educators. The assumption is that, by making schooling compulsory, we are saying educators can do it better than the parents, on average, and I take that very seriously.

Steen: And, at the very same time, the Danish school system, at least, but you also have it here, it had a little kind of opening towards free schools where people can do . . .

John: . . . educational experimentation. Yes, we still do that here in Australia . . .

Steen: . . . and parents, they can organize their own schools. You have your Catholic schools here, and properly also Summerhill schools, Steiner schools, sport and art schools, etc.

John: The Catholic schools and the state schools look very similar. Indeed once in a classroom in this country it would be hard to say if it was Catholic, state, or independent (except that more money is spent in independent schools on the buildings and facilities – but the teaching is similar).

Steen: In Denmark they also look pretty similar, but the idea was that, even though the state has said or the official educational 'logic' declares that the state can do it better than the private and narrow-minded parents themselves, there is still a legal and legitimate opening for the parents to organize schools and to get some economic financial support from the state to run the schools.

John: You're right, and there are two things we need to consider. First, if you look at Larry Cuban's work, who is a US historian of teaching, he looks at how teachers have changed over the last 200 years (Cuban 1984). And his argument is that 85% teach in a similar manner, 10% teach more effectively but in a similar manner, as we did 200 years ago. About 10% are different and 5% are dramatically different. And so every time when I look around the world and Larry looks around the world, and you look at people who have engaged in experimentation, that 85, 10, 5 seems to hold. We see it across Australia – and so much attention is given to the 15% but it has not changed the mainstream of schooling.

In this country, there's a school out near the airport here that's run by quite a famous teenage author – John Marsden. It is very, very different, stunningly different (Marsden 2019). Very much like Summerhill – which was Bertrand Russell's school Candlebark. And it is based on probably the world's biggest school campus: more than 1,100 acres just north of Melbourne, Australia, and it uses this gift fully. Everyone is on first name basis, extensive use of peer teaching, and is a true community of learners. But it requires a gifted, fully committed leader as it is so much harder to commit to teaching in this environment with this ethos. It is unlikely to become the norm.

Further, across Australia during the past 20 years we have swung the pendulum too far to support parents' rights to choose schools. This has led to a very unhealthy debate about school differences, maximizing beliefs and branding about how school x differs from school y, and competition between state and independent schools. One state reinvented many of its public schools as 'independent public schools', so much money is spent by all in advertising, and too often principals consider a good school to be one with a large enrollment, thence stealing students from the schools next door. Here in Melbourne over 60% of students pass their local school to go to their school of choice.

There is just not the evidence that the variance between schools is that large in Australia. Sadly, it is increasing, but this is also leading to residualization effects in some state schools as the grass is always greener in the independent schools (the 'real' choices). There is little evidence, once you control for input variables like prior achievement, that state, Catholic, or independent schools differ much on achievement or progress.

The information parents have to choose is minimal. There is information about average achievement scores on the government website, but it does not consider prior achievement or socioeconomic resources of the home. It does report a minimal amount of progress information, but that is harder for parents to find than average scores – which are often better indicators of house prices. But I am not implying parents are irrational when they make choices, and so often they choose schools where there are students they want their children to be friends with.

But this overplay for the rights to choose has led to more money being spent on the wrong things – what I call the politics of distraction in contrast to the desired politics of collaborative action. I wrote two papers with these titles to make this contract (Hattie 2015a, 2015b).

Steen: Okay. There seem to exist two extreme positions at stake here, viewing and conceptualizing the state very differently. One is stating that the state needs to have ambitions also for socialization, upbringing, cultural heritage, canonical subjects, whatever. And the other is that the state has to reduce its influence and then we should let the market and the consumers (parents, taxpayers) decide.

John: I'm not a fan of the latter. I would like the local school to be the best in the neighborhood, and the best school in the neighborhood is also the one next door. But this is a little naïve in this day, although the differences between schools is not as large as many believe or would advocate.

Parents can also decide to homeschool, and there are about 30,000 students in Australia who call Mum or Dad, teacher. There is much research that the achievement of these students is quite high. But then the average student who goes into homeschool typically is performing at about the 85th percentile. The education in homeschool is only as good as the teacher. Certainly for me, my boys deserve better than me, need to learn to interact with others, and have the variety of experiences that regular schools can offer.

My sadness with all this debate is that I do think that the debates revolving around school choice are distractions. We should not be so obsessed with structural questions about the nature of schools, the grouping of students, class size, buildings, and similar. It detracts from the needed focus and investment in excellence and expertise, which every student is entitled to. Our mantra is students deserve great teachers by design, not by chance.

Take the penchant to set up different kinds of schools – charter schools, trust schools, academics, and so on. I have news to these advocates – within six months of setting up these new-fangled entities – you are running a 'school'!

Steen: Yeah, and there are certain rules about running a school.

John: It's no secret that we've kind of worked out the fundamental ways of running schools. There are deviations and there are differences, but you go to any school in the world and you could walk in and understand them immediately. They might have different systems and different kinds of leadership structure.

Steen: You have uniforms here in Australia, and school-kids and students do not wear uniforms in Denmark.

John: Uniforms, oh, my goodness, they have zero effect on students' learning, which means I don't care whether you have them or you don't have them. Just get over it and make a decision. Any system that's obsessed about those things is obsessed about the wrong things. And, unfortunately, there are a lot of wrong obsessions. This comes back to the politicians. Sometimes they like those obsessions. Bill Clinton demanded they have uniforms and we had a whole debate about it. What a destructive debate, because it wasn't a debate about learning and about the moral purpose of schooling, which matter so much more.

The purposes of education – once again

John: Steen, I suggest that we maintain our wide-ranging talk about the purpose of education. So far, I would argue we've been privileging those who can embark in the kind of aspirations and ideals that we had been talking about for education. But there is a group of students out there, and they're going to struggle, because their intellectual abilities may not be as advanced, and they more likely to lose out. We could argue we have to educate them to the best of their ability. Not good enough. How does *Bildung* apply to those students? Do we just do it to them and enforce it, and hope? But that is just too limited for me.

Steen: Well, of course, we couldn't have enforced *Bildung* upon people, first of all because *Bildung* also demands a will of you own to be *selbstgebildet*, as you would say in German, meaning 'self-formatted' in a bad technical translation. But if some pupils and students are getting sick and tired of too close a contact to the educational system, there might be a good reason for them, or a freedom they should have, to drop education. You cannot and ought not force people to everything. Formal and lifelong education cannot be mandatory for everyone – but a 'standing' offer and an option. And who knows, maybe they return to the educational institutions later in life after having gained other deep and formative experiences.

John: And is it okay that they drop schooling?

Steen: Never, it's very bad that people drop schooling at the age of 10 or 12, but what was good in the 1960s and 1970s and 1980s was that the educational system in, for example, Denmark provided you with flexible logics, so you could come back and take, for example, a gymnasium high school exam when you were 34 or even 50, or having just a ninth grade exam from boarding school you could come back 20 years later and continue at another level. I think that societies should offer people all kinds of ways to become wiser and more cunning, but of course you cannot – and shall not – enforce that on people. Probably you're right that we couldn't just say everything is nurture. There is also nature. All of us are complex creatures of mixed nature–nurture patterns, and some people have a hard time wiring their 'educational' synapses and a harder time building up their 'intellectual' neuro-plasticity and hopefully their craftsmanship than other ones. But all this has also to do with the stimulation from your background. As you stated earlier in our conversation, the vocabularies of a three-year-old in one family and in another family are tremendously different. The same counts for questions of whether or not you are free to play with and build up your own role, and if you're reflective, and you are afraid of your dad coming home and bashing you, or afraid of losing your mother's love tomorrow, and so on. A basic insecure position, socially, psychologically, and economically, will also not foster intelligence. And you can destroy people's intelligence if you limit their nutrition and enslave or intoxicate them. There are many ways to destroy plasticity of the brain (Fuchs 2018; Larsen 2013a). So, you are of course right to point to the existence of all kind of systems and steps that have to be taken to help people to navigate alongside these biological and social conditions for students and adults to learn to practice and become wiser and, in your vocabulary, to learn.

John: The purpose of education is not only all those positive attributes that we were talking about before but it's also to make sure that those negative attributes are not dominant.

Steen: And, of course, it also has to do with basic skills that a schooling system should provide.

John: I take a very strong line on that. Many argue for excellence, but I start with the minimal, the non-negotiables that *all* students should have the right to have delivered from an education system.

Steen: And I think that the claims or the ideas of what people should be able to do have been raised dramatically through the last decades.

John: Over the past 20 years, the increase in children receiving schooling has been the most dramatic in our world's history. While there are too many vicious inequalities and there is still much to do, educators have much to celebrate. Yes, much is basic, but it is the foundation.

Steen: In the old days, it was maybe enough to train people to be able to follow commands like "Listen!"; "Write your name on this contract!"; "Press your finger here!" Well, it doesn't work like that any longer. Fortunately, we seem to have become wiser in many educational institutions around the world.

John: Yes, we need to build the bases, in our country usually by about age eight, otherwise students get left behind. A young German student, Max Pfost, came out and spent six months here with me and we did a meta-analysis on the Matthew Effect in reading (Pfost 2014). The argument is that by age eight, if students have a minimum quality of reading (say Level I in PISA), then they continue to grow and flourish across many school domains. If they don't get the minimum by that age, they rarely catch up. Hence the Matthew Effect, the biblical notion that the rich get richer, the poor stay poor.

  Initially, Max's argument was that the Matthew Effect was related to the complexity of the language you had. We looked at the German, Finnish, Chinese, but it turned out that wasn't the case at all. The Matthew Effect was across all these languages.

Steen: In our neighborhood, there is a school where the pupils have brain damage and/or serious physical problems and they are . . .

John: I'm not talking about those students. That's another story, and we should come back to them. There are so many children that come to school at age five and every teacher knows those students are struggling well before age eight. They're real people with real names. But they still have below acceptable skills at age eight. Why? Why aren't we doing something for these students? If the Matthew Effect is indeed as we describe, we are failing these children from the day they start school.

Steen: In Denmark, you have had special schools for exactly those students – for example, students with different diagnoses like ADHD and Asperger, but these schools used about 20% of the resources spent on all schools in the country. In 2012, the former minister of education, the social democrat Christine Antorini, and a broad majority in the Danish parliament passed an inclusion law. The expensive special schools were closed down and inclusion of all students in 'normal' school classes became compulsory.

John: No, that's not fair. No, that's very unfair. Going from one claim, exclusion, to the other, inclusion, may not necessarily be the most optimal schooling environment. Yes, I know many of the parents demanded it.

Steen: You are right, but many parents with students with special needs also criticized the closure of the special schools.

John: There were quite a few very big advocates to move to inclusion, in some cases well before the teachers were ready and equipped to work with these students. One of my PhD students, Chris Forlin, investigated this factor and showed that those teachers who could collaborate with fellow educators were most likely to best work with these students (Forlin 1996). For others, seeking help was seen as a sign of failure.

Steen: Yeah, and it was claimed that the law would help to integrate and include students with special needs in normal schooling. But, as I said, there were a lot of parents also stating, "This will be a catastrophe for my son because the special school helped him."

John: Yes, and now there is a move back to opening some of these special schools as more optimal environments for these students to be educated.

Steen: So there were all of these different debates, but what has been the result is actually that it is very, very tough now to be a teacher, because if you have two or three of these students in the class and they need complete attention one to one – then the 'normal' school risks falling apart.

John: There is a recent meta-analysis that shows that the other students are impacted positively – small but positive (Szumski et al. 2017). But the greatest problem is that so often we introduce amateurs, such as teacher aides, to keep these students distracted or worse do the work for these students while the teacher works with the other students (Blatchford 2011). The students who most need the expert get the amateurs!

Steen: If I dare to make a summary here, it seems to me that you think that the *Bildung* concept that I promote, favor, and try to do my best to revitalize could risk highly prioritizing and highly privileging a certain group of youngsters out there.

John: I worry about that.

Steen: You worry about that it could be a kind of an upper class or elitist logic. Another critique could be that it would be an enforcement by the state if the state made *Bildung* as a mandatory program and thereby tried to decide and 'design' the future for students. If you make a *Bildung* plan this way – a masterplan for the 'production' of the formation and character-building of the pupils' subjectivities – it will be enforced *Bildung* by the law, and I think that is a wrong way to do it. This whole top-down logic is definitely not my cup of tea (Larsen 2015b).

John: But that's the beauty of *Bildung*. It kind of defeats the point if you legalize it.

Steen: Yeah, that's right. The Humboldt version was that one thing was making a law of education, another thing was *Bildung*, and *Bildung* couldn't be enforced by law. But you could, of course, fertilize it or try to promote it. Humboldt's idea was that all the different sciences should debate with and fertilize each other, and for him *Bildung* came through interaction with science as we stated earlier during our talk.

The brothers Wilhelm and Alexander von Humboldt were two very talented guys, knowing many languages, philosophy, botanic, mapping, arithmetic, theology, history, and anthropology, and I don't know what. . . . They possessed all these multi-talents, they were encyclopedic people. Their overall idea was that the actual process of the ontology of education could create and 'grow' *Bildung* by and for itself.

Maybe we could talk about two critiques, two reservations. Either you make it a part of the curriculum, which would be wrong, or you make it part of an elitist program, which would be exactly as misleading. So my argument will be: "No, *Bildung* does not have to be elitist, neither does it have to be legislated." Besides, *Bildung* is not a canon of holy or profane national texts serving identity-political reasons and self-mirroring demands.

In my perspective it is better to think about *Bildung* as a highly contested concept that's always there, when we debate and form educational programs, giving voice to all that which is not a part of instrumental learning or qualifying you to manage a future job task.

And, therefore, we never get rid of it. But I have just presented three different versions of *Bildung*, dealing with knowledge, citizenship, and formation of the character. Of course, there is much more to say, and the content of concept has to be debated and it may be changed.

John: In Australia and New Zealand, the public claim is we are very tolerant and accept multiple views. And New Zealand had a debate about what the attributes of New Zealand are, and it went nowhere. I was involved in a TV program about the 'normal' kiwi, and the major answer was that they were adventurous, and that's a desirable trait to have. Our most famous New Zealander, and the one that every New Zealander bar none loves, is Sir Edmund Hillary. Not just because he climbed Mount Everest, but because he spent the rest of his life giving back to the Sherpa people. Australia has this concept of itself as the open country, the sunburnt country. Dorothea McKellar wrote a poem widely cited about this: "I love a sunburnt country, A land of sweeping plains, of ragged mountain ranges, of droughts and flooding rains."

We claim to tolerate many views. If that's the case, how can we then have *Bildung*?

Steen: I see the problem but first of all, it's probably not correct that Australia is such an open and welcoming country any longer.

John: Perhaps not, but that's the claim, that we are open.

Steen: Okay, that's the claim, a kind of a national myth.

John: It may be, and therefore, we can't have the first aspect of your *Bildung*.

Steen: Why not? But I find it utmost problematic if there is a kind of a canon or a curriculum that you have to study, maybe even be forced or indoctrinated to embrace, accept, and love. My idea of a substantial *Bildung* vision also contains the ongoing examination of the ideals and the heritage of the enlightenment – for example, a critical 'reading' of the national history and the myths of the country. It implies that we also have to teach people about the romantic critique of modernity and the conservative life perspective, but also not forget the peasants', workers', women's authors', and artists' centuries-long fight to come to live a decent life and to gain freedom of expression, etc. You also have to teach people about populism, identity politics, and self-destructive logics of economic growth and capitalism. So, in a way, instead of a kind of a glorious and self-satisfactory or self-praising way of dealing with *Bildung*, it should absolutely also be a critical gain or invitation to study the inner conflicts and dilemmas of society. But the problem about this *Bildung* concept in the Danish horizon was that the leading politicians in the government and the parliament made and enforced a national canon from 2004 and onwards. They proclaimed, "These 15 works in literature and these 15 historical events of Danish history are mandatory for you to learn." Thereby, one national narrative was canonized, and they even had people from the cultural scene, writers, authors, scientists, architects, and so on to back them up. Asking what the 15 most important architectural classics in Denmark are supposed to be, and so on, and that was definitely the wrong way to go. First of all, it was stupid because it was national. In such a little nation as Denmark, nearly everything that's going on has been influenced by events and 'actors' in Germany, France, Italy, England, Sweden, the US, etc.

Is there a purpose of education, many purposes – or none at all?

Does the world need education?

Are we as educators and educational scientists in need of a philosophical anthropology?

How does the purpose question relate to the revitalization of the heritage of *Bildung*?

XI. IS IT POSSIBLE to UNDERSTAND
PEDAGOGY as an ART of DECENTERING?

IF A LEARNING goal is MANDATORY, how DO YOU DECENTER yourself FROM THINKING that YOU ARE THE CENTER of THE UNIVERSE and the ONLY one ABLE to REACH AND FULFIL the GOAL?

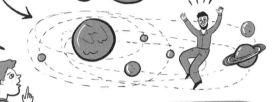

THIS IS WHY WE NEED to TEACH STUDENTS to DARE TO ANALYZE and QUESTION THE VALUES and NORMS of SOCIETY, to JUMP a LITTLE bit TO THE SIDE and ASK:

- HOW DID WE BECOME these PEOPLE with THESE VALUES?

- HOW WERE WE FORMED TO BECOME these VALUE-HONOURING PEOPLE?

- WHY DO WE THINK THIS WAY?

- WHY DO WE CLASSIFY THE THINGS THE WAY WE CLASSIFY them?

THIS IS WHY WE NEED TO reflect THROUGH THE EYES of OTHERS. ESPECIALLY the EYES of

- STUDENTS · COLLEAGUES

- and EVIDENCE

WE SHOULD have THE POSSIBILITY and RIGHT to BECOME SURPRISES **TO OURSELVES.**

DON'T BE so OVER CENTERED that we fail TO RESPECT OTHERS.

Steen: Biesta concludes his terse oeuvre, *The Rediscovery of Teaching*, empha-
          sizing that it's important for the teacher to be driven by the idea that
          teaching matters and is necessary for "our existence as grown-up sub-
          jects in the role but not in the center of it" (Biesta 2017: 98). Meaning
          that the teacher must be driven by the idea that all humans come to
          know how to decenter themselves. Schools and universities must be
          open to and welcome **the art of decentering** through daily practices,
          and I find that pretty interesting in relation to the strong educational
          political tendency to enhance and 'petrify' learning goals. If a learning
          goal is mandatory, how do you decenter yourself from thinking that
          you are the center of the universe and the only one to able to reach and
          fulfill the goal? Is the art of decentering also a part of your thinking?

John: Oh, totally. This comes back to my fascination with reflection and get-
          ting this concept right, because too often reflection is not decentered.

Steen: It's centered then?

John: When we ask, "What did I do?" the emphasis is often so much about
          reflecting as recall. But this is not so worthwhile. I often use *Alice
          Through the Looking Glass* to illustrate the issue (Carroll 1871). Alice did
          not look in the mirror and reflect, consider, tell, or comment on what
          was reflected back to her – and this too often is what 'reflection' is in
          teaching. Instead, Alice touched the mirror and her hand went through,
          and she fell onto the other side. The rest of the book is a parable about
          how others see her through the looking glass. In the same way, I want
          teacher reflection to be less post-hoc justifications and recalls about
          what they did, but how can you seek other (e.g., from the students)
          perspectives of what they experienced when you did what you did.
          Hence, the mantra of *Visible Learning*, seeing teaching through the eyes
          of students.

Steen: Yeah, you seem to enter an endless circularity about your reflection, and
          to be absorbed in your self-reflection.

John: Yes, but I need your help here because as you know I'm not a specialist
          in the different philosophical and sociological ways of grasping what
          reflection is and can be.

Steen: I'm very much in favor of what the Germans call *Dezentrierungskunst*
          (the art of decentering; see also Ziehe 2004). For example, it is very
          important for students in schools to learn to dare to analyze and ques-
          tion the values and norms of society. Several reflection processes can start
          if you jump a little bit to the side and dare to ask: How did we become

these people having these values? How were we formed to become these value-honoring subjects? Why do we think this way? Why do we classify the things the way we classify them? With heavy inspiration from Friedrich Nietzsche, the French historian of ideas Michel Foucault began to ask all these profound and critical questions in the 1950s to 1980s (Nietzsche 2009/1989; Foucault 1980). Foucault also asked: How did we become these kinds of subjects? How do we talk about the objects? What is the relationship between knowledge and power? How does language, discourse, 'create' subject and object positions and different truth regimes?

John: Yes, we can learn much from this, and while I listened to my colleagues, like Michael Peters, talk about these ideas, I still struggle (Peters 2013). Take centering . . . there is a smile on my face as my son went to a Quaker school, and he was often a very naughty boy, and one of the concepts they have in the school was centering. And what that meant was that he had to go and sit in a place in the classroom to center himself, to get a sense of his self and consider his actions – it was a very effective method. He is now 33, if he does something we don't like, we say:

Steen: Go center!

John: Yeah, but maybe they should have decentered him: How did he understand how he affected others?

Steen: I think philosophers like, for example, Foucault open our eyes and emphasize ways of being in the world that contradict the strong narratives about the sovereign and competitive subject. Such an ideal or standard subject does everything to center him- or herself, invents strategies, wants the best self-presentation, and a unique personal branding. For the centered subject it is of major importance that other people think you are a smart guy. But schools and universities could be places for decentering, and options for experiments of self-forgetting and self-transcendence.

John: I would welcome both, and yes, there can be different skills, different knowledge, but this reflection or 'know thyself' requires looking through the mirror both front on and from the other side of the mirror.

Steen: But if you are out there to fight for your selected purpose in the name of being a centered and strategic subject, how can you then be both?

John: Yes, we indeed need to be taught to be both. I'm reading a biography of the world-class golfer Tiger Woods at the moment, which is really interesting (Benedick & Keteyian 2018). And what he did in competition is that he centered himself so much when his competitor did him a favor, he wouldn't even acknowledge it.

Steen: Wow, he was obsessed with the golf game . . .

John: Yes, he tried not to be disturbed by distractions, but it came across to his other golfers that he was not behaving as a nice person. There was a famous incident where he was going for his third amateur title, which had never happened before. On the second-to-last hole the two players were both equal. He picked his ball up, as you're supposed to, because it was in the way of the other one, and when he put it back down, he put it down on the wrong place. His competitor said to him, "Tiger, remember you've got to move it across." Now, if he hadn't done that, he would have lost the competition because of two piddly points. He never thanked him. He never acknowledged that . . .

Steen: Bad style. He would have lost without the friendly warning.

John: . . . because he was so centered. He didn't acknowledge the other person. Now that's fundamentally rude. He was over-centered, or at least centered around only one aspect of the game. There are skills to be learned about not being distracted, and when to be distracted. Indeed, distractibility is one of the core functions of executive control, and I am sure teachers know many students who have not learned (or been taught) the skills of not being distracted inappropriately. Yes, there are moments when we need to be centered, and moments when we need to be so centered as to miss learning and respectful opportunities from others around us.

Pedagogy in two triangles

Steen: Let us move towards another theme. Let me try to describe pedagogy – the depth of education – in two triangles (Larsen 2016a). As you know, I strive hard to give the concept 'pedagogy' flesh and blood. The first triangle tries to grasp what happens when a kid begins in public school. In a limited perspective, you can understand this entry as a mixture of a private customer–system relation, embedded in a twofold logic and placing commodities on both ends of the spectrum. The kid (and parents behind the child) gets a good service from the system (the state provides the education) and the payback is to 'produce' good marks throughout the years to come and to earn a good degree in the end to become a sales-worthy and productive part of the workforce.

But, thinking only in this way, you make a categorical mistake while you tend to forget that the first and foremost thing that happens when you enter a school and pass the threshold to a public institution is formation to become an active and knowable citizen. So the pedagogical triangle has an utmost important third angle. So a kid–school relation can and should never become a 'pure' marketized relation. Maybe the kid as a youngster or an adult will take part in radical attempts to change the educational system. The clue is that we don't know and shouldn't know if that will be the case. The endeavor with the school must be an open(ended) one for every one of us. Through schooling, every one of us has to become qualified to take part in public life (to be engaged in *res publica*).

John: I absolutely agree.

Steen: The logic of the first triangle is that you have the right and the opportunity to become a citizen of the world and a citizen of the community. You have to take part. If you buy a tomato or a car – you normally do not have to take part in more than a transaction. A pupil is much more than a private consumer of education or an object subjected to state control. Of course, the teacher – as a state representative – is giving you something and you are yourself a private and interested subjectivity. But, in a way you are also addressed by and raised by a logic that transgresses and challenges the state–private axis. Becoming a *res publica* agent, the schoolkid thereby incarnates a third angle in this first pedagogical–educational triangle.

  Another triangle gets established when class starts and you realize that the teacher and you as a pupil are not only taking part in a twofold communication. There is always a substance matter in between, a case, a subject, a task, a theme, a problem field. So both of you have to do your best to comprehend – and present interpretations of – the subject matter, no matter whether it 'contains' and offers grammar exercises, historical events, volleyball smashes, or multiplication tasks. The 'in-between' content can be labeled magic of the third.

  So my idea is basically that we ought to fertilize, foster, and defend these two triangles, implying that we have to become citizens, and we have to be knowing and autonomous thinking subjects.

John: Stop. Five-year-olds are citizens.

Steen: Yeah, but also have to, you know, be trained to take part in society. They have to practice to become world citizens . . .

John: Yes, but they do it. This is Dewey's notion. They do it by being it. Now. Our role as educators is not to create students for future experiences, future jobs, future societies. Our role is to educate students, so they create their futures (Dewey 1933).

That astronaut teacher (Christa McAuliffe) said it best: I touch the future, I teach.

Steen: Yeah, I agree, and at the same time you also have to learn to decenter yourself from immediate needs. Because if you are a customer and you want to have gasoline for a cheaper price, you go to the next gasoline station. But a school can never, ever be like that. It can never be a market relation. So, what I really dislike is that this new public management logic has transformed the two triangles into a more or less simple two-pole communication logic.

First, you depict the citizen as a private customer in the educational market place, and he kind of gets a commodity from a state education provider. Then, you provide somebody interested in mathematics with the best mathematics available, donated by 'learning agent' (formerly called a teacher). So this two-pole communication logic has in a way erased the triangular logics ... and I think that you and me and other educational philosophers and people debating this stuff, we should maintain the two triangles ...

John: I see merit in that. But, then, not only have you got the child, the teacher, and the content, you've got the social context.

Steen: Yes, of course.

John: And, certainly, as I've tried to do as a father, I want my students to be students. I'm not a great fan of looking to the future. My argument is that they create the future.

Steen: The French and the Japanese style in which you're very busy making a five-year-old become an adult and take part in the competitive society is also not my cup of tea ...

John: But I acknowledge there are some parents who want that from their children and I respect that. I don't.

Steen: Then there's probably also a third triangle at play, stating more or less that you have this kind of identity, this character that you have, and you think that the system here should give form to the right new character. But my idea is that the formation of the character can be understood as a neverending process of becoming, an 'eternal' inter-being and an inter-play, or as you would say in German, a *Bildung* process (Koselleck 2006). There is no fixed identity (no mandatory *Bild*, image) to receive or to expect from the educational system.

So, instead of thinking that you should go from A to B, you should think about building up character also as a triangle. Where you're always decentering yourself, as Thomas Ziehe, the German educationalist from Hannover, states in German, *Dezentrierungskunst* – **the art of decentering** (Ziehe 2004). **Ziehe**, as the Danish philosopher Søren Kierkegaard, is always emphasizing that human beings should have the possibility and right to become surprises to themselves (Kierkegaard 1959/1843). The identity work takes place in the field that opens you towards the world and new ways to be. In 1793, the German philosopher and educational reformer, Wilhelm von Humboldt, gave a tenable description of *Bildung* as the richest possible "*Wechselwirkung*" (interplay, interaction) between the world and the human being in order to fertilize "*die Veredlung seiner Persönlichkeit*" (the improvement of his/her personality) in his text *Theorie der Bildung des Menschen* (Humboldt 1960/1793; see also Klafki 2000).

John: But, again, the difference between when you went to school and now is that now we expect schools to take more responsibility for that. And I have no problems with that.

Steen: The predominant view is to take for granted that schools should more or less be a part of and directed by the societal economic logic . . .

John: Much more, now.

Steen: . . . and the competitive logic of the nation state. And I think that has deprived the school institution – and the university, too – of their autonomy, as the French philosopher Jacques **Derrida** proclaimed in his famous and eye-opening lecture *The University Without Condition* (Derrida 2002/1999; Larsen 2019c).

John: Yes, I would agree here, but I would want today's schools, parents, and society to take more responsibility for developing respect for self and respect for others. This, more than most things, is what I want my students to learn. This then leads them to wanting to learn more to give back more.

Steen: Of course, but we also have to understand and discuss, as you said, the overall social setting around the school.

John: That's the bonus.

Steen: And we also have to know how to criticize it. The nature of thinking is to dare to think critically and differently (Larsen 2018b). What often happens at the institutional level is that the habits and conventional ways of doing and understanding things become canonized in themselves, even behind the backs of the people 'inhabiting' the institution – that is, professional teachers and pupils. We have to remember that the educational institutions and their logics and procedures are only based on arguments, and they can be always scrutinized and questioned.

John: You're right. I cannot recall the number of graduation speeches I have heard where the speaker implores the graduates to forget what they have been taught, and now create new ways of knowing. The critique, the strategies to learn anew, the curiosity to wonder why are indeed powerful.

Steen: Institutions are argument-based spheres, not just physical buildings or state properties.

John: But that's why I welcome you here today. Critique is the essence of our business and should be the essence of business in universities.

Is **the art of decentering** a school task?
Does pedagogy take place in two triangles?
Is self-forgetting necessary to come to know the world and how to think?
How do we learn to become citizens in school?

XII. HOW to DEAL with NEUROSCIENCE

THE VISIBLE LEARNING STORY is in THE OVERLAP of THE MANY influences, AND HAS BEEN REFINED OVER THE PAST 25 YEARS.

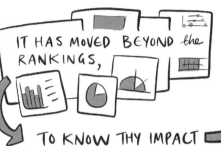

IT HAS MOVED BEYOND the RANKINGS,

TO KNOW THY IMPACT

TO THE ESSENCE of EDUCATOR EXPERTISE ENCAPSULATED in EVALUATIVE THINKING.

THERE is A SCIENCE, EVEN a NEUROSCIENCE OF LEARNING.

NO, WE CANNOT MAKE the BRAIN'S LEARNING VISIBLE

'LEARNING' MUST REMAIN A MOST CONTESTED WORD.

YES, WE CAN AIM TO MAKE the LEARNING PROCESSES and WHAT WE KNOW MORE VISIBLE:

• TO OUR STUDENTS

• TO OURSELVES

• and TO COLLEAGUES.

Steen: Let's now try to deviate from the present discussion and enter a new field, filled to the edge with great expectations: neuroscience. But when it comes to the dual relation between educational research and neuroscience, it seems necessary to be able to estimate what goes on when we learn in billions of different synapses (connection of brain cells, neurons) at the same time, if you want to come to know how we learn. Meaning that you ought to have a very strange and wide-ranging mathematic, not the least a mathematical brain, shouldn't you?

John: Of course.

Steen: Because just to have one, two, or three parameters that's interrelating while measuring them is already complicated mathematics. But then you have to deal with approximately 13 multiplied with 10 in 12th 'learning' neurons. How can you ever translate that to a neuro-image on a screen? How can you tell your story in the midst of all these ungraspable constellations?

John: You're absolutely right. It is indeed complicated.

Steen: And that is, in a way, what I think is really misleading, and in the worst case wrong, science, if you reduce a complex phenomenon to a simplistic explanation and a colorful and seductive image.

John: But that's why people have looked at the league table I created, often misinterpreted it and assumed each is unique, and then question why I have not attended to the overlap!

Steen: And they're not separate?

John: No, and that league table, I actually introduced it in at the very end of writing *Visible Learning* to try and bring some kind of overview. But many people see it as the starting point and they forget that the story wasn't the league table. In the sequel, I won't have a league table.

Steen: Because, it could be that factor, down here, rank 38 (teaching outlining and summarizing) and factor 1 (teachers' collective efficacy), and factor 15 (presence of success criteria), they are closely interrelated?

John: Absolutely. And that's why it took me 20 years to write that story. It's all about the overlap. Now Chapter 3 and Chapter 10 is where the story is, but perhaps it wasn't bold enough. I now have over 20 books on implementing and reinterpreting *Visible Learning*. The aim is to try to get the message across. It's the story. It's the story. The data are the mechanism to get to the story. But then, when I read some of the criticisms they seem all about the data, the league table, and hardly even do they critique the story, hardly ever do they acknowledge the existence and claims about interpretations and implementation in the other books.

Steen: But tell me then, now you worked in this field since 2009, what have you accomplished?

John: I completed my first meta-analysis in 1978, started the collection and thinking about the synthesis of meta-analysis while on a study leave at the University of Washington in 1983, and published the first attempt in 1992 (Hattie 1992b). The editor of this journal wrote to me rejecting the first draft of article, noting that there was not much of a story (thanks Richard Smith, the then editor) – and that led to the quest for the story – so really it is more like 25 years of thinking, plotting, planning, rejecting, and building the fundamental interpretations. I had the luxury of this think time, as it was not my main research area but more a hobby. In the meantime, I lived in my main world of measurement.

Steen: And have your stories changed through the 25 years, or do you still stick to one mega-narrative?

John: The story has changed a lot. As I said, the first article I ever tried to publish was rejected for the right reason. It was just data, there was no interpretation, and that was a real eye-opener to me.

Steen: There was a time when there was no story?

John: Correct.

Steen: Okay, and then there was a story, but then, was it the same story?

John: No way. I took a long time to work out the story.

Steen: Because it seems to me that you have this, in a way, positive view that, for example, people from not privileged backgrounds should have the possibility to have the highest support and the best teaching that could help and stimulate them to come to live a life in freedom and prosperity. With all your *Visible Learning* programs, do you want to contribute to their social jump?

John: Absolutely. That's the point of education.

Steen: And teachers should be able to reflect upon their practices and do better. So, there are some components building up your narrative. Am I right?

John: Correct.

Steen: And these components have been stable – one might even say universal and pre-given – through the years?

John: Some of those, yes. Not many, but some.

Steen: There was at least two: improving and reflecting. And there also seems to be a third thing: the right to make mistakes and to learn from failures (*Fallibilismusbewusstsein*, the consciousness of **fallibilism**, as the Germans call it). This probably has also always been a part of your grand narrative.

John: Yes, in the sense that I made many mistakes during the building of the story. No, in that the research on learning from failure has been a more recent research focus, as I have come to see its importance particularly for those often not privileged in our schools.

Steen: That's much more recent? So the narrative changes?

John: Yes.

Steen: Would you say that the narrative also changes and has to change in relation to the contextual, societal, and historical logic around you? Maybe the narrative is even related to and challenged by political and academic critique of your endeavors?

John: There has been so much misinterpretation and misunderstanding of the work, especially as it enters the political space. Simple interpretations, like just using the ranking, picking off some favorites which do fit a person's individual mission, get in the way of a more nuanced discussion. But that is politics – but it is the critics inventing the slogans and then critiquing the work because of their inventions. I met many politicians and nearly all, perhaps without exception, are much more detailed in their knowledge of the work and its interpretation, they do not see the slogans, but genuinely want to understand the work. But political space is not just politicians.

But I won't resile from the interpretations of the evidence just to fit a political climate, to win points with politicians, or to appease those who want different answers. One thing I have learned from the political debate is to see the immense power of the 'narrative'. In many ways this narrative is opposite the care, conditionals, and considerations of the academic – for example 'Know Thy Impact' was aimed at making a powerful simple narrative – with a focus on asking educators to understand their impact, to debate what we mean by impact, to ask what impact would look like – all core questions.

Right now, in Australia, I am speaking in the narrative of 'expertise', as I see the amateurization of education as one of the biggest threats to our profession. An immense proportion of salaries in schools is now going to teacher aides – who everyone seems to love but the evidence is they have a zero to negative impact on student learning. But they are cheaper, loved by parents and teachers, and seem to provide 'individual attention' – and surely the students who most need the experts should not get the amateurs. I see the dumbing down of teacher education, taking in more with little attention to quality as major dog whistles opposed to what really matters – the expertise of educators.

Here in Australia, I have joined the dark side – I am appointed by the Federal Cabinet as chair of their Australian Institute for Teachers and School Leaders (AITSL). This gives me a platform, access to senior officials and ministers, and backed by stunning board members and a tremendous staff within AITSL. They have used social media superbly to reach to the profession, provided stunning resources, devised the Australian professional standards for teachers and school leaders – and so much more. I thoroughly enjoy this role, as it is a little out of my comfort zone as an academic. It certainly means I interact with political people, critics, the profession, and see the enormous power of the narrative, the keeping to the message, the ways to appeal for support for initiatives, the ways to structure briefs, policy papers, and the critical nature of how to convince the various hierarchies of systems to be with the story.

Of course, I only chair AISTL, but this means I have to learn to listen to the board – which are the world's best critics. And this is, surely, the essence of all our debates.

As to academic debates – it is critique. I have no troubles with academic critics, indeed thrive on it. From day one, I prescribe probably the best critic article (Snook et al. 2009) as a text for all my courses where I mention *Visible Learning*. I have learned a lot from the critics, and certainly have changed some of what I have written and said in light of their claims. I have resisted engaging with back-and forth-articles with critics, as I do not want to be seen as overly defensive but want to be seen as encouraging critique (as if I could stop it!). Of course, I ignore all the personal barbs, and, wow, there are too many of these from academics (and bloggers). I have written about 'being a public intellectual' as this seems a dwindling role, and indeed the very notion is seen now as elitist (Hattie 2010). We have recently released a White Paper summarizing all the criticisms we could find (minus the personal attacks) with a response aiming to further this debate (Hattie & Hamilton 2018).

I do keep a file of as many critiques as I can find, and some bloggers help here with spending inordinate amounts of time compiling them. I am writing a blog with a reaction to these but know it will not appease those who do not like the story, and because I will only react to the ideas in the criticism this will not be welcomed by those who want personal fights. And I will ignore the ridiculous, the personal, and many of the claims that are so left field as to be not worthy of reifying with critique – I will leave that to others. It is humbling, to see books and articles of critique about one's work, and I trust this helps advance the ideas. There is solace in the maxim that one's success may be measured by the number of arrows in one's back.

Critique of neurocentrism

John: And then you criticize our view of the human brain in a book I wrote together with Gregory Yates, *Visible Learning and the Science of How We Learn* (Hattie & Yates 2014).

Steen: The background is that I actually studied neuroscience for many years, from the sideline, in a philosophical, sociological, and body-phenomenological perspective, and that means that you look at the brain and the plastic and synaptic connections in the brain as embodied and embedded phenomena (Larsen 2013a; Sheets-Johnstone 1990; Fuchs 2018). So when I read and reviewed your book I thought that it had a kind of instrumentalist approach and thought that you can navigate with the brain in a way that you could steer it. That we could be on top of the brain logic, steering the brain to have observations of certain types. And I think that's against the logic and insights of modern neuroscience (Larsen 2014c). Both scientists and philosophers have criticized the neurocentristic approach to and understanding of the brain.

John: There is no sense that you can navigate the brain such that you can steer it. And there is a reductionism in here – when you replace the word 'brain' with 'student' it usually shows if you're saying something new or different – "you can navigate the student such that you can steer it" – I think not. We know a tremendous amount about the brain, but we cannot operate on the 'brain' as we work with the student who has a brain (and heart, and hands . . .). It is not directly affecting the wiring and firing in the brain, but seeing how students develop ideas, relate them, use them, and explore them – which can lead of course to wiring and firing.

Steen: Yeah, in those days when I was reading that book, I found your perspective very limited. Therefore, for me, it was a great surprise – as I have already stated – to read your and Klaus Zierer's newest book *10 Mind-frames for Visible Learning* (Hattie & Zierer 2018) because I found that was much richer and opened the argumentation towards the humanities and towards the *what* question. In this work, it seems you had to change your approach (Larsen 2018a).

John: Not really changed, but elaborated. I fought very hard to get away from the notion of what works. The simplistic notion is that all you need is 'evidence' that you can enhance learning and then all is okay. Nearly everything works, almost. I'm much more interested in what works best. And one of the major underlying differences between those influences in the top from bottom half of the distribution relates to how educators think – the mindframes.

Steen: That's also what you put forward in the book, and you didn't stress that so much in your 'older' books. Now you say: "It's not what works, it's what works best." No, it's not being defensive. You have actually clari-fied some of your argumentation in the newer books.

John: Yes, you are right.

Steen: As I told you, I recently published a critique of your work, called "Blindness in Seeing – A Philosophical Critique of the Visible Learning Paradigm in Education" (Larsen 2019a). My argument is that learning is not immediately visible to the learning subject. It demands and deserves a qualitative lifelong perspective and an autonomous reflection to come to know and acknowledge what learning is and can be in an existential perspective. We cannot see in the brain, and I continue to make a case for *Bildung*, noting that teaching is much more than a method to 'pro-duce' learning, or to reproduce learning goals. So why do you say that learning is a visible phenomenon?

John: Mostly learning is not at all visible, hence the title of my work is about aiming to make learning more visible. This can be done in many ways – teaching students to think aloud, watching them perform various parts within a task or problem, privileging their voice as they are solving problems. In many ways we need to teach students to help make their learning visible, so we know our impact, what we have taught well, what conceptions and misconceptions may need attention, and hear the errors and the success of our teaching. Of course, this involves much talking to the learners.

We (Hattie & Yates 2014) never aimed to convince you "that neuro-learning processes can be managed and transformed into a willful field of intervention for designing neuro-enhancement processes in learning institutions," as you state it. We have never claimed that learners can know what is happening in their brains, and just because any person talks aloud about how they are thinking need not be 'how they think'. This is why we need teachers with expertise in the science of learning strategies to triangulate what the student says with what the student does, test their beliefs about how the child is learning, and seek 'second opinions' either from similar or transfer tasks or by working with colleagues – for example, through cognitive task methods.

Steen: Thanks for the clarification, but as you know, my position is that learning is a highly contested notion.

John: You have already cited another Dane, Knud Illeris, who has provided some of the best research in the world on the concept of learning, and his work certainly shows the contested notion of 'learning' (see Illeris in Larsen & Pedersen [eds.] 2011: 380–381; Illeris 2004; and I have contributed articles to his edited works: Hattie & Donoghue in Illeris [ed.] 2018 as part of this contestation). Learning will continue to be a polymorphous word, it should be contested, and we still have much to understand about how we learn (in multiple ways usually).

I agree with you that "learning can never be an instant, simple and visible phenomenon," and that thinking is much more than learning. I agree *Bildung* is a powerful notion that should have much traction in the English-speaking world, as it is more than education and can go directly to the important debates about character formation (which is more important than the C21st Skills, the knowledge, and the strategies of learning). And throughout this book it should be clear I agree with you that the purpose of education is much more demanding and challenging than enhancing visible learning processes and results.

Does educational science need a strong narrative – that is, a story?

What does **fallibilism** mean, and can it help science to become more humble?

Is educational research in need of neuroscience? Or is neuroscience in need of education?

Why and how is learning a highly contested concept?

XIII. HOW TO DEAL WITH CRITIQUE

CRITICISM of IDEAS is the ESSENCE OF ACADEMIA.

To be CRITIQUED is an HONOR.

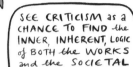

SEE CRITICISM as a CHANCE TO FIND the INNER, INHERENT, logic of BOTH the WORKS and the SOCIETAL CONDITIONS YOU AIM to TRANSGRESS.

KARL MARX

HOW to REACT to CRITICS:

 SEE HOW YOUR IDEAS ARE BEING IMPLEMENTED and RECLARIFY YOUR CLAIMS.

ACKNOWLEDGE and FIX ERRORS.

CRITICISM INVITES YOU TO OVERCOME and TRANSGRESS WHAT YOU COULDN'T SEE and TO INVENT ALTERNATIVE ways OF THINKING.

STRENGTHEN YOUR OWN ARGUMENTATION.

OPEN your HORIZON to OTHER WAYS OF THINKING.

 DO NOT GIVE OXYGEN to ad hominem CLAIMS.

DISTINGUISH BETWEEN:

 LEARNING IDEAS (SURFACE)

 RELATING IDEAS (DEEP)

and TRANSFERRING IDEAS (TRANSFER)

CONCEPTUAL HISTORY (ie. THE KNOWLEDGE of THE HISTORICAL SHIFTS IN THE MEANING of CONCEPTS LIKE LEARNING, BILDUNG, CREATIVITY, INNOVATION etc.) IS A MOST FERTILE TOPIC TO TEACH.

CREATIVITY is the BRINGING TOGETHER of TWO or MORE SEEMINGLY UNRELATED IDEAS.

ARTHUR KOESTLER

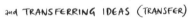

WE CAN HAVE misconceptions, mis-concepts, malconcepts, AND BEAUTIFUL RISKS.

PHILOSOPHY IS THE COURAGE TO INVENT NEW CONCEPTS.

GILLES DELEUZE

FÉLIX GUATTARI

PHILOSOPHY is a COURAGEOUS ACTIVITY - 'demanding' THAT YOU DARE TO INVENT CONCEPTS and THEREBY BRING SOMETHING NEW into THE WORLD that WAS NOT THERE BEFOREHAND.

THOUGHTS WITHOUT CONTENT are EMPTY INTUITIONS WITHOUT CONCEPT are BLIND.

IMMANUEL KANT

Steen: Probably you also learn from your critics.

John: Criticism of ideas is the essences of academia. I read lots of the critics' commentaries. In my own classes, I include some of these criticisms, especially the very first by Ivan Snook and colleagues (Snook et al. 2009). It was among the most respectful critiques, focused on the ideas, not me as a person, and raised some important issues. To be critiqued is an honor.

Steen: That is the famous falsification way of Karl Popper once again, and that's probably what we agree upon as a minimum condition to follow for being able to make and defend valid science in the empirical study realm (Popper 2002/1953). There's of course no use in being defensive.

John: One of the criticisms is that the title of my breakthrough book is misleading – how can learning be 'visible'? Yes, learning is rarely visible, but the focus is how can we make the thinking of students, teachers, school leaders, and policy people more visible. Tough as it is – how do they think, process, strategize, have misconceptions, make connections, transfer learning, and so on. One condition is the necessity to build very high trust between you and the student, and between the students, and then 'hear' their thinking, talking aloud, and create opportunities to learn from what we don't know.

Steen: Okay, but even though we have touched upon this several times already, I still struggle to understand this message – and, not the least, the argumentative and scientific implications of this message – that you present in your newest book: that 80% of what's happening might be something we cannot make visible! That might limit a *Visible Learning* program's chance to grasp and expose learning in toto, I guess?

John: No, I didn't say that. I was – as I have stressed – citing Graham Nuthall's finding that 80% of what happens in their classroom the teachers do not see or hear (Nuthall 2007). Thus, to the contrary, we need more ways to help teachers see what is happening in their classes, to make the learning of all students more visible.

Steen: Okay, the teacher doesn't see it with his or her normal eyes, and you seem to think that the teacher needs training and maybe some Hattie reading. My argument here could be, or my question is, could it be that there exist at least three reasons for this invisibility (see, e.g., Larsen 2019a, 2019b)? One is that learning as such is an embodied phenomenon.

John: Correct.

Steen: But a whole bodily perspective cannot be studied – nor set free – in a school system where everybody is sitting still.

John: Correct. Or when they are moving about in continuous motion.

Steen: And, by the way, you're also having (i.e., incarnating and living) a full-fledged bodily approach to knowledge when you leave school. You embody the knowledge both in- and outside school, and of course the teacher can't see or harvest the honor for all this in a 1:1 perspective.

John: That's correct.

Steen: And the second 'thing' is, we cannot look directly and immediately into the human brain as you point out . . .

John: Correct. Well, you can in a very technically complicated way, but it doesn't help.

Steen: Even though neuroscience has tried to come closer to real life outside the lab, the whole setting of a complex class interaction between 20 to 30 pupils and their teacher(s) hasn't been brain scanned yet in a detailed and proper way.

John: We're doing it. We have built a classroom here at Melbourne and in Brisbane where this is now possible, and it is possible to see the interactions between the brain functioning of students as they work together, and the effects of one student on another.

Steen: Yeah, we probably will do. But until now, you still normally fixate humans in order to scan them, which would be a very artificial version of a vivid class in action.

John: You can put on these fMRI helmets and we can see all the interaction wiring and firing, but you get swamped with data and it doesn't tell you much (yet). You get pretty pictures. But there are important advances in this neuropsychology.

Steen: The third one is that a teacher can happen to be blindfolded because (s)he only wants to see what (s)he knows, and only wants to see on behalf of the concepts and the mindset (s)he has to see through. So the mindset risks to blindfold the teacher. Do you also envisage these three reasons, or do you see more explanations to the question why 80% of what happens in a class doesn't come through to the teacher? And do you find that one of them is more important than the other(s)?

John: I certainly agree about the self-confirmation biases, we humans have to explain what is happening in front of us. But I want to go back to the second one you stated, and that is that not only do you not see a lot of the interactions that are going on in your class, you also don't often hear the private talk among students. This was Nuthall's major claim (Nuthall 2007).

Steen: And as you say about universities, the most important thing is happening around the coffee machine . . .

John: Exactly, today's gossip is often tomorrow's problem.

Steen: . . . where colleagues are exchanging rumors, jokes, and 'evaluations' of leaders and colleagues.

John: Less so with the students, but we are trying to understand how the students think and talk with each other because peers are very powerful with each other – both in terms of the language they use with each other and how they talk to their peers. And both are hard for the teacher to hear. This is partly why I am not a great fan of observing teachers and the current desire to have checklists, principals, or inspectors sitting in the back of the room, watching videos of so-called best practice – all suffer.

Steen: They had the inspectors traveling around in the UK?

John: Well, yes, worse than that. You have the principal sitting in the back of the room filling out a 'Danielson' or 'Marzano' (Danielson 2011; Marzano 2018). Both these frameworks aim to capture the core notions of effective teaching in domains. The Danielson is based on four domains: Planning and Preparation, The Classroom Environment, Instruction, and Professional Responsibilities. The 'Marzano' has many more domains, such as set goals, provide feedback, presence of simulations and low-stakes competition, engagement, maintaining class rules, relations with students, communicate high expectations. They were never invented or promoted as methods for some person sitting in the back of the room, ticking boxes as to whether they are present or not.
        Or you get a teacher to create a video and send it in to be looked at, or coded. And I strongly object to that methodology because, once again, you're watching the wrong person – the teacher. Once again, you're privileging the teacher's views of the world only – both the teacher in terms of the on-looker and also in terms of watching the teacher. How can a 60-year-old principal sit at the back of the room and understand what it means to be a 6-year-old in that classroom? How do they know the evaluative thinking the teacher is using to make

the moment by moment decisions in the classroom? Instead, we should over and over again be asking how we teachers come to see this other 80% of what is happening in their classrooms. That is the ambition and my hope. At best, we should be looking at the impact on the students and helping teachers understand their impact on all the students.

Steen: It also risks producing a situation of mistrust and surveillance of the teachers . . .

John: That could happen, yes. And of course this reduces the power of the observation, privileges the observer and their mindsets, what they saw or not, and diminishes the teacher's evaluate thinking.

Steen: . . . so by watching, rehearsing, or indirectly examining them, you might force them to stage and show glorious positive interactions between the teacher and the pupils. Of course, every teacher will protect him- or herself against being fired, against being scandalized.

How to react to criticism and critics

John: So, how should I react to criticism and critics?

Steen: How you should react? There are probably four different ways to react to critics. One is to strengthen your own argumentation if you feel that they point toward a weak point, and that's probably what you are up to all the time. But another thing is to think that, "Wow, I must add something to my argumentation." Not to say that this curious side-glance will strengthen your perspective and protect you against future remarks and critique. But you might say to yourself, "Maybe I should look towards what actually Niklas Luhmann or Wilhelm von Humboldt wrote or try to think with the German concepts *Bildung* and *Erfahrung*."

John: I like that.

Steen: Okay, while procedure number two means opening your horizon to other ways of thinking, the first one is primarily a way to re-polish your own argumentation, so it becomes comprehensible, clearer, and not too easy to misunderstand. Number one is probably active for you, because you often realized and stated, "Well, I should have stressed that in my first volume, and I also learned that they read it wrongly and I wasn't arguing in the right way," "I placed the impact figures in a lead table, that came to look like a hierarchy, showing the first factor as the best and most important, and that was not my intention."

Facing critique form number three, I guess you will say, "This is a pure *ad hominem* argumentation, so I don't want to listen or reply to this stupidity because they're not really addressing anything else than my person."

John: I have refused to give any oxygen to these *ad hominem* claims. I was taught to critique the ideas not the person. Do you ignore those?

Steen: Yes, I try to ignore such attacks. A fourth way to react could be that you have come to think that now you have done this research which is written in a certain research code language, but then you realize that people implement your work and results wrongly in all kind of other spheres – for example, as ideology for a party's educational politics, trade union members' interests, principals of schools in need of a branding strategy for legitimizing visible and mandatory learning goals, or whatever. While science deals with validity and truth claims, the code of politics is power, and the code of economy is profit.

John: Certainly, this is what I have tried to do in the 20+ books since, in my speeches, in the implementation of *Visible Learning*.

Steen: Summarizing: Number one, two, and three belong to the internal science logics, but the fourth one contains all the delicate implementation dramas. Who knows, you could maybe come to state for yourself, "One thing is my academic argumentation. Another thing is I'm going to make it more precise, which kind of limits the risk to implement this in different societal, political, ideological contexts. And I maybe have to have a chapter in my next book dealing with these obvious limitations and restrictions, as I see them." It could maybe be something that looks like an extended version of number two, that when you're adding a new perspective, it could happen to become so profound that you have to readdress your collected production and standard scientific narratives.

And that was, in a way, how I read *10 Mindframes for Visible Learning* (Hattie & Zierer 2018). Before you wrote it, you might have said to yourself, "Well, until now I did only deal with 'how' questions. But now, I have to go deeper and ask the both 'what' and 'why' questions, implying the ontology question of: What is it to be at all? And the existential, normative, and the political questions: What is man's role in education, and why does education matter in a society? All these very big questions have to be posed." So patiently transforming yourself, from being a statistician to a completely new – or expressed more modestly, a different type of – human being, maybe a quasi-philosopher, maybe a quasi-sociologist – as I have claimed many times during our 'chat', maybe a transdisciplinary old wise man with a lot of talents who could not only welcome change, clarify, and add things but also manage to readdress his way of thinking, arguing, and writing. And that must be the radical fifth way to reply to criticism and critics.

John: I trust I am evolving in this thinking, and we saw a major gap (yes, you and colleagues had often raised it) about the *how*. But our thinking was that too many were still looking for the *Visible Learning* recipe for teaching, for structuring schools and classrooms, for our answer as to what they should adopt as 'impact'. I have resisted addressing these issues, but did decide to write this mindframes book showing that I had more to present than *how* thoughts. There are particular ways of thinking that led to the expertise to truly make a difference to the learning lives of students. It is the thinking in the moment, in the adaptations, in the reacting to students knowing and not knowing, in the ways they redress what is happening in their class – all these are a function of *how* teachers think.

Well, let me then mention a sixth one, indeed an easy one. There are errors that I and others have noted. The answer to this is easy – fix them. In the first book I thought, how do I come up with other ways of interpreting the effect–size? So I used the common language effect (McGraw & Wong 1992). It took five years for a group of Norwegian students to find that I had made a transcription error. They emailed me, but I was travelling and said I would get back to them, which I did soon after. I had transposed the wrong column from my Excel master file into the page proofs. I fixed it immediately and the publishers updated the appendix. I think the message is clear. After five years, no one has seen the error or paid attention to the common language effect-size. But the critics out there went ballistic . . . oh, my gosh, they went overboard in terms of criticizing me because I made an error. It never changed one iota of the story, it was positioned as an additional way to interpret the effects, it had no bearing on the message; but the Twitter feed, the blogs, and indeed some journals published personal attacks on me for this error. Yes, I regret making it, but fixed it when it was pointed out. And I welcome any other errors and will also fix those.

Steen: Now, I think that in the last years . . . and especially in *10 Mindframes for Visible Learning*, I acknowledge a more open attitude to my critique and other persons' critiques of your work (Hattie & Zierer 2018). So, the fifth critique form I emphasized before you mentioned and fleshed out the kind of 'easy' sixth one, is full-fledged and full-fleshed academic and takes place in changing atmosphere in a societal and scientific historical context. Was it written before the First or Second World War? Was it written before or after the breakdown of the wall, before or after the Vietnam War? There is always a bigger societal context around you and your word. And now and then you have also to think about whether or not your work gains success due to different types of power logics out there.

John: Well, I feel more responsible.

Steen: And I think that, much to your surprise, you also couldn't forget about the hyper-conditioned score and also that it's wonderful to be read, and it's great to have half a million copies in circulation out there. Or it's great to be invited to all kinds of places in the world. This is a kind of reputation, high self-esteem, and all that. It's a part of it, for everyone. Not only you, but in principle for everyone. Nearly every academic wants to be read and in this way to become 'famous' . . .

John: No, no, it's scary. I have a long way to fall.

Steen: Scary, but probably also great, okay? But if you move that a little bit to the side, and try to decenter yourself from your reputation, the *Visible Learning* business, the clapping hands, and 'honorable Mr. John Hattie', you could say. "What was it in the time, the zeitgeist that actually loved me? Why could they use my argument?" You might experience becoming loved to death and at the same time misinterpreted. And maybe they love you so much because they need you for another table of content than you could ever have thought of – for example, this Danish minister of education in 2012–2013.

She's probably not reading your work, and I guess she does not understand it. She's applying it to another kind of fight they have in which they actually wanted 60,000 teachers and their union leaders not to be a part of the political game, and ex post dictating them their work standards, and change the rule of the law for the whole school, and create a new school based on *Visible Learning*, understood as mandatory and explicit learning goals. So in that sense, they needed a kind of research legitimation of a type, and they found your work (Skovmand 2016, 2019a, 2019b).

So, that is also something that you have to know about while you're receiving both critique and political hurrahs, and I think that you can study a lot of this from reading Karl Marx. He said that in a way, critique, from his standpoint, was also to find the inner, inherent logic of both the works and the societal conditions that you had to transgress (Marx 1976/1867; Larsen 2014b, 2014d, 2018b). That's why he read the economists of the late 1700s and early 1800s United Kingdom, Adam Smith and David Ricardo the most, to state that they didn't understand the concept of labor, the delicate and utmost real connection between living labor and commodified labor power, surplus value production, exploitation, and accumulation of capital. They only understood the concept of labor. They didn't know about how value was created, through exploitation of surplus value, and all that damned serious jazz. So by reading the classics, he could see their failures, and that provoked him to form another way of thinking, analyzing, and conceptualizing.

John: Oh, yeah, I can see that. In the article on the public life of an intellectual, I addressed most of these critiques (Hattie 2010). Yes, I could spend my whole academic life dealing with my esoterica, and indeed until 2008 I was doing that – in my world of measurement. I have been president on the International Test Commission, edited measurement journals, given keynotes at measurement conferences, taught numerous courses in measurement, been head of school in measurement departments, supervised students in measurement theses, and written books and papers in my areas of measurement and statistics. I see my contribution as using sophisticated and appropriate measurement procedures to answer interesting educational questions. In am proud of this. My hobby was *Visible Learning*, but yes, the publication changed the trajectory of my career.

But I did not want to spend the rest of my career speaking about work I have done 10 years ago. So I decided to stay in the laboratory and let others deliver and implement, and I am most grateful to these stunning professionals. I give 30 days' travel only a year to speaking about *Visible Learning* and have maintained a lively and fun research program and team.

This means that I continue to grow, to learn, and to refine the *Visible Learning* messages. I have corrected errors; I have aimed to strengthen my own argumentation where they pointed toward a weak or contested point. I have opened my horizon to other ways of thinking, learning from many critics and colleagues, in subsequent 25+ books and many articles I have tried to re-polish my own argumentation so it becomes comprehensible, clearer, and less easy to misunderstand. I have continued to add to the database in attempts to falsify the underlying story and theory within *Visible Learning*, and remain staunch to not react to the *ad hominem* attacks.

I must say I am surprised at some of these attacks – they most often are made by teachers, in letter snail mailed in handwriting, and rarely signed. I just wonder what must happen after they have released, in some cases, vitriol against me, when they then walk into classrooms – heaven help their students who disagree with them. But they are the minority.

I am so pleased that there are learned critiques about my work – what an honor. To be critiqued by you, Biesta, Snook, and so many others of this ilk is a privilege. I am the beneficiary of their critiques.

Steen: That's probably also how you work.

John: Yes, critiquing literature, which means other academics' work, is core business, and I trust I do it with the respect that is so necessary in academia. That's I like to think how I work, yeah.

Steen: In criticizing the predecessors or their argumentation, it already invites you to overcome and transgress what they couldn't see and to invent alternative ways of thinking.

John: Yes, developing new ways of thinking, new explanations, and new relations between ideas is what it is all about.

Conceptual history as fertile way of thinking

Steen: In the German tradition, where I was brought up, you honor *Begriffsgeschichte*, conceptual history (the knowledge of the historical shifts in the meaning of concepts like learning, *Bildung*, creativity, innovation, etc.) as being a very, very strong part of the capacity for students to be enlightened and to think (Koselleck 2006; Larsen 2015c, 2016a).

John: Of course.

Steen: Conceptual history is, for example, that you know that the actual and very broad use of the concept competences was not a reality in the 1600s or 1700s because in those days it was only the king having the competence, or maybe the military or the police. Because it was very much aligned with the monopoly of using violence and not with the modern ideas of empathic, social, innovative, creative, personal, flexible, robust, resilient, etc.

John: And that word is not used in English.

Steen: But during the last 20 years we have witnessed that the competence concept was exploding in a broad and former unseen semantical plurality. And it ended up being embedded in a six- or seven-layer competence profile for every individual citizen in Denmark and many other European counties. Therefore, you have to know the history of the concept of the words.

John: Of course. Yes, I would agree with that.

Steen: But how do you actively work against the disappearance of that knowledge while you pile up analyses and data. And how do you pay respect to conceptual historical knowledge in the *Visible Learning* program?

John: Because people like you and I need to acknowledge that. I have mentioned that I'm a great fan of a story on Larry Cuban, who's an American historian (Cuban 1984). He's looked at how teaching has changed over the last 200 years. And his – and my – argument is that if a teacher from the 19th century came back today, he could walk into a classroom and teach. Alexander Graham Bell could not do that with the telephone. He would look at an iPhone and say, "Nay, that's not a telephone."

Steen: No, of course not.

John: And on the one hand, that's a statement of what is. On the other hand, it's not necessarily a bad thing. We've kind of worked out that the 'tell and practice' model kind of works. We've worked out how to teach in classes of 25 to 35. That's not a defense of that class size nor of 'tell and practice'. It's an acknowledgment that, as adults, we have actually been very effective in working around the barriers that have been placed before us. If anyone came to earth and looked at our current schools, which are very much like egg crates, with 30 to 35 students broken up by year group, broken up by teacher, it's madness. But it has worked. Doesn't mean to say it's good enough.

Steen: No. You're right. But there, I detect a kind of a paradox in your way of thinking. Because if your dream is that learning students should have a will of their own, freedom to change the directions in which they're told to go, have their autonomous capacity of thinking, why then not talk to them? I simply don't understand. Why are you not interested in their first-order appearance in your field of research?

John: I am.

Steen: Yes, but not in your big book about *Visible Learning*.

John: No. Because that wasn't directly about the students gaining the capacity of thinking.

Steen: Wow, I would of course love if you'd dare to write a thick book about students' will and capacity for thinking critically, but the fact is that you are now world famous for this *Visible Learning* book (Hattie 2009). And it seems to me that now you're still saying, many years after, that now we have even more data than in those days, and we have even more meta-analysis. First, it was 800, and you tell me it is 1,600 now.
    Yeah, but it's still in line with your original approach and, harshly speaking, depriving the pupils and students of their voices.

John: The publishers want me to do a second edition because it's 10 years ago since it was published. I'm not going to do it.

Steen: You're not going to do it?

John: No, I don't want to write the same book again. Done that, been there. The story has not changed, and critics will get stuck on the data, the changes in the data, and ignore that the extra data has reinforced the major *Visible Learning* messages.

But I am working on a sequel. And part of the sequel is writing about the kind of things you're talking about. Putting the student into perspective. I'm struggling with the writing, but it is a fun struggle. I go on study leave for six months and the whole point is to write this sequel.

The differences between knowing and thinking

Steen: You often emphasize the differentiation between surface learning and deep learning. Was that also there 30 years ago in your mind, or 25 years ago, or is it a recent insight?

John: Yes, this has been a feature for a very long time. Because when I started as an academic, Bloom's taxonomy was the rage. The original taxonomy was based on classifying learning objectives into six levels: knowledge, comprehension, application, analysis, synthesis, and evaluation (which in a second edition was changed to remember, understand, apply, analyze, evaluate, and create). Even today, when I ask audiences how many know and use Bloom's taxonomy, the vast majority indicate yes. I've walked into many classrooms, and there it is – like Maslow's hierarchy of needs (and interestingly Maslow never drew the needs triangle!). Many years back, Nola Purdie and I hunted for every article ever written evaluating Bloom's model – and surprisingly there were very few (Hattie & Purdie 1998). Most were by philosophers, like you Steen, who had major concerns from an epistemological perspective; and some showed there was indeed no hierarchy. It is fascinating that one of the most used aids in the business has so little evidence to support it.

A major aspect of Bloom is that it's a mixture of how we think and what we think about. Knowledge and understanding on the one hand, and analysis and synthesis on the other. In the year 2000, the originators of Bloom came out with a new model. And they slightly changed the order of their six, making create higher than evaluate, although surely the skills of evaluation supersede those of creativity. But they also added a new dimension: factual, conceptual, procedural, and metacognitive knowledge. That is, they finally acknowledged that there was a complexity or depth of knowledge.

This new dimension is somewhat akin to the SOLO model. This is a model developed in the 1970s by John Biggs and Kevin Collis – two Australians (Biggs & Collis 1982). They put cognitive complexity at the heart of their model. It has five levels: pre-knowledge, one idea, many ideas, relate ideas, and extend ideas. (Yes, it has fancier language than this: uni-structural, multi-structural, relational, extended abstract.) Basically, the idea phase is the surface and the relate phase is the deep, and the extension is the transfer phases of thinking and knowing.

I have used this model in my measurement work since it was developed. For example, we write items at each of these levels, we score tests for content and also for surface and deep. I consider John Biggs a good, personal friend, and we have worked together, and enjoy our sessions. For example, we were working on a meta-analysis on study skills trying to sort out the interpretations and I recall the afternoon in his house in Hong Kong when the lightbulb went on – of course, if you classify study skills along the surface to deep – and then many things suddenly fell into place.

The other beauty of SOLO compared to Bloom is the falsifiability claims. You cannot be wrong with Bloom – everything fits, nothing is excluded. That is certainly not the case with SOLO – you can fail in an item you think is deep but students only need surface knowledge to answer it. This is why when I see the Bloom list on class walls, I think, "Oh my gosh. They're using it to justify their status quo. Nothing can be wrong." You can be wrong in SOLO.

Steen: Okay, thanks for the long explanation. But does surface not deserve a non-pejorative vocabulary? I guess that immediate ignition of the awareness of the pupil or student (the aha trigger) can be called surface in its own right?

John: Yes, I struggle with the word 'surface' – too often it is interpreted as superficial, but it is not. You need knowledge before you can relate and extend knowledge. I often hear, you don't need knowledge anymore, as Ms. Google has it all. But success means not only knowing lots but knowing the relations between knowledge and using it in context. Those who are successful in our society not only know lots but know how to use and relate this knowledge. Although nowadays they also need to know how to interpret for others, work in teams, and have social sensitivity to apply knowledge along with others. Perhaps a better word than 'surface' would help – any suggestions?

Steen: How many different types of knowing do you have in mind while investigating?

John: I'm not so worried about the distinction between an idea and ideas (within the surface factors), or between relating the ideas or extending them (within the deep factor). But I'm deeply interested in the difference between knowing stuff (surface) and thinking about stuff (deep). Of course, they overlap, but my measurement self is not satisfied. The key question is: How do you create assessments able to deal with both challenges? And my teacher self asks the questions (which have hardly ever been researched): What is the right proportion of surface and deep? Should you best teach surface then deep, or excite by the deep then attend to the surface? And what is the right proportion? And is there an optimal moment to move from surface to deep? Now, of course, the answer to the right proportion is that it depends on what you're doing and when you're doing it. But I think those are the right kinds of narratives and questions that we should be asking.

One of the dilemmas is that above-average students tend to prefer the surface – they know how to play the game of knowing lots, asking for more, and are often applauded because of how much they know. So, teachers tend to prefer surface knowledge. Students prefer it. Bright students prefer it. Parents prefer it. Society prefers it. Our measures prefer it. And I worry about surface being so dominant. I worry that students think that school success is about knowing lots.

Let me give you a specific example. We were asked to develop an assessment in science, particularly for elementary or primary school. I refused to do it on the grounds that the only assessments I could come up with to fit the model at that moment were multiple choice closed–item tests. And my worry is that not that you can't use those items to measure science – but that students would think that's what science was, and it's not.

Steen: Yes, it would be a very narrow-minded view on science.

John: Yes, so I refused to do it. And I think, today, if you asked me, I'd probably do it because we can now use computer-based testing, you can get students to do simulations, and get involved within experiments and situations, and do so much more about the participating, evaluating, and experimenting in science assessment. Much more than you could 15 years ago. But getting that balance right at the right time is what drives me. There would of course be science knowledge as well.

To let the text come alive

Steen: What I now and then in glorious and rich moments experience with students is that when their text, their assessment paper, their dissertation is piling up papers and so, and suddenly, instead of them writing the paper, then their paper is telling them what to write in the next chapter. Then, suddenly, the text becomes alive somewhere within the enigmatic communication with them and their own way of writing. And in a glimpse they are pretty close to becoming artists because, then, it's not so much me demanding something, or them trying to live up to a certain ideal out there or honor the course goals, but then the text in itself is stating where the next argument should come from.

John: If you ask my students, what is the most common thing John says to you, the answer will be: "What's the story?"

Steen: Yeah, and I think the story gets born within the midst of their process in writing it. And that gives both the text a very concrete style, like a hands-on essay, and at the same time a meta-view. In the very same moment two texts are being born as one.

John: Exactly, and too many students think doing a thesis is collecting data. It's not.

Steen: Well, it's not enough.

John: No. In fact, when I was in the US, I wouldn't let most of my master's students collect data. They had to use secondary data to try and get them away from thinking that collecting the data is the hard part. Yeah. It's hard. Things go wrong. But that's not thinking. That's not interpreting. That's not developing and defending a story.

Steen: And another force, could it be this one. We have all these people studying educational anthropology at my university, and they do fieldwork. And when you are out there, you have big masters to look up to and learn from. You have **Malinowski**. You have . . .

John: Margaret Mead.

Steen: . . . yes, and Mary Douglas. You have many people who were out there before. Lévi-Strauss, too. And the students learn to use and gain inspiration from all their concepts. And so it could also be more modern thinkers then, like for example, Erving Goffman, or Norbert Elias. And they take all these concepts and try to organize the empirical study due to well-known concepts. It could be tribalism, impression management and presentation of the self, civilizing norms, recognition theory, etc.

But the real clue of where you start to produce something as a student is where you try to, on behalf of your own empirical research, produce new concepts. You might even 'create' conceptual neologisms and manage to surprise the teacher. For example, I had a student, and she was dealing with stigma in her fieldwork done in an institution for drug addicts and prostitutes. Of course, these people often were stigmatized due to their bodily features. And, for example, if you are using narcotic drugs, and you are sticking needles into your own veins, you risk getting scars and exposing yourself to bodily stigmatization.

John: Correct.

Steen: But you can also be stigmatized in other ways, due to spelling mistakes or whatever. You can also be stigmatized in the eye of the peers. For example, suddenly, the so-called stigmatized group has, within itself, criteria of stigmatizing each other. Meaning that the street whore, for example, is lower in the hierarchy than the urban hipster amphetamine (ab)user. So he is, in a way, stressing her, attributing even more stigmatized ideas and concepts to her, or fixating her than maybe the Canadian micro-sociologist Goffman had ever seen or described. So this student of 'mine' wrote this dissertation, including all kinds of new autonomous stigmatization concepts developed in relation to her empirical work. And I find that very talented, when the students themselves, based on their own investigation, invent – what you will call it – new stories – and I would call – new ways of conceptualizing and thinking. They demonstrate the will and the courage to produce new concepts not seen in the literature they were trained to digest.

John: As I have stated earlier, I really like Arthur Koestler's definition of creativity as the bringing together of two or more seemingly unrelated ideas (Koestler 1964). That can happen with a 5-year-old or a 15-year-old, and for them it is the first time they make these connections (even though someone may have related these ideas before). That's creative thinking. That's core to education. It is also the fun, pleasurable part of much learning, when it seems to 'come together'.

Steen: "Philosophy is the courage to invent new concepts," the French philosophers Gilles Deleuze and Felix Guattari wrote more than 20 years ago (Deleuze & Guattari 1996/1991). And I really like that because the clue of successful teaching and learning could be that the pupils, the students, dare and know how to invent new concepts, not just coming from the teacher.

John: And for all students, that should be a regular occurrence.

Steen: Yeah, it should be, and we have to do our best to fertilize such events, both as practitioners and educational thinkers.

Agreeing with Immanuel Kant

Steen: Let's move to another theme. I feel the urge to bring a very famous quote forward, written by Immanuel Kant in his so-called first critique, *Critique of Pure Reason*, in 1781. He states, "Thoughts without content are empty, intuitions without concept are blind" (Kant 1999/1781).

John: How could you not agree?

Steen: How do you view this quote in relation to both the teacher's and the pupil's perspectives in schooling?

John: Well, it's the notion you often have often stressed during this conversation. You don't learn, you learn about. There's always a content to which the learning relates. I can see the togetherness of thoughts, concepts, intuition, and concepts. For a thought, you need a content; for an intuition, you need a concept. We need both.

Steen: And content could also be a whole subject, with all its branches, all its attachments . . . all these welcoming narratives and inter-correlations. For example, history, sociology, and pedagogy are very big subjects.

John: Why are you asking it when I think the answer's obvious?

Steen: Because the Kant quote is very thought-provoking, stimulating, valid, and of current interest. At the same time I also wanted to hear if you'd agree that we need concepts when we try to fertilize our intuitions?

John: Yeah, but given the Popper in me, a concept should say more than what it is, and there should be reason to consider that it could be wrongly conceived. Take 'self-concept'; it would have been so much better if this had been labeled 'self-conception', as this highlights even more that we could have wrong, inconsistent, inaccurate conceptions about our self.

Steen: Yes, we have to do our best not to end in self-deception. So, basically, you seem to be critical towards a conceptual realistic way of thinking that seeks and favors a 1:1 relation between the concept (epistemology, theories of acknowledgment) and what is (ontology, questions concerning our being in the world)?

John: Am I?

Steen: Yes, because conceptual realism will honor the point of view that the concept sums up and equals one-to-one what's out there. But as I have shown in the aforementioned article in *Danish Yearbook of Philosophy* with the title "A Critical Essay on the Exercise of Critique: On the Impossibility of Reconciling Ontology and Epistemology," hermeneutics, phenomenology, and Critical Theory – 'loaded' with very convincing arguments – all question the positivist and conceptual realistic claim that is no problem to reconcile and – so to speak – 'fuse' ontology and epistemology together (Larsen 2018b).

John: No, I want more.

Steen: I don't quite understand, John, because I've just said and claimed a lot, maybe even too much at the same time. Do you want me to strengthen my argumentation?

John: I think a concept should also have some predictive power to cover more than it was derived to explain. This is partly why I would have preferred to talk about conceptions: because we could then talk about misconceptions. We don't have a word for misconcepts, and there are a lot of misconcepts out there. Or even (grammatically worse but higher in meaning) malconcepts.

Steen: Yeah, that's probably what I'm criticizing all the time, when I think that, for example, malmanagement or very bad governmental governance politics where they use learning as a kind of steering concept. I think that's a malconcept.

John: Yeah, yeah.

The courage to invent new concepts

Steen: How do you actually view and 'judge' the tandem philosophers Deleuze's or Guattari's idea I have just presented for you, that philosophy is a courageous activity – 'demanding' that you dare to invent new concepts and thereby bring something new into the world that was not there beforehand (Deleuze & Guattari 1996/1991)? Do you 'incarnate' a congenial approach?

John: Totally agree, and this is akin to Biesta's beautiful risks (Biesta 2013) and Koestler's act of creation (Koestler 1964).

Steen: I know, and you always have the right and the chance to interpret all this differently.

John: Yeah, exactly.

Steen: Moreover, you might come up with new research into the origin of Second World War, of the French Revolution, etc. You can also go back to old sources, and read and use them in new ways. History is not over – or proclaimed with other words, history is never finished with itself – as Gadamer, the hermeneutic philosopher, and Bloch, the warm-blooded Marxist, never forget to stress and to tell us (Gadamer 1989/1960; Bloch 1986/1954–1959).

John: Australia has a horrific recent interpretation of history. It's only in the last 30 years that we've discovered that the Aboriginals had stories and they had views and they actually fought back against the white person. I recall when a friend, Eric Wilmott, was writing a biography of Pemulway, one of the Aboriginal warriors that resisted the Sydney invasion. He was told: "it was too early for this and it would not be believed or accepted," so he turned it into a novel (Wilmot 1987). This was in the 1980s.

Steen: Yes, I have seen the memorial marks on buildings and in parks around University of Melbourne that this was once Aboriginal property. But, then, when it comes to 'build' narratives, for example, at least in Denmark, the teachers are under pressure. The teachers were, for example, depicted to be too over-encumbered with their experiences and prejudices. They ought to wave their own experience goodbye and instead believe in science, *Visible Learning* programs, and educational statistics. That has, for years, been the 'argument'. So I have this question for you. Is there another language in which teachers can express their valuable experiences? You're also talking about what they have gained after 20, 30, 40, or so many years, as teachers and practitioners. What happens to their valuable experiences, if the language – jargon – of *Visible Learning* and 'Know Thy Impact' is mandatory to use in order to express experiences? Or is it just kind of an open offer for them?

John: Yes, their 20 to 40 years' experience can also be considered 'evidence' as long as it is open for critique, falsifying, and collaborating. Every teacher has often strong theories of teaching and 'their' teaching. And they have a language for their teaching. And certainly not understanding that, and not privileging it, is the fault of many professional learners and academics. Not acknowledging it is guaranteed to reduce any impact, to upset the teachers, and more times than not nothing will happen, nothing will necessarily improve if you do not start by understanding the worldviews and theories of teachers.

There are some valuable experiences in some instances of theories of teaching that I don't think are good enough. And yes, I would want to question and change these. Do the theories have to be the jargon of *Visible Learning*? Of course not.

Steen: Okay, I think the way you could surprise the world of readers out there, have maybe another half a million copies sold of a book, could be to write a book about the vast experiences of teachers as professionals. Such a book could give voice to all these different languages in which teachers express their experiences. How does this proposal sound in your ears?

John: I would certainly read such a book, and would love to be part of a team to embark on such a worthwhile activity. Bring it on.

Steen: Because some of your works and activities seem to have a bad reputation here and there in Europe. You may find that, for example, this critique is based on prejudices: "Here's this guy, Hattie. He has power and he's depriving teachers of their experiences because he wants them only to talk in jargon." So, if you wrote a book, showing the world the giant field of very different types of experiences and interpretations from teachers, and listened carefully to them and studied and conceptualized their expertise, then you'd demonstrate the courage to tell new stories and maybe also invent new concepts.

John: As long as you'd allow me to have a normative aspect to it. Not all experiences are equal. I would not want it to be an unedited, uncommented upon compendium of beliefs. But if it could be done in a respectful way, I could see a kind of Wikipedia of theories, interpretations, critiques, associated evidence, and much more.

How can we learn from critique and critics?
Is conceptual history able to inspire educational thinking?
What is the difference between knowing and thinking?
How do you differentiate between a good concept and a 'malconcept'?

XIV. IF SCHOOLS didn't EXIST
— WOULD WE MISS THEM?

WHAT if WE CLOSED ALL SCHOOLS?

YOU DON'T HAVE to LIVE, WORK, and THINK LIKE YOUR PARENTS, and YOU HAVE the CHANCE to BREAK up FROM YOUR 'TRIBE' and LEAVE THEIR BACKGROUND NARRATIVES BEHIND.

SCHOOLS in PRINCIPLE SHOULD be CLASS-BLIND. THEY SHOULDN'T HAVE an UPPER CLASS, A LOWER CLASS, or A MIDDLE CLASS PERSPECTIVE and SHOULDN'T PRIORITISE the TRADITIONS and TASTE SYSTEM of A CERTAIN CLASS. INSTEAD, SCHOOLS SHOULD INVITE EVERYONE IN.

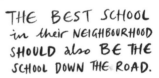

THE BEST SCHOOL in their NEIGHBOURHOOD SHOULD also BE THE SCHOOL DOWN THE ROAD.

THERE ARE STILL SAVAGE INEQUALITIES that SCHOOLS REIFY and REINVENT in the NAME of EDUCATION— and THIS IS INDEFENSIBLE!

TEACHING IS A SUBVERSIVE *activity*

CHARLES WEINGARTNER and NEIL POSTMAN

RATHER THAN STARTING from WHY SCHOOLS and TEACHERS FAIL,

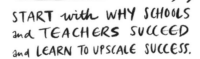

START with WHY SCHOOLS and TEACHERS SUCCEED and LEARN TO UPSCALE SUCCESS.

Steen: Once, I interviewed Thomas Ziehe, a German educationalist from Hannover, an important writer and thinker, widely read in Denmark since the 1980s (the interview is to be found in Ziehe 2004). Ziehe was born in 1947, and ever since 1968 he has analyzed the delicate relations between the emancipating social and cultural possibilities and young people's identity work – that is, their diverse formations of character in the ever-changing modern society. According to Ziehe's view, you don't have to live, work, and think like your parents, and you have the chance to break up from your 'tribe' and to leave their background narratives behind. He states in his writings that schools, in principle, should be class-blinded. They shouldn't have an upper-class, a lower-class, or a middle-class perspective, and shouldn't prioritize the traditions and taste system of a certain class. Instead, the schools should invite everyone in.

John: I agree. We should be responsible for every student who is crossing the school gate.

Steen: So everybody can come to know about whatever: arithmetic, English spelling, Plato's dialogues, the 30-years war in Europe, the atomic bombing of Hiroshima and Nagasaki, etc. And that is independent of whether or not the parents would ever manage and like to bring these things up in front of their students at home. So the school's job is to introduce everyone to the highest culture and the achievement of modern civilization and to the most awkward and awful things that has been done to mankind, often in the name of the very same culture and civilization. Schools must be able to compensate for the fact that everybody comes from very different homes, very different social backgrounds, and the school's task and challenge is to be this common denominator. Do you agree with Thomas Ziehe?

John: Yes, and what bothers me is the in-school class systems. I take tracking, streaming, and the effect-size supporting; these are very small indeed. But the equity issues are frightening. It's reinventing the class system within the school, separating those who have and those who have not. In many schools, you can walk the classrooms and count the color – and the race discrimination via ability grouping is just not defensible. Nearly any one in the lower SES track is denied the challenging material, and when some students boost their investment and start to make progress they can often never catch up as they have been denied access to the more challenging material. This is indefensible in our society.

Take also retaining students back a year. I was involved as an expert witness in a Supreme Court case in the US for The National Association for the Advancement of Colored People. They were taking the case not because 80% of the students who are held back in America are boys, but because 80% that are held back are African American and Hispanic. This should disgust us. And schools reify this when they continue to track. They're reinventing that class, and so many schools claim to be growth-mindset schools and continue and support tracking – the hypocrisy is outstanding.

I'm really struggling, as tracking can have dramatic implications in terms of the haves and the have nots. Jonathan Kozol wrote about the savageness of the inequalities that schools reify and reinvent in the name of education – and this is indefensible (Kozol 2012). So I'm not a fan of tracking because that is mimicking social class in another way. Retention dramatically mimics social class in another way. The school choice debate does it dramatically by allowing those who have the option of choice to make and enact these choices – but it residualizes many of our local schools, and then we say these local schools do not have 'high achievement' and all kinds of negative aspersions are cast at the educators in these schools. I think the best school should be the school in the neighborhood or the school down the road in the neighborhood. As our mantra says: Every child should have a great school and teacher by design, not by chance.

Steen: Yeah, and in a way I think that any school should be the best school. They should all be good schools. That's at least what you could hope, because what happens now is that you have some schools in so-called underprivileged areas, and they are being deprived of resources, the best teachers, and that can be devastating.

John: No, I don't agree that they're deprived of resources, and when you look at the evidence, and particularly in this country, that's not necessarily true. They're deprived of expectation. They're deprived of ambition. Like, go to the five schools from the lowest socioeconomic areas in New Zealand I was talking about before. They had incredible resources. But those teachers gave those messages to those students and to those parents that they were never going to go on to a university. Now, I'm not saying university is the aim of everyone, but none of them? By the age of nine or ten, they had killed that opportunity? That is immoral. It's not necessarily a question of resources.

If the school did not exist

Steen: Have you ever dealt with the question that we only have schools in order to keep the students away from the real societal power structures – for example, the job sphere, the roads, the fields, the military, whatever? So we have schools as a compensatory device, as a substitute to 'real' life.

John: Yes.

Steen: There was this guy from Norway, a criminologist and sociologist called Nils Christie. In 1971, he wrote a book, in Norwegian, called *Hvis skolen ikke fantes?* (*If Schools Didn't Exist*; Christie 2020/1971). He provoked many readers when he stated that we should, as a thought experiment, consider closing down the educational institutions and letting the students get out in real life to take part their parents' work life. Let them have the right to become active in the political life and maybe even change the fixated power structures, instead of being 'imprisoned' in school institutions, blocked off from society.

John: Here's a political problem for you. For all kinds of capitalist reasons and for all kinds of other reasons, we want to allow our adults to earn an income. And over the last 30 years, the biggest change is the acceptance that females can enter the workforce with the same rights and ways as males which, as we know, wasn't true 50 to 100 years ago. We also know that schooling as we know it started in the 1800s, and it was very much an agrarian- then industry-based model of schooling in terms of school hours and school times. When you ask about not having schools – then who 'babysits' the students – can you imagine if they turn up to our work place – we would then be responsible for educating, entertaining, and managing them – so we reinvent schools but in the workplace. When I hear people talk about the future of schools and they say it can be accomplished anywhere, any place, I wonder then who will supervise and oversee? I think we will have expert adults in this role, and this is the essence of schooling. Until we solve the issue of working with students who do not want to be so involved in learning ideas and topics that they are not interested in, who do not know by themselves where to go next, and who cannot get into the zone of proximal development by themselves (a contradiction given Vygotsky's argument), then we will need expert others as teachers (Vygotsky 1997). So yes, schools may change, but teachers will be needed.

I note also the advance of robotics and AI. I visited a class recently being taught by a five-foot-tall robot. What was fascinating is that the students loved it *because* there were no relationship issues. Like our GPS, you can ask the robot ten times the same question and they do not get flustered or annoyed. You can reboot and start again and the robot has no memory of failed prior attempts, and because of this lack of relations the students are much more experimental, much more likely to admit they did not get it first time, and loved that the robot intentionally did not recall their behavior from before. Imagine if my GPS person said, "Silly fool, I told you to turn left," "How many times do I have to tell you to do a U-turn," "Idiot, you did not follow my instructions." I would not use it, I would probably talk back to it, and clearly this is not the best way to get to my destination.

So we may see changes in who is a teacher, but we will need institutions where students go and learn that which they would not learn if there were no schools.

Like your Norwegian friend, I can see merit in the idea that students should be free to do what they want. Yeah, we should close schools down. So everything's going to be on the web, etc. And both parents are working. Who babysits?

Steen: The basic question here was: Do we need specific enclosure institutions for students, to lock them in six to eight hours a day?

John: Yes, we do. Although it does not have to be for so many hours, or locked!

Steen: And we have reserved a certain space for students because we don't want them to take part in society.

John: No, that's not true.

Steen: But that's Christie's argument.

John: We don't want them to take part in society without restrictions or constraints. They're not as free to go out in society because who looks after them? Who feeds them? Who nurtures them with both parents at work? Who is responsible for advancing their learning? Who manages their behavior, especially with others? And so, all these arguments that the future of schools is going to be on the web, ignores the fact that adults need to be there for some kind of supervisory role at minimum. And given that, why don't we do something decent with them whilst they're in institutions? Teachers are much more than babysitters.

Steen: Okay, I was only trying to test an argument, which I don't necessarily find attractive. By the way, some bilingual Danish-American PhD students I know, Lucas Cone and Joachim S. Wiewiura, recently realized that the nearly 50-year-old Christie book was never translated in English. And soon their translation will hit the international market (Christie 2020/1971).

And actually, it is interesting and worth thinking about, that if you go back to that time shortly after the 1968 movement, the zeitgeist was dominated by a critique of institutions, which as you probably know, was a harsh critique of bourgeois and capitalist institutions and all that.

And the left-wing people, they were so much opposed to petrified institutions, so they simply played with the alternative and anarchist idea: "Let's dissolve and get rid of the institutions, the sooner the better."

But now, 47 years later, the leftist movements, at least in Denmark and Norway, but also in Germany and France, those are the ones that are most in favor of protecting the welfare institutions against being dissolved, cut down, or even privatized. And the danger could be the market logic or neoliberal governance or whatever. So now, the left-wing of 2018 has transformed itself to become a vivid defender of public welfare institutions, especially schools. The refrain sounds: Let's enhance investments in schools, have more teachers in schools, etc. So the social democrats, the social liberals, and the extreme left, they all favor of investment in daycare institutions, schools, and universities. How do you comprehend and interpret this transformation? Isn't it interesting?

John: I just find your analysis fascinating and interesting.

Steen: Is it the same here in Australia?

John: Oh, yeah. And so the fascination for me is can you imagine what it's going to be like in 40 years' time? In one sense, what we do know is that it won't be the same. On the other hand, we've been saying that the last 200 years of schooling have remained the same in many ways. The difference, as we have talked about, is the extra responsibilities we now ask of educators – to be more responsible for emotional and welfare issues of the students, to build respect for self and others, to attend to teaching the strategies of learning by one self and with others, and so much more responsibility.

Steen: But here in Australia, you have a wild and vivid experiment going on that we don't know of yet because you have this private enterprise of education, meaning that this whole town, Melbourne, wherever you go, also in Box Hill, there are people from many nationalities all coming over specifically for schooling or university study. Thus, there are many from middle-class families with enough money to go there to buy education and then one day return to their home country to be the smart guys and girls at home.

John: Yes, Australia has one of the highest percentage of students in private schools, about 35% to 40%, and yes there is heavy investment in attracting overseas students; and this increases the more schools become responsible for their budgets, and this is the case for government schools as well. But it will not be long before the reverse happens – and it is already starting at the university level – of students going to China to their fast growing tertiary sector. We have much to learn from the Asian learner, and there are some great books on this topic (Watkins & Biggs 2001).

Indeed, I was involved in some of these studies comparing Asian students in East Asian counties, Asian students in Australia, and Caucasians in Australia. The seeming paradox is that they use a lot of memory and other skills to overlearn, but the difference is that the Asian students use memorization and so on to overlearn *so* they can then move to the deeper understanding. Whereas too often we use memorization to pass tests and thus see memorization as bad. We miss the point. This is why I am so invested in using cognitive task analysis that asks what thinking skills are desired and how are they reflected in the tasks and assignments we ask of students, and how do our assessments mirror the proportion of surface to deep.

So we have much to learn from the Asian student – but too often they are seen as marketable products to make money from.

Steen: So, you have marketized educational business here to the far extreme.

John: Yes, absolutely. It's the fourth-largest income earner for the Australian economy.

Steen: But you see, in Denmark we haven't gone very far in that direction. Most of the schools are still public schools, and we don't have much private enterprise in schools and universities, even though private funding to a considerable and growing extent decides what goes on in 'free' research projects.

John: Thirty-five percent of students go to a private school in Australia.

Steen: In Denmark it is approximately 17%. But we don't have private universities in Denmark. None. But 'foreigners' from non-EU countries have to pay to enter the universities.

John: We have a private and many church universities, but that's another question, Steen, and I think it's outside our realm here, which is more focused on schools. My view is, living in a democracy, the state systems have to be the best possible systems. I have no trouble with independent schools, with Catholic schools, but unfortunately in Australia the branding is such that people think they're better; and when you account for prior differences when students enter these schools, it is hard to find evidence that they are better. No question they have better facilities – more green grass, sweeping driveways, lovely buildings, swimming pools – but no difference in the quality of teaching; the former structural issues are often used to claim the latter without cause. My worry is the residualization in state schools. The parents who can't move, who don't have the options to move, stay in the state schools. And when you look at the movement here in Australia, and I can show you the data, it's the brighter students who drift to the independent schools and private schools. So the not-so-virtuous cycle continues.

Steen: Also the brighter teachers?

John: There is evidence of that, yes. One of our worries as we promote highly accomplished and lead teachers (HALTS) is that, once identified, we do not want them to be captured by the private system, or even to congregate in the more wealthy public school areas. This is why I like the South Australia model, where positions are allocated to schools in need, in low SES areas, for HALTS and only HALTS can apply, with an increase in salary. It has been quite successful to ensure a more even distribution of excellence.

Steen: You have seen that in US, too?

John: Yes, but they have far fewer students in private schools (about 10%).

Steen: And so you end up having schools with very poor standards in poor neighborhoods.

John: Which is why I'm very much, philosophically and empirically, against things like screening and tracking, because there is a residualization. But then it goes back to the fundamental reason why parents choose schools. They want to choose schools on the basis of the friends they want their students to have.

Steen: My dad, who died last year, 85 years old and an ex-engineer, always said, "We have the public schools where we can get the chance and have to meet people from all classes."

John: I agree. Schools need to be core to the great civilizing effect in our society, especially for children.

Steen: The old man also made this argument, and it has been a proper argument in the majority of the middle class for many years. We should come to learn about different life situations, family structures, and different views on society's development, and at least we would get that important knowledge and insight from mutual schooling. Maybe also from sports or from other places where you meet, but in school, you have an obvious chance to come to experience, feel, and maybe understand society's complexity of lifeforms.

John: Going back to my argument right at the beginning is that if you look at countries, particularly, in the last 100 years that have been successful, it's usually 20 to 30 years after mass immigration. Bringing in diversity enriches a country, gives a push to be creative and entrepreneurial. Richard Florida makes the argument about creative cities, and one of their markers was the tolerance of diversity (Florida 2005). He got into big troubles at one point because he said, "One of the indices of great cities is whether they accept gays and lesbians." And it wasn't about gays and lesbians, it was about the proficiency to accept diversity. The best cities in the world he showed do welcome, use, and promote diversity. When you look at some countries, and I see places across Europe and America closing down debates and action related to diversity, and you think the future for them is not rosy. Maybe we need a similar index for schools (see deWitt 2012).

Steen: This fight is going on right in the midst of many big European cities in this very moment, also in a metropolis like Copenhagen, between the governments, the financial interests, and especially the market for houses on one side, and the poor and underprivileged people, the refugees, and the asylum seekers on the other side. Diversity seems to be okay if people have high income.

If you gain high income, you are welcome and more than tolerated. You can be lesbian, you can be gay, whatever you like, you can have a Hindu belief or loving Norse gods. But we don't want people with low performance, low skills, and low income from African and Arab countries and 'we' don't need Muslims. That's the utmost depressing standard narrative all around Europe.

John: All they are doing is building barriers, excluding people, and missing the opportunity to grow.

As a human in the world, this bothers me. The nationalism and xenophobia are just a disaster in terms of this world. It is not the message I would want our students to learn about the world they are living in.

Steen: I most certainly agree.

School number 2,365

Steen: Here is an observation from a street very close to University of Melbourne. Here, walking from my hotel to your office, every morning

281

I see school building number 2,365, founded in 1880. My question goes like this. How could it be that today nearly every school has to have its own array of its own branding? Now, it is normal practice for a school to 'say', "This school is a specific, maybe even a special school, with a genuine self-branding ideal." But once in Australia, and maybe also in the rest of the world – and not very many years ago – people would say, or maybe it is more correct to say 'take for granted', "This is state school number 2,365 and it is exactly as good as number 2,600, or 2,364, and 2,366." It has the same quality as the others.

One might think that this common numerical logic was something that happened in China, maybe North Korea or Russia. How could it be that those people were thinking that one school had exactly the same quality as any other school and that they gave them numbers? How do you explain that?

John: When we started this business called mass schooling in the 1800s, then the aim was to have kind of an interchangeable sense of quality. All schools were exchangeable, quality was evenly distributed, and no matter which school you went to the aim was to be the best school. But as we've got more and more into the debate about school outcomes we also got into the debates about parental rights to choose schools, and we've got branding. We started giving more management and funding responsibility to schools, and given that the level of funding was closely tied to the number of students, we created a market for principals to brand their schools to attract students to come. Most of the branding is about, "Come to this school because we have pretty students, pretty buildings, pretty cultural events, pretty sports." Only once in my career have I ever seen a school say, "Come to this school because we have great teachers."

I supervised a doctoral thesis here a few years ago on branding in state schools, and every principal emphatically said they didn't do it – while they engaged in so much branding.

I was involved in the television show 'Revolution Schools' where a TV crew followed a high school here in Melbourne that went from the bottom 10% to top 10% in the state. It was the principal and school leaders that resolutely and doggedly evaluated their impact, whereas I was merely the commentator that linked the three-part series. What was fascinating was the last episode where Michael Muscat (the principal) and I were looking over the change data for the past few years . . . indeed impressive. But the last word was – so what is the one thing that shows you this was all worth it – and the answer was, "We have 100+ more students than usual enrolling this year." Success is stealing from neighborhood schools – sad, but this is the game. I think success was the evidence of impact that they were having on their students – more staying in school as it was a safe and inviting place to come and learn, teachers and school leaders passionate about maximizing their impact, robust discussions among the adults about what they mean by impact. And, not least, asking how they would know this impact is being realized, and building a community for students and parents to be involved in the pursuit of progress to higher achievement.

Steen: But these schools probably want to have their own profile, and in Denmark a lot of gymnasiums (high schools), vocational schools, and universities spend a lot of money on advertising.

John: Yes, I see no problems with schools building and having pride in their profile. Unlike the private schools, which have branding companies, many government schools were engaging in branding by coming up with claims about their school, and of course every August in Australia, when parents make decisions where to send their students, it's a massive mass market.

          Today, the New Zealand government announced that any school that has more than 50% of students outside the enrollment area will not get resources to accommodate them anymore. They're not going to give them new buildings; and this is an attempt to stop the branding and stop the poaching of students from other schools. Now my argument was, why don't they just make a decree saying you can't have that many students out of zone. But they can't do that when you've got self-governing schools, autonomous schools, when you have principals who are expected to run their school, when you have funding so tied to student numbers – you create the market for this kind of branding.

Steen: I guess, they also compete in a very similar market.

John: . . . and that by having a branding that says, "This is how we're different."

Steen: Okay, but would it be ideal for you to apply the *Visible Learning* programs, so we could have a lot of visible schools with numbers? They could be exactly the same.

John: Yes, exactly the same in terms of the focus on the thinking of the adults, the evaluation capacity of adults, the debates about impact, etc. But this does not mean they have to then look the same.

Steen: So you know, wherever you go, it has high quality. So it could be called state school number 2,365.

John: Yes, the best school in their neighborhood should also be the school down the road.

But as I've mentioned to you a few times, and what fascinates me, is that we don't have a literature, a narrative, or a discussion about scaling up success. Instead, we say we've got these problems and here's how I could fix them, which has led to the kind of branding exercise. It leads to every time a principal goes to a new school, they say, "Oh. I'm going to listen for the first six months, and then I'm going to change it," as if change is what we need when things are going well. Yes, we always need improvement.

Steen: We all seem to live – as we have touched upon earlier in our talk – in the midst of enforced develop*mental*ism. And apparently both the mental and physical structures have to adapt to dynamic changes of the zeitgeist.

John: Like McDonald's, we want every store/school to be similarly high quality. Ikea does this. You name it, they are obsessed about quality control and coming across in their branding as excellent. I ask, "How do they do it?" My colleagues in that business were very clear. You use franchising/licensing, and in licensing you are obsessed about quality control. You're obsessed about a legal contract that says, "If you don't do this, you're out and you take nothing with you." We don't have any of that in education because we are a care business. We care for our principals. We think that by giving them local control and having a school that's unique, we will drive the system up. Instead we have driven the system apart, create a jungle of dog-eat-dog or steal students from neighboring schools. No wonder the equity issue is huge and hard to solve when it is built into the fabric of schools and into funding models. We need to see this funding and branding as a serious problem.

Harsh critique of the state

Steen: From my point of view, from my angle of observation, it's like all rhetoric connected to a state is related to some kind of idea and critique of totalitarianism and pressure from above. Besides, the 'blood' of the state is framed as the tax-burden for the citizens - that is, as something enforced upon the poor people from the outside. In sharp contrast every kind of semantic related to market is being portrayed as dynamic, full of flexible attitude, individual choice, whatever. So this mess you are talking about, might it also have to do with the lack of respect for a state semantic or a state linguistic? It seems to be very easy for the market to fight back and portray the state as ineffective and in principle in vain.

John: Yes, there are competing claims. There is struggle when the top decrees, then allows flexibility in the middle, but then gets upset when the middle usurps the top! Charles Weingartner and Neil Postman in 1971 had the best title of a book in our history: *Teaching Is a Subversive Activity* (Weingartner & Postman 1971). Viva the subversives. 'Tis a pity, however, when the state is seen as the enemy.

Steen: It's seen as the enemy, but you see the state as a kind of savior or at least a high-quality securing guardian.

John: Yes, they are responsible for quality assurance, but by supporting schools to meet the assurance quality standards and not standing back and 'measuring' them or collecting the data. If they are to move into outcomes of schooling then they should also be evaluating the support they give schools to do their work. I think the state has a responsibility for some quality assurance with the profession.

Steen: So you're up for a state with high ambitions? A state caring for the whole population's access to public goods and the right to strive for *Bildung*, not just education?

John: Yes.

Steen: Okay, let's leave that theme, but I find it interesting looking at that building, which by the way is the Victoria Department's center for professional learning. But they haven't changed the façade – and I see it every day, "2,365" – and I think it's a damned interesting sign in the urban jungle that makes me wonder and reflect.

John: In the 1800s in Victoria, they hired this guy as the builder of schools, an architect. Yes, he argued schools should be impressive edifices and help define a community. So, Bastow designed many schools in this impressive Victorian image. It screams order, efficiency, sturdiness, adornment, and rigor. He did build splendid buildings.

Steen: Yeah.

John: It is amazing how many schools start with glass and then have to invest in curtains to cut out the light! These scream functional, efficient, orderly, hey we may look different but this is the façade, and a sense of ease. Yes, a bit of over generalization, but we do not have the sense that schools are core to the community, but more that they stand apart. Sad.

Steen: And they have high-quality. The old schools were built of the solid red bricks.

If schools didn't exist – would we miss them?

Is the state school in principle blind to class differences and open for everyone?

Can any state school be the best school?

Why do market solutions – for example, private schools – seem more 'sexy' when it comes to schooling?

XV. WHY ARE WE LONGING
for PREDICTABILITY and SECURITY?

WHEN I STARTED in UNIVERSITIES the ACADEMICS RAN the UNIVERSITY.

BUT *now*, UNIVERSITIES are MORE RUN by PROFESSIONAL ADMINISTRATORS, the BUDGET is KING LEADING TO MORE CASUAL STAFF and LESS INVESTMENT in LONG TERM CAREERS.

THE BEST DISCRIMINATOR OF ACCEPTED OVER NOT ACCEPTED JOURNAL ARTICLES is WHETHER there is A WORTHWHILE STORY in the CONCLUSIONS.

 WE NEED to FIGHT AGAINST the INERT IDEAS,

 THE HOLY STATUS of PRAISING YESTERDAY'S *ideas*,

 and JUST PILING UP UNNECESSARY knowledge FROM THE OLD DAYS,

 BUT we HAVE TO INHERIT the PAST in ORDER to CRITICIZE, TRANSGRESS THEM and to FOSTER the NEW

RESEARCHING has TO BE a RISKY and COURAGEOUS ACTIVITY because THE STORY MUST be TRUTHFUL and AUTHENTIC,

and the STORY has TO HONOR the RESEARCH EXPERIENCE and THE PARTICIPANTS of THE RESEARCH.

Steen: Let's enter a discussion of the prevailing quest for security in our unstable and ever-changing society. The problem is that if you, for example, don't have a kind of a security while you are working at the university and you get stuck there with bad working conditions you risk not to be willing to experiment and to question authorities and accepted 'truths'. Maybe you become too protective and conservative.

John: I would like to think I've been reasonably good as an academic. My first 17 years I did not have a single funded research grant. I had the luxury of trying things, experimenting, and exploring. You can't do that now.

Steen: It is much harder now.

John: I look at people who on their first year expected to have paid their wages by lots of teaching, bringing in research funds. That is more a servant than a growing role. By legislation in New Zealand, academics are supposed to be the 'critics and conscience' of society, and while younger academics are on short-term contracts, playing the grant game, often answering questions imposed by outside funders than from their own curiosity, over-teaching, and joining the journal impact publication game – how can they take the necessary risks to be critics!

Steen: You also look upon the young academics now and they are forced only to have focus on one question, and not to try to answer two or three questions. It's too much and not strategic. And then in a way today the horizon gets narrowed. For example, the students are told now, "You are not allowed to present new knowledge after your conclusion." And I say, "Where is that written? It's not written in any scripture." "But, that's what the teachers tell us when we come to the courses." And I say, "Just be sure that what you write in your master's thesis is fulfilling the mandatory claims of the study guideline." Is it stated anywhere that they are not allowed to add new stuff to the text as a final, new, and opening perspective? No, it is not stated there, so they could do it. "Oh, we're advised not to do it." So students are very insecure these days about living up to the regulations and 'good' advice from protective colleagues.

John: Yes, this is what worries me about the future of academia. Universities are more run by professional administrators, the budget is king, leading to more casual staff, less investment in long-term careers, and the seeking of more than building reputation. As we are paid by the taxpayer, I believe we have a responsibility to speak about our expertise in the public, in the media, and when asked by reporters. Younger academics are never taught to speak to reporters, shy from the media, and are scared of their own reputations being sullied by negative comments about media commentary.

Further, throughout my career I have had the opportunity to move into many areas – yes, I would argue the common theme is excellent measurement models applied to fascinating educational questions. For example, we have a 20+ year program in loneliness, adolescents in prisons, well-being, national parks, early childhood, ethnic identity, breakfast in schools, police standards, speech language, evaluation of US Marines, elite sports, paraprofessional counseling, and left-handedness. A reviewer once commented I could be world famous if I had stuck to one topic. A newer colleague would struggle to move too far from a core set of topics.

Steen: Students are told that master theses should be not more than 80 pages. In the old days, it could be 300, 400, 500 or even 600 pages, depending on your skills, ambitions, and, not the least, what you wanted to scrutinize and dwell on. Now the papers are composed and written in a predictable style including a method chapter, a state of the art chapter, presentation of the empirical stuff, presentation of the theoretical concepts, and then the conclusion. So it's more or less a kind of a straitjacket that's already there before they even start to study and investigate. But the self-imposed prison is apparently very popular. Therefore, an ideal template and master plan(!) for the master thesis is often wanted and delivered, too.

John: I love the study by Fiske and Fogg. They took few hundred articles, which had been submitted to APA journals – that is, very good journals – and knew which ones were accepted and which were not. They asked which part of an article was most predictive of being accepted (Fogg & Fiske 1993). Was it the title, the department, the affiliation, the introduction, the literature review, the methods, the results, the conclusions, or quality of the references?

Steen: What were their conclusions?

John: The conclusions were that if you hadn't got a story, why would you care about how good your method, analysis, results, etc.? It's all about the convincing power of the story (yes, the other parts lead to the credibility of the story, but if you are not saying anything then why should we care about design and results?). And I say to my students, "Read the conclusion first. If there is no story there, don't bother with decoding the rest of the article." Similarly, I over-emphasize the last chapter of their theses – it is never a summary, never a treatise on limitations, it is telling a story (carefully of course). Say something. The same every time I met with the students: "What's the story today?"

Steen: There also seems to be a presentation format. The medicine and natural science way to write an abbreviated abstract has now become the new global norm. The conclusion has to take less space and attention than ten lines, and then you are supposed to have all other areas of the academic world to fit into this abstract format and to accept the rhetoric style: the humanities, social science, philosophy, etc. You should always be able to make an abstract and condense all you have to say in a few lines and put it up front. My favorite philosopher, Theodor Wiesengrund **Adorno**, one of the founding fathers of Critical Theory (also called the first-generation Frankfurt School), would have hated this imprisonment of freethinking in academia. He wrote that in philosophy, every sentence is important and can never be abbreviated to something else. Philosophy is not journalism (Adorno 2004/1966, 2005/1951).

John: Well, that's not true with most academic articles.

Steen: Another credo of Adorno is that every sentence in a philosophical text is as far away from the center of the argument as any other sentence or else it is not worth anything. If you can summarize philosophy, it would not be philosophy, but something else. So he'll probably not be accepted in any magazine because he would never be able to say one clue out of his 100 pages or something and make it into a little paragraph of an abstract. He was strictly against that logic and I agree with him. We can also fear that the enforced and narrow science narrative model ends up as a new straitjacket. It might also have to do with the commercialization and commodification of knowledge in an attention economy being highly depending on new thoughts and ideas. In this sense, we have become knowledge producers in a cognitive capitalism, as the French economist and philosopher Yann Moulier Boutang 'labels' 'our' contemporary capitalism (Moulier Boutang 2011/2007; Larsen 2014b). What do you, by the way, think about Adorno's argument?

John: Well, I agree to a point. With the proliferation of articles and journals, I do want the writer to help me decide whether the 100 pages+ have a convincing story to like to read the text. I want the abstract to suggest more than the article says because that's how you're going to be wrong. Let's be bolder.

Steen: Oh yeah. That could be a good document. But more or less, the most abstracts, they just identify and 'coagulate' (i.e., condense) what is the content of the whole article.

John: Yes, but the boldness matters. For example, in *Visible Learning* I provided some 'bold' conjectures as to the underlying themes, which increased the chances I was wrong. If I had stuck to summarizing the data, then this is less likely, but surely not as enticing to read (and critique).

The biggest trend in the education of the moment is oversight by the big societies – the American Psychological Society, the American Education Research Association, and others. Many of them have joined and are about to demand and make it compulsory that every time you submit an article, you submit all your data. Now, there are all kinds of issues in this decision, but it would mean that meta-analysis will die – as you will have access to all the data in the primary study (and this could be a good death). It also means that the focus will revert back to the data and maybe less the big ideas.

Steen: Your problem would be that you should send the whole box of stuff to people.

John: You're right, it's going to be a huge issue. If you go to your examples of physics and chemistry, they do that now. We do need to ask why we are spending so much time re-collecting data, because we believe that class and that subject and that the teacher is so unique. Of course, they are, but whether their impact is different is the key empirical question.

Steen: But if you go back to, for example, the Plato dialogues, then one should be forced to summarize the dialogues into an abstract. I think that would go against the nature of the good, rich, and multi-faceted Plato dialogue? An example could be the approximately 2,400-year-old **Cratylus** dialogue on the origin and function of language (Plato 1989). You have three different voices – you have Cratylus, Hermogenes, and of course Socrates himself. And while you read what they discuss, they all more or less represent a language philosophical approach that's still here: one is more or less a conceptual realist (Cratylus), one is a nominalist (Hermogenes), and one is a more pragmatic and communicative one (the role of Socrates). And when you learn to dwell in the text and interpret these three voices, you are not only being born as a thinker, you also come to realize that today's discussions of the status of language has a long, interesting, and winding history. The midwife logic of the dialogue (also called *maieutics*) donates the reader a chance to begin to interpret the different arguments for the three different legs of philosophical language approaches in an autonomous way. And of course I hope that Plato's dialogue has more to give than this brief summary of mine might indicate. The dialogue has the power to ignite free interpretations, and we haven't heard them all.

291

The quest for predictability

Steen: I think that it is a big problem that many people want the teachers and what goes on in schools to be predictable. Meaning that they could serve and present some packages, or they could give us some things that we think they should give our students. These claims are extremely problematic because the teacher without any doubt faces a bigger challenge, or maybe even an obligation, to be unpredictable and to come up with things that you could never know that he or she will invent, present, and deal with – and thereby 'fertilize' pupils and students far beyond a mandatory master plan for a school.

John: But that's why – as I stated earlier in the conversation – I'm very attracted to the 'thin' and open New Zealand curriculum. For every age, for every subject, it's just 39 pages. There's a dramatic amount of responsibility for the teacher and each school because they're saying, "These are the kind of competencies and skills that we want the students to have. Now, if you want to use Germany as your study, or Ancient Egyptians, or Maori in New Zealand, good luck to you," whereas so much curriculum is deciding on that content. As we know from history, the minute you get into a content-based curriculum, it explodes – we love to shove more and more in. And so, I'm a great fan of giving the teacher a lot of freedom to choose the content, but I'm not sure I'd necessarily give them the rights all the time to choose the progressions or necessarily the level of impact, because if teachers choose badly, the students suffer. This is why we need the notion of collective impact – each teacher's concepts of impact and progression needs to be contested, and who better to be involved in that than their peers, moderated by cross-school considerations.

Steen: I have just read the copy of this very famous speech or sort of text you generously gave me, written by Alfred North Whitehead in 1916 about the dissertation in which he fights against the inert ideas, the holy status of praising yesterday's ideas and just piling up all this unnecessary knowledge from the old days (Whitehead 1959).

John: It's a wonderful text.

Steen: It's a text worth reading also today, 102 years after it was written, but I also have some reservations. It is no great secret for you that I favor that it is indispensable to come to know 'old' knowledge and traditions in order to be able to transgress it in a critical, autonomous, and inventive way.

John: But the problem today is that students above average are great at playing the learning game of learning inert ideas – they know the way to do this, they know this game – just tell what you want me to know, and I can tell you it back. There is indeed a grammar of surface learning endemic in too many classrooms.

Steen: So you think that students are the most conservative?

John: …'among' the most conservative … particularly above-average students. They learn to play the 'game', know how to be compliant, want teachers to talk more, favor the facts as they know how to play this game, and sometimes want to retain the world they know. Students below average can be less conservative. They can be the radical ones. They want help to interpret, to understand, and learn more. They question the value of 'so much' stuff that is so often incoming noise to them. If they don't get the ideas, build the relations between ideas, they are more likely to turn off. When we ask so many students who's the best learner, too often they say, "It's the kid that knows lots, who gets it easily, and can answer all the questions." And I think, yeah, if this is a good learner we've got a real problem here because knowing lots isn't my answer.

From 'knowing lots' to robotics

John: Historically, I understand why you wanted lawyers and doctors to know lots. They didn't have the technologies. They didn't have the collaborations. But those days have changed. I remind you that 'evidence-based' medicine is a very recent phenomenon, and ironically it was most opposed by the 'experts' who claimed they knew the truth and did not need evidence!

Seeing the change in lawyers is a classic example. We used to train lawyers, and then we sweated them in their first five years to do all the background research, get all the stuff in the library, the precedents, and write the background reports. Whereas now, robotics does a lot of that stuff, and there are moves in the legal profession to reduce the length of law degrees as the firms want to engage more in the development and teaching – particularly as many firms have become specialists. Moreover, right now in Australia, we have so many unemployed legal graduates.

Steen: Not yet in Denmark.

John: Well, it is here. Because the old days, where we wanted lots of lawyers at the bottom level to do all that grunt work, have changed.

Steen: In Denmark, the leading politicians, managers, and media powers tell people to become engineers, economists, administrators, lawyers, biotech-experts, and doctors . . . and we often hear about prospering jobs in medicine and pharmaceutics of all types, supplemented by the daily ideology about the breadless humanities.

John: I will predict that in 10 to 20 years' time, it will be almost impossible to get a job as a surgeon (if you trained today) because robotics will take over. Being a nurse will always be a needed profession, but as artificial intelligence advances, I can see many roles, teachers currently do, being replaced. Yes, some say the relationship is critical, but as we noted earlier, in many situations students prefer to not have humans recall their past behaviors and hold them against them or use it to color their interactions. They want the chance to ask, again and over again, without the sigh of exasperation by the teacher or by their peers, and they try different options to see the best ways to progress.

Risk-aversive terror management

Steen: In addition, we envisage a kind of a double movement in state politics. Many politicians find that the market solutions are better and more effective than the state solution. But at the same time, the majority of the leading politicians 'say', "We have to be certain that we get value for money; that we provide the best and cheapest services and standards; that the learning goals in education get fulfilled, and all that." How does it come that states and politics are immensely involved in security management, when the nude fact is that the market is, in principle, itself insecure and creating insecurity?

John: There's an argument within psychology called 'terror management'. The claim is we do things to reduce the terror of the negative consequences. This can lead to avoiding and certainly never confronting new ideas, risky situations, and continually seeking explanations in terms of what we currently think. Different is terrifying.

A simple example is that the number of parents who drive their students to school for safety reasons is inversely related to the safety of the community that they live in. But they have believed about the terror that might occur *if* they did not do this. Similarly, many serious crimes in many countries, particularly the US and Australia, have been dramatically decreasing over the last 20 years. But the rhetoric has gone up about how evil it is and how crime is terrible and increasing, because we're trying to assure the parents that they are perfectly justified in driving their students to school – imagine the alternative.

Steen: That's also a part of schooling management, isn't it?

John: Yes, in terms of how we manage the rhetoric about schooling. Take school shootings. What's the probability, if you're a kid in any school in the United States that you're going to have a school shooting in your school? Once in 33,000 years. But everyone's obsessed about school crime. If you want to be safe in the US, run to a school. There is ten times more likelihood a teenager will be shot in a restaurant, but we never hear about arming cooks and waiters – this does not fit the way some want to manage the sense of terror. We can have robust talks about free trade, but often resist debates about immigrants or refugees and their rights to free trade.

Steen: Another thing is, of course, that it's not only school management or national school policies but also the lack of parents', teachers', and students' approvals. They all seem not to be out there to tolerate great risks.

John: No, because they haven't got good mitigation strategies.

Steen: But how could you understand that, because when we were young – even though you and I don't have the same age – there were hitchhikers all around in Europe, and probably also in Australia and New Zealand, and now there are nearly no hitchhikers in the roads any longer. It has nothing to do with real risks and dangers, in spite of warnings like, "Well, it's too risky. You'll be robbed or raped." At the same time, school management could say, "Without learning goals, without strict regulations, we have no secure and trustworthy school."

John: Yes, our sense of the probability-of-terror reactions have ballooned.

Steen: How do we describe that? It's probably also due to the intensified globalization of the economy, the intensified technological development that might diminish or even abolish jobs, and intensify automation. Maybe it is possible to relate the security agenda to these tendencies. It seems to be so that educational politics and institutional schooling are destined or doomed to become inscribed in this importunate and protective logic.

Towards a closed society?

John: And, again, it relates to the concept of society and what it is. And the society is, particularly in the country I live in, it's becoming a much more closed society. Can I go back and ask you to read Karl Popper's book *The Open Society and Its Enemies* (Popper 1945)?

Steen: Yes, I have read it. It's a very interesting post-Second-World-War book written as a harsh critique of totalitarianism and the dangerous and destructive enclosure of societies around the globe.

John: He wrote that when he was in New Zealand. He was a refugee to New Zealand during the war, as I stated right in the beginning of our conversation, and he was appointed to the University of Canterbury. I know it is not in the flow of our discussions right now, but there is one story I love. When he'd finished the book, he was summoned to the vice chancellor's office, and he had to defend that he never used any paper, any typing, any pens, any resources of the university, because research and writing books was not in his contract. How our universities have changed in their contingencies.

Steen: Thirty-three years ago, Ulrich Beck, a sociologist from Germany, wrote a famous and highly influential book, called *Risk Society* (Beck 1985). He's unfortunately dead now. I met him and had lunch with him, together with a bunch of colleagues at University of Copenhagen. He was a great guy, but he suddenly died in the split of a second in 2015. Beck had the idea that in the old days risks were related to natural catastrophes: ice ages, earthquakes, big storms, floods, avalanches, exploding volcanoes, lava, and so on, causing death, illness, famine, forcing people to become refugees. During the last 30 to 40 years we have entered – what he calls – the risk-manufactured societies, in which we produce giant risks – for example, pollution, radical climate changes, dramatic inequalities, weapons of mass destruction, global financial crises, wild traffic jams, etc. Basically, he claims that we are living in a paradoxical risk-producing society, while we are trying to compensate for the risks we have produced ourselves.

John: Oh my goodness. I have this friend who's a principal of school just outside of Melbourne airport. I think I mentioned him earlier – John Marsden (Marsden 2019). He's is a very, very famous writer of teenage fiction, but he's also a principal of a school, which is much more like Summerhill than Eton. It is on a farm with much bush and the children are encouraged to be in the wild. But he gets letters from the department about what he can and cannot do: "No, students aren't allowed out into the bush unless there is the right ratio of parents to children present." And he wrote this reply to the department that is beautiful. He didn't just go and contest them or point out the absurdities like I would. He used his world-class writing to show the nonsense and inconsistencies with the philosophy of the school (which they had approved). He can now still invite students to go into the bush and not be enveloped by the presence of adults.

Steen: We also now and then see old teachers and journalists in Denmark writing feature articles in newspapers where they state that: "Well, when we were youngsters, we were playing in the harbor areas. We were jumping over very risky things, from heights, and crawling on lifts and in high trees. And we did all kind of wild things, far away from the gaze of the parents, like diving in the sea, sailing on ice-flakes, making big fires, and so on, and now our own students are not allowed to do anything."

John: Exactly, in my 20s we used to have this – oh I cannot believe it – have this argument when we were mountain climbing. If you live to 30, you didn't go to the edge close enough. How stupid looking back, but it did lead to some great risks.

Steen: But you survived.

John: I did, and had some great times in the mountains around the world. When I was 32, I fell off Ama Dablam, one of the most magnificent Himalayan mountains. I survived, with only a few broken ribs, and decided then that I had risked the gods' favor enough and it was time to stop and enjoy.

Steen: I read that you, during an interview conducted by your Melbourne colleague, Maurizio Toscano, stated that researching has to be a risky and courageous activity because the story must be truthful and authentic, and the story has to honor the research experience and the subjects of the research (Hattie & Toscano 2018).

John: However, the story has to say more than just a summary, and yes, this should be risky. Take meeting you, Steen. That I'm prepared to talk with you, it's very risky. You have written negative reviews of my work. I had emails before you came from quite a few colleagues and some I did not know saying, "Don't talk to him. Don't privilege him. Don't give him oxygen." The reason I talk to you is that in your writings, with some exceptions [laughter], you don't make personal statements; you critique the ideas. I admire the kind of philosophy that was behind that, as a greedy academic, I want to learn. But as I look around my colleagues, some are not as risky and some are not courageous, they won't speak out, they tend not to build models, they keep too close to the data, like not to create and defend narratives, and dislike taking their messages to the profession and the public. And I think that's a not defensible, given we academics are paid by the taxpayer.

Steen: I am happy that we met face to face.

But I wonder, how does research differ from life in general? Life can also be risky and challenging.

John: Well, I suppose love is risky and courageous, but there are some times you do have to stop and smell the roses.

Steen: I think my view is that all humans have to invent and present stories, while they find themselves to sense, experience, and listen to the world and other people and then attempt to decipher and donate these life patterns meaning . . .

John: We do.

Steen: . . . and teachers, students, pupils, parents, and whosoever, also do that. So we're all inventing and all taking risks, in principle, when we are presenting something the way we see it. But do you think that researchers are engaged in a specific risk-taking in their presenting of a story?

John: Look, I think that's a fundamental role of academic researchers, that we're supposed to do the things that are hard, ask the questions many consider not easily answerable. And if we don't, then I don't think we're doing our jobs. Of course it has to be risky.

Why are we longing for predictability and security?
Are we living in a risk-producing society?
Which tendencies point towards a closed society at the moment?
Do we have to think and act like world citizens in the future?

XVI. THE CONVERSATION STOPS
but MUST CONTINUE

CAN the EXPERIENCE of IMPACT be POSITIVE EVEN though THE IMPACT was EXPERIENCED AS BEING negative?

YES, ONE of the PURPOSES of SCHOOLING is TO ENABLE STUDENTS to CRITIQUE and SOMETIMES PROTEST about their INTERPRETATIONS of THE TEACHERS' PLANS.

IS YOUR BASIC IDEA that HUMANS are SENSE-MAKING creatures?

YES, BUT WE ARE ALSO PREDICTING CREATURES, WE HAVE VARIOUS LEVELS of RISK TOLERANCE for PREDICTIONS, WE LIKE TO be APPRECIATED, WE ARE PRACTICING and IMPROVING CREATURES, and WE SHOULD be ABLE to WALK in OTHER PEOPLE'S SHOES and SEE their WORLD.

REFLECTION is more like LOOKING into THE MIRROR. IT IS a KIND of thinking THAT CONSISTS in CONSTRUING A SUBJECT OVER in the MIND and GIVING it SERIOUS thought, IT CAN lead TO A STATE of DOUBT, UNCERTAINTY, or DIFFICULTY.

JOHN DEWEY

IT involves COMING BACK and THEN coming BACK in A NEW WAY.

LET'S KEEP talking

LAD OS FORTSÆTTE VORES SAMTALE.

Steen: As we already have stated, in German and in Danish we have two words that you only have one word for in the English-speaking world: experience. The first meaning of the word is related to things happening all the time. I see and experience a movie, experience the protagonist in a novel, experience the taste of the beer, etc. And this experience form is called *Erlebnis* in German and *oplevelse* in Danish, but when you elaborate and reflect profoundly upon your experience and they become embedded in your life story, you call the experience form *Erfahrung* in German and *erfaring* in Danish.

How you grasp and interpret the most-often unforeseen events in life become – so to speak – 'inscribed' in your conscious and unconscious, mental and bodily structure of your profound experience – qualifying your "body-thoughts", as my friend, the Danish philosopher Ole Fogh Kirkeby, would express it (Kirkeby 1994). As an enigmatic and unforgettable echo of a great quote of Deleuze, Kirkeby proclaims that it is a task for every one of us to make the world worthy of what could happen to it – and not the least to us (Kirkeby 2004; Deleuze 1990/1969: 149–150).

With these differentiations on the table, I have a question for you which I find pretty interesting, and nearly cannot wait to hear you reply. Can the experience (*Erfahrung* in German) of impact be positive even though the impact was experienced (*Erlebnis* in German) as being negative? Meaning that what happened in class could provoke – as an example – students to protest against the teacher's plans, ideas, and arguments. Meaning that the impact is low – or even negative – because the student or the pupil did not realize the expectations of the educational set-up. But the impact should actually be high – or positive – because the student really learned something that day.

John: That certainly does happen, and so often we can derive the positive from the negative experience. Particularly if the experience leads to negation of previous beliefs, learning about how to adapt and improve next time, and consider the conditions that led to the negative experience. One of the outcomes of schooling at every age is to get students to critique and sometimes, therefore, they may have to protest about their interpretations of the teachers' plans.

The critiques need to be framed with the respect required for them to be heard. We also have to be careful about the degree of certitude or confidence that we have of our beliefs and critique. We certainly know from the psychological research that if you go into an argument with incredible confidence and you turn out to be wrong, the learning is much more profound.

I hear the two different meanings of experience and can see the claim that the former is more the stories and histories we create, but

I would still see these as the basis for our interpretations — that is, the evidence.

Steen: Yes, but my idea is, now, when you go back to your league table — and for example to your figure 0.40 — and your clue that everything we do has influence and an impact, it can be hard to put in that kind of positive negativity in the decimals, and thereby validate 'real' experiences.

John: Why don't you think of it as an outcome?

Steen: If we state something like not fulfilling the plans, coming up with other alternatives, building up a critique of the rules of the school as I stated, I think, you're not really opening for these things in your *Visible Learning* program. You're much more asking in a way where you apply positive taken-for-granted entities — for example, the teacher role, the learning plan goal, two teachers helping one another, the size of class, etc. But how do you bring an invitation for the positive negative into your field of educational statistics? Meaning, for example, in the everyday life-world — outside schools and universities — that you can learn the 'lesson' being rejected by a woman and maybe find someone you love better. You can even learn from being harmed by someone or by reading very demanding, indigestible, and 'tough' theoretical texts.

John: Obviously, you're stretching the argument here because if you look at some of the methods that are very successful on the *Visible Learning* work, they encourage that. Or take some of the low effects; they should scare us into action. So often a low effect is misinterpreted as of no value, but the low effect should cause us to question. For example, the low effect of teachers' subject matter knowledge certainly has spurred me into action to ask why it is so low. Some of the other effects actually encourage you to do exactly what you are asking for.

Steen: They encourage that?

John: . . . For example, by reciprocal teaching. It encourages questioning. It encourages summarizing. It encourages clarifying, and encourages critique. It is based on teaching the students the strategies of enquiry, questioning, seeking evidence, experiencing particularly in the second sense of the word.

Steen: Yes, but I guess the normal way to think will be, "Here we have a class and we have some goals, and we know what they should achieve. If you don't achieve the goals, it's bad."

John: If you go to that example, you're right, and this is why I'm a fan of Michael Scriven's argument about goal-free evaluation (Scriven 1991). The teacher can have all those goals, but as the person coming in as the evaluator, I don't want to know what those goals are. I want to see what the students actually do and say. Can I see the goals manifest in the actions, behaviors, and in the voices of the students?

Steen: So actually, you think that straight and definitive goals, they can be both positive and negative, so to speak.

John: Yes, that is indeed what I mean.

Steen: So it's the same value of the different so-called factors that you're bringing in. But my worry is, I would say, and I can see that these negative experiences – that are actually being positive – and all these open critical tensions and dilemmas, they risk vanishing and not to be invited in school planning.

People as sense-making and practicing creatures

Steen: I have been wondering about this question. Is your basic idea that humans are sense-making creatures, that humans are destined and doomed to meaning as a *conditio sine qua non* (an indispensable condition)?

John: Yes, but not only sense-making, we are also predicting machines. We like a sense of predictability, but we also like to predict (some more cautious and some ambitiously so). It comes back also to our notion of tolerance of risk. Some people can tolerate risk and ideas much more than others. The more important thing is that we like making sense of our world, we like explanations, we like predictability. But then there's a problem as it is that which we do not know, it is questioning and adapting (and sometimes discarding) our narratives about the world that is the essence of education. We do not go to school to learn that which we already know. In that sense the brain is a great predictor of errors, and grows and thrives because of what we do not know. Yes, some covet predictability and their sense-making so much so that they are closed to opportunities, never allow critique, and just keep piling in the facts – oh so often this is the case with the students we label 'gifted'. And then, usually in their early teens, when new ideas open up, when they are asked to learn new domains, they can collapse as they do not have the learning strategies or openness to fail, to be wrong, and to learn from these errors.

I think we need a better word than 'sense-making' and 'predictability'. We also need a sense of appreciation, and this is where respect for self and others comes in because I may be a sense-making creature, but if I don't understand and explore how you (the other person) make sense, I'm missing an opportunity of me being a sense-maker. It helps if I can walk in your shoes and see your views of the world. I think the notion is learning to be your own teacher.

Steen: We then seem to have three different views on man: sense-making, predicting, and appreciating others. And then there must be also a fourth one, that we are practicing creatures. More or less all the time we're trying to improve what we are doing, as individuals, and as humanity.

John: Exactly.

Steen: Over and over again we try to do it better. We try to change, shift gears, maybe we have the courage and need to experiment ...

John: Also understood.

Steen: We try to improve the argument, or playing the guitar, or throwing a ball in Australian football, or whatever. So you are probably also a practicing, exercising, and training social creature – not the least in education, meaning that *Bildung* and *Übung* (German for practicing; see also Sloterdijk 2013/2009) are congenial both as concepts and as lived educational experience. In practicing, we enter self-qualifying feedback-loops, changing us a little bit all the time.

Final thoughts on reflection

John: And I still don't understand Luhmann well enough and I want to. Reflection is pretty essential to sense-making. And it's probably the most misunderstood concept since the American MIT philosopher Donald A. Schön wrote *The Reflective Practitioner* 35 years ago (Schön 1983). And when I go back and read Schön, I think he was actually pretty reasonable. But people have misinterpreted it and see reflection as more like looking into the mirror. Schön was more nuanced than this, and he introduced the notion of reflection-in-action and reflection-on-action.

He argued that reflection-*in*-action is like 'back talk' where teachers put a plan into action, and the introduction of this action then 'talks back' or provides the source of reflection to the teacher. This involves the ability to think on your feet and making the moment-by-moment decisions that teachers make during their teaching. Reflecting-*on*-action so as to engage in a process of continuous learning. This involves reliving the experience, noticing what was going on, critically analyzing the situation, and reframing to capture new understanding.

Steen: I have to re-read that.

John: Dewey considered reflection as the kind of thinking that consists in construing a subject over in the mind and giving it serious thought; it can lead to a state of doubt, uncertainty, or difficulty (Dewey 1933). Your 'mate' Habermas also saw it generating knowledge (Habermas 1971). Then along came Schön, and as Moon claimed his notions of reflection had been subject to no better testing and had no more claims to be right, despite the widespread adoption of his work over others (Schön 1983; Moon 2000).

   Most of the reflection work in education can be traced back to Schön, especially his distinction between the processes of reflection-in-action and reflection-on-action. I think it is a hard ask to consider reflection-in-action in busy, buzzy classrooms, and too often reflection-on-action occurs when something does not go according to plan (which of course is a good notion). But something going wrong depends on the mind-frames of teachers, on their sense, who is responsible for the doubt (the teacher or the student). But far too rarely are these reflections shared, contested by or informed by others, and are only 'seen' by the teacher who often then claims privileged viewpoints.

   That's where all this 'teacher is a reflective practitioner' comes from, and the intent is great, but the operation has often become too narrow. Too often, it is reflection in the sense of looking back. Given so much in the classroom is not seen or heard by the teacher, our main interest in such reflection is: Why did they recall this rather than that? And there are then so many biases in our reflecting, most of all confirmation bias.

Steen: What is actually interesting about *reflexio*, from Latin, is that it both has to do with lights and sounds and how they come back – so to speak – but also deals with, for example, how bending branches and trees can be followed by a situation where they 'manage' to be flexible and return to their original shape and position. So, as a word, *reflexio* also possesses this recursive logic, to recreate the same form.

   But then, the thing is that you can also talk about a second- and a third-order reflection, as Luhmann does in his communication theory of observational logics – and philosophers and sociologists can also debate intensively and for years whether or not reflection's fundamental place is the individual human mind or consciousness (Luhmann 1998).

John: Yeah, that's good.

Steen: This utmost delicate relation between maintaining, qualifying, and reshaping the form makes you in a way able to stand up, experience, and encounter the world in ever new ways. So *reflexio* is this doubling of coming back and then coming back in a new way.

John: Yes, especially the coming back in a new way – but so often we need others to help us reflect, as we have but one view, and often a very selective view of what happened. We are spending a lot of research time experimenting with ways to help the teachers 'see' what happened so they have more data to thence reflect. Take, for example, when we ask teachers what percentage of time they talk in classrooms. The modal answer is 'too much', followed by about 40%. But it is almost double this percentage. They ask 150 to 200 questions a day, talk about 80% to 90% of the time, and this talk and questions are dominated by surface-level comments (about the facts, the details, the already known content). Why would we care about teacher reflection on the 20% only they recall – especially if they have strong confirmation bias.

This experience of content-dominated teacher talk is what the students experience, but too often the teacher reflection is anecdotes where the student does some interesting, deeper comment, and so on, and this gets generalized inappropriately. We have built an app (Visible Classroom: https://visibleclassroom.com/), so that teachers can get a transcript (with high levels of accuracy) immediately; and automatically coded for some critical factors – and it is instant. They can also get their talk transferred straight to the students' laptops or whiteboard, so students have more than one chance to *hear* what the teacher has said and requested, and students can rate their learning to then feed back to the teacher to begin to *hear* their impact. After about ten hours we can see and come to know some major enhancements in how then teachers interact. Right now, there is an RCT in place in the UK with this tool, and we continue to improve it.

My point is that I struggle with the usual reflection based on simple recall.

Steen: In 1943, French philosopher Jean–Paul Sartre defined reflection (*réflexion*) this way in his "Key to special terminology" to one of his main philosophical works: "The attempt on the part of consciousness to become its own object. 'Reflection is a type of being in which the For–itself is in order to be itself what it is'" (*Being and Nothingness* 1998/1943: 634).

One might probably say that the self-reflective processes in today's society are becoming self-referential and that they are 'lifted out' of the inner conscious field of the individual's mind and take place – and therefore have to be scrutinized and studied, thoroughly – in different communication spheres. The privileged focus point is not destined and doomed to be the individual consciousness after the linguistic turn in the second half of the 20th century, and the rise of reflexive sociology, intersubjective communication theory, and system theory.

Inspired by Luhmann's concepts of first-, second-, and third-order observations – but also reflecting(!) upon our **vivid, pluritopic, multilayered, and unforeseen** exchanges on the purpose of education during the last days – one might say that we have both used first-order observations as take-offs (what is happening in education around us, how are governments 'policing', and pupils, students, and teachers 'doing'); second-order observations (what is stated in our and others' books and articles, etc.); third-order observations (including attempts to interpret, challenge, and critique each other's observations and arguments); and fourth-order observations (attempts to find common ways of reasoning and/or consensus on dissensus – now and then even doing our best to try to revitalize the heritage of the German *Bildung* concept and wide tradition and let it have a profound encounter with the empirical turn in education [like meta-studies, *Visible Learning* programs, impact figures, etc.]).

That was indeed a long sentence, maybe too long and dense.

A fifth-order observation probably has to come from you, dear reader.

So here is a colon: . . . To be continued.

References

Adorno, T. W. (2004/1966). *Negative Dialectics*. Taylor & Francis E-Library.

Adorno, T. W. (2005/1951). *Minima Moralia. Reflections on a Damaged Life* (e.g. Appendix IX: Procrustes). London and New York: Verso Books.

Alexander, P. A. (2000). Research news and comment: Toward a model of academic development: Schooling and the acquisition of knowledge. *Educational Researcher*, 29(2), 28–44.

Alexander, P. A. (2004). A model of domain learning: Reinterpreting expertise as a multidimensional, multistage process. In: D. Y. Dai & R. J. Sternberg (eds.). *Motivation, Emotion, and Cognition: Integrative Perspectives on Intellectual Functioning and Development* (pp. 273–298). Mahwah, NJ: Erlbaum.

Anderson, C. (2008). The end of theory: The data deluge makes the scientific method obsolete. *Wired* (magazine), 16(7), 16–17.

Arendt, H. (1958). *The Human Condition*. Chicago: University of Chicago Press.

Arendt, H. (1971). *The Life of the Mind: One/Thinking*. New York: A Harvest Book.

Augustine, S. (1876). *The Confessions*. Edinburgh: Clark.

Barber, M., Moffit, A. & Kihn, P. (2010). *Deliverology 101: A Field Guide for Educational Leaders*. Thousand Oaks, CA: Corwin Press.

Batchelor, D. (2008). Have students got a voice? In: R. Barnett & R. Di Napoli (eds.). *Changing Identities in Higher Education: Voicing Perspectives*. London and New York: Routledge.

Beck, U. (1985). *Risk Society: Towards a New Modernity*. London: Sage.

Benedick, T. & Keteyian, A. (2018). *Tiger Woods*. Ossining, NY: Simon & Shuster.

Berckley, J. (2018). *What Are the Observable Correlates of the Aha! Moment, and How Does This Moment Relate to Moving from Surface to Deep Thinking?* Unpublished doctoral dissertation, University of Houston.

Bernstein, B. (1971). *Class, Codes and Control: Theoretical Studies Towards a Sociology of Language*. London: Routledge & Kegan Paul.

Biesta, G. (2013). *The Beautiful Risk of Education*. New York: Routledge.

Biesta, G. (2017). *The Rediscovery of Teaching*. New York: Routledge.

Biggs, J. B. & Collis, K. F. (1982). *Evaluating the Quality of Learning: The SOLO Taxonomy (Structure of the Observed Learning Outcome)*. New York: Academic Press.

Blatchford, P. (2011). *Reassessing the Impact of Teaching Assistants: How Research Challenges Practice and Policy*. London: Routledge.

Bloch, E. (1986/1954–1959). *The Principle of Hope*. Cambridge, MA: MIT Press.

Caplan, B. (2018). *The Case Against Education: Why the Education System Is a Waste of Time and Money*. Princeton: Princeton University Press.

Carroll, L. (1871). *Alice Through the Looking Glass*.

Christensen, S. & Krejsler, J. (2015). *Evidens – kampen om 'viden der virker'*. PUF's skriftserie Nr. 2. København: FOA.

Christie, N. (2020/1971). *If Schools Didn't Exist*. L. Cone & J. S. Wiewiura (ed. & trans.). Cambridge, MA: MIT Press.

Clay, M. (1991). *Becoming Literate*. Portsmouth, NH: Heinemann.

Clay, M. (2005). *Literacy Lessons Designed for Individuals: Why? When? and How?* Portsmouth, NH: Heinemann Educational Books.

Clinton, J. M. & Hattie, J. A. C. (2005). *When the Language of Schooling Enters the Home: Evaluation of the Flaxmere Project*, June. Final report to Ministry of Education. www.educationcounts.govt.nz/publications/schooling/10001.

Clinton, J. M., Hattie, J. A. C. & Nawab, D. (2018). The good teacher: Our best teachers are inspired, influential and passionate. In: M. Harring (ed.). *Handbook for School Pedagogics* (pp. 880–888). Munster, Germany: Waxmann.

Cook, T. D., Scriven, M., Coryn, C. L. & Evergreen, S. D. (2010). Contemporary thinking about causation in evaluation: A dialogue with Tom Cook and Michael Scriven. *American Journal of Evaluation*, 31(1), 105–117.

Cuban, L. (1984). *How Teachers Taught: Constancy and Change in American Classrooms, 1890–1980*. Research on Teaching Monograph Series. ERIC Document: https://eric.ed.gov/?id=ED383498.

Danielson, C. (2011). *Enhancing Professional Practice: A Framework for Teaching*. Alexandria, VA: ASCD.

Danielson, C. (2012). Observing classroom practice. *Educational Leadership*, 70(3), 32–37.

Deleuze, G. (1990/1969). *The Logic of Sense*. London: The Athlon Press.

Deleuze, G. & Guattari, F. (1996/1991). *What Is Philosophy?* New York: Columbia University Press.

Deming, D. J. (2017). The growing importance of social skills in the labor market. *The Quarterly Journal of Economics*, 132(4), 1593–1640.

Derrida, J. (2002/1999). *The University Without Condition*. Cambridge: Cambridge University Press.

Dewey, J. (1933). *How We Think: A Restatement of the Relation of Reflective Thinking to the Educative Process*. New York: DC Heath.

DeWitt, P. (2012). *Dignity for All: Safeguarding LGBT Students*. Thousand Oaks, CA: Corwin Press.

Dochy, F., Segers, M., Van den Bossche, P. & Gijbels, D. (2003). Effects of problem-based learning: A meta-analysis. *Learning and Instruction*, 13(5), 533–568.

Durkheim, É. (1956/1922). *Education and Sociology*. Glencoe, IL: University of California, Free Press.

Ehrenberg, A. (1998). *La fatigue d'être soi: dépression et société*. Paris: Éditions Odile Jacob.

Fadel, C., Bialik, M. & Trilling, B. (2015). *Four-Dimensional Education: The Competencies Learners Need to Succeed*. Boston, MA: Center for Curriculum Redesign.

Flexner, A. (1939). The usefulness of useless knowledge. *Harpers*, 179, June–November.

Florida, R. (2005). *Cities and the Creative Class*. London: Routledge.

Fogg, L. & Fiske, D. W. (1993). Foretelling the judgments of reviewers and editors. *American Psychologist*, 48(3), 293.

Forlin, C., Douglas, G. & Hattie, J. (1996). Inclusive practices: How accepting are teachers? *International Journal of Disability, Development and Education*, 43, 119–133.

Foucault, M. (1980). *Power/Knowledge: Selected Interviews and Other Writings, 1972–1997*. New York: Pantheon Books.

Foucault, M. (1984). *The Foucault Reader*. P. Rabinow (ed.). New York: Pantheon Books.

Freire, P. (1970/1968). *Pedagogy of the Oppressed*. New York: Herder and Herder.

Fuchs, T. (2006). Neuromythologien. Mutmaßungen über die Bewegkräfte der Hirnforschung. *Jahrbuch für Psychotherapie, Philosophie und Kultur No. 1 & Jahresschrift für skeptisches Denken*, 36.

Fuchs, T. (2009). *Das Gehirn – ein Beziehungsorgan. Eine phänomenologisch-ökologische Konzeption*. Stuttgart: Verlag Kohlhammer.

Fuchs, T. (2018). *Ecology of the Brain: The Phenomenology and Biology of the Embodied Mind*. Oxford: Oxford University Press.

Fuchs, T. & De Jaegher, H. (2009). Enactive intersubjectivity: Participatory sense-making and mutual incorporation. *Phenomenology and the Cognitive Sciences*, 8(4), 465–486. www.klinikum.uniheidelberg.de/fileadmin/zpm/psychatrie/fuchs/Enactive_Intersubjectivity.pdf.

Fullan, M. (2015). Leadership from the middle. *Education Canada*, 55(4), 22–26.

Gadamer, H.-G. (1989/1960). *Truth and Method*. London: Sheed & Ward.

Gage, N. (1991). The obviousness of social and educational research results. *Educational Researcher*, 20(1), 10–16.

Gardner, H. (1983). *Frames of Mind: The Theory of Multiple Intelligences*. New York: Basic Books Google Scholar.

Gilligan, C. (1982). *In a Different Voice*. Cambridge, MA: Harvard University Press.

Glass, G. V. (1976). Primary, secondary, and meta-analysis of research. *Educational Researcher*, 5(10), 3–8.

Goffman, E. (1959). *The Presentation of Self in Everyday Life*. New York: Doubleday Anchor.

Golding, W. (1954). *Lord of the Flies*. London: Faber and Faber.

Gorz, A. (2010). *The Immaterial*. New York: Seagull Books.

Griffin, P. & Care, E. (eds.). (2014). *Assessment and Teaching of 21st Century Skills: Methods and Approach*. Rotterdam, Netherlands: Springer.

Habermas, J. (1971). *Knowledge and Human Interests*. London: Heinemann.

Habermas, J. (1989). *The Theory of Communicative Action*. Vol. 2. Cambridge: Polity Press.

Habermas, J. (1991). *The Theory of Communicative Action*. Vol. 1. Cambridge: Polity Press.

Haig, B. (2014). *Investigating the Psychological World: Scientific Method in the Behavioral Sciences*. Cambridge, MA: MIT Press.

Haig, B. (2018). *The Philosophy of Quantitative Methods: Understanding Statistics*. Oxford: Oxford University Press.

Hardt, M. & Negri, A. (2009). *Commonwealth*. Cambridge, MA: The Belknap Press, Harvard University Press.

Hart, B. & Risley, T. R. (2003). The early catastrophe: The 30 million word gap by age 3. *American Educator*, 27(1), 4–9.

Hattie, J. (1992a). *Self-Concept*. Mahwah, NJ: Erlbaum.

Hattie, J. (1992b). Measuring the effects of schooling. *Australian Journal of Education*, 36(1), 5–13.

Hattie, J. (2009). *Visible Learning: A Synthesis of Over 800 Meta-Analyses Relating to Achievement*. London: Routledge.

Hattie, J. (2010). On being a 'critic and conscience of society': The role of the education academic in public debates. *New Zealand Journal of Educational Studies*, 45(1), 85.

Hattie, J. (2012). *Visible Learning for Teachers: Maximizing Impact on Learning*. New York: Routledge.

Hattie, J. (2015a). *What Doesn't Work in Education: The Politics of Distraction*. Open Ideas at Pearsons. www.pearson.com/hattie/distractions.html.

Hattie, J. (2015b). *What Works Best in Education: The Politics of Collaborative Expertise*. London: Pearson.

Hattie, J., Brown, G. T., Ward, L., Irving, S. E. & Keegan, P. J. (2006). Formative evaluation of an educational assessment technology innovation: Developers' insights into assessment tools for teaching and learning (asTTle). *Journal of Multi-Disciplinary Evaluation*, 5(3), 1–54.

Hattie, J. & Donoghue, G. M. (2018). A model of learning: Optimizing the effectiveness of learning strategies. In: K. Illeris (ed.). *Contemporary Theories of Learning*. Oxon: Routledge.

Hattie, J. & Hamilton, A. (2018). *Cargo Cults Must Die*. www.visiblelearningplus.com/groups/cargo-cults-must-die-white-paper.

Hattie, J. & Marsh, H. W. (1996). The relationship between research and teaching: A meta-analysis. *Review of Research in Education*, 66, 507–542.

Hattie, J., Myers, J. E. & Sweeney, T. J. (2004). A factor structure of wellness: Theory, assessment, analysis, and practice. *Journal of Counseling & Development*, 82(3), 354–364.

Hattie, J. & Purdie, N. (1998). The SOLO model: Addressing fundamental measurement issues. In: B. Dart & G. Boulton-Lewis (eds.). *Teaching and Learning in Higher Education*. Herndon, VA: Stylus Publishing.

Hattie, J. & Toscano, M. (2018). John Hattie on interpretation, the story of research, and the necessity of falsifiability: In dialogue with Maurizio Toscano. In: J.

Quay, J. Bleazby, S. Stolz, M. Toscano & R. Webster (eds.). *Theory and Philosophy in Education Research: Methodological Dialogues*. Oxon: Routledge.

Hattie, J. & Yates, G. (2014). *Visible Learning and the Science of How We Learn*. New York: Routledge.

Hattie, J. & Zierer, K. (2018). *10 Mindframes for Visible Learning: Teaching for Success*. New York: Routledge.

Hedges, L. V. & Olkin, I. (1990). *Statistical Methods for Meta-Analysis*. Orlando, FL: Academic Press.

Hegel, G. W. F. (1979/1807). *Phenomenology of the Spirit*. Oxford: Oxford University Press.

Hirsch Jr., E. D. (2010). *The Schools We Need: And Why We Don't Have Them*. New York: Anchor.

Humboldt, W. V. (1960/1793). Theorie der Bildung des Menschen. In: *Schriften zur Anthropologie und Geschichte*. Werke in Fünf Bänden I. Stuttgart: J.G. Cotta'sche Buchhandlung.

Hunter, M. C. (1982). *Mastery Teaching*. Thousand Oaks, CA: Corwin Press.

Hyldgaard, K. (2017). Pædagogikkens placebo. In: T. A. Rømer, L. Tanggaard & S. Brinkmann (eds.). *Uren pædagogik 3*. Aarhus: Klim.

Illeris, K. (2004). *The Three Dimensions of Learning: Contemporary Learning Theory in the Tension Field Between the Cognitive, the Emotional and the Social*. Denmark: Krieger Publishing Company.

Illeris, K. (2018). *Contemporary Theories of Learning. Learning Theories . . . In Their Own Words*. New York: Routledge.

Imms, W., Cleveland, B. & Fisher, K. (eds.). (2016). *Evaluating Learning Environments: Snapshots of Emerging Issues, Methods and Knowledge*. Rotterdam, Netherlands: Springer.

Kane, T. J. & Staiger, D. O. (2012). *Gathering Feedback for Teaching: Combining High-Quality Observations with Student Surveys and Achievement Gains*. Research Paper. MET Project. Bill & Melinda Gates Foundation.

Kant, I. (1971/1803). *Education*. Ann Abor: The University of Michigan Press.

Kant, I. (1999/1781). *Critique of Pure Reason*. Cambridge: Cambridge University Press.

Kant, I. (2007/1795). *Perpetual Peace: A Philosophical Essay* (Zum ewigen Frieden. Ein philosophischer Entwurf). Minneapolis: Filiquarian Publishing, LLC.

Kant, I. (2008/1790). *Critique of Judgement*. Oxford: Oxford World's Classics.

Kauffmann, O. (2017). Usynlig læring. In: *Turbulens*. http://turbulens.net/usynlig-laering/.

Kennedy, M. M. (2005). *Inside Teaching*. Cambridge, MA: Harvard University Press.

Kennedy, M. M. (2008). Contributions of qualitative research to research on teacher qualifications. *Educational Evaluation and Policy Analysis*, 30(4), 344–367.

Kierkegaard, S. A. (1959/1843). *Either/Or*. Vol. 1–2. Princeton: Anchor.

Kirkeby, O. F. (1994). *Begivenhed og krops-tanke. En fænomenologisk-hermeneutisk analyse*. Aarhus: Forlaget Modtryk.

Kirkeby, O. F. (2004). The eventum tantum: To make the world worthy of what could happen to it. *Ephemera, Critical Dialogues on Organisations*, 26, October.

Klafki, W. (2000). Didaktik analysis as the core of preparation of instruction. In: I. Westbury, S. Hopmann & K. Riquarts (eds.). *Teaching as a Reflective Practice: The German Didaktik Tradition* (pp. 139–159). Mahwah, NJ: Erlbaum.

Knudsen, H. (2017). John Hattie: 'I'm a statistician, I'm not a theoretician'. *Nordic Journal in Studies of Educational Policy*, 3, #3. www.tandfonline.com/doi/full/10.1080/20020317.2017.1415048.

Koestler, A. (1964). *The Act of Creation*. New York: Macmillan.

Kohlberg, L. (1981). *Essays on Moral Development.*Vol. 1. San Francisco: Harper & Row.

Koselleck, R. (2006). Zur anthropologischen und semantischen Struktur der Bildung. In: *Begriffsgeschichten. Studien zur Semantik und Pragmatik der politischen und sozialen Sprache*. Frankfurt am Main: Suhrkamp Verlag.

Kousholt, K. (2016). Testing as social practice: Analysing testing in classes of young children from the children's perspective. *Theory & Psychology*, 26(3).

Kozol, J. (2012). *Savage Inequalities: Children in America's Schools*. New York: Broadway Books.

Krejsler, J. B., Olsson, U. & Petersson, K. (2014). The transnational grip on Scandinavian education reforms: The open method of coordination challenging national policy-making. *Nordic Studies in Education*, 34(3), 172–186.

Larsen, S. N. (2004). Evalueringsfeber. *Dansk Sociologi*, 1.

Larsen, S. N. (2011). Der er ingen evidens for *evidens* – refleksioner omkring en magtfuld illusion. *Dansk pædagogisk Tidsskrift*, 1.

Larsen, S. N. (2012). Is capitalism dying out? (review of André Gorz. *The Immaterial*). *Ephemera*, 4.

Larsen, S. N. (2013a). The plasticity of the brain – an analysis of the contemporary taste for and limits to neuroplasticity. In: *Neurolex . . . Dura Lex*. Wellington, New Zealand. www.victoria.ac.nz/law/nzacl/PDFS/SPECIAL%20ISSUES/NEUROLEX/CP%20Neurolex%20Book%20Web%20Alpdf.

Larsen, S. N. (2013b). *'Know thy impact'* – kritiske tanker i forbindelse med Hattie-effektens evidente gennemslag (review of John Hattie. *Synlig læring – for lærere.* Frederikshavn: Dafolo 2013). *Dansk pædagogisk Tidsskrift*, 3.

Larsen, S. N. (2014a). Efterskrift: Hvordan undgå at læring bliver til en kliché? In: C. Aabro (ed.). *Læring i daginstitutioner – et erobringsprojekt*. Frederikshavn: Dafolo Forlag.

Larsen, S. N. (2014b). Compulsory creativity – a critique of contemporary cognitive capitalism. *Culture Unbound*, 6. www.cultureunbound.ep.liu.se/v6/a09/cu14v6a09.pdf.

Larsen, S. N. (2014c). Evidenstænkningens videnskabeliggørelse som videnspolitik (review of John Hattie and Gregory Yates. *Visible Learning and the Science of How We Learn*. London and New York: Routledge 2014). *Dansk pædagogisk Tidsskrift*, 3.

Larsen, S. N. (2014d). Kritik – et essay. *Social Kritik*, 140.

Larsen, S. N. (2015a). Blind spots in John Hattie's evidence credo. *Journal of Academic Perspectives*, 1. www.journalofacademicperspectives.com/back-issues/volume-2015/volume-2015-no-1/.

Larsen, S. N. (2015b). Top-down university governance eradicates thinking and good teaching. In: E. Westergaard & J. S. Wiewiura (eds.). *On the Facilitation of the Academy*. Rotterdam. www.sensepublishers.com/media/2288-on-the-facilitation-of-the-academy.pdf.

Larsen, S. N. (2015c). *Dannelse – en samtidskritisk og idéhistorisk revitalisering*. Munkebo: Fjordager.

Larsen, S. N. (2015d). Evidens – 19 kritiske aforismer. *Social Kritik*, 143.

Larsen, S. N. (2016a). *At ville noget med nogen. Filosofiske og samtidskritiske fragmenter om dannelseog pædagogik*. Aarhus: Turbine.

Larsen, S. N. (2016b). Runddans på missionshotellet (review of John Hattie et al. *Visible Learning into Action*. London and New York: Routledge 2015). *Dansk pædagogisk Tidsskrift*, 1.

Larsen, S. N. (2016c). Hvilke konsekvenser har målstyringen af (ud)dannelse for universitetsansatte og -studerende? In: M. Friis Andersen & L. Tanggaard (eds.). *Tæller vi det der tæller. Målstyring og standardisering i arbejdslivet. Moderne Arbejdsliv # 5*. Aarhus: KLIM.

Larsen, S. N. (2017a). Biestas blinde vinkler. In: L. Grandjean & O. Morsing (eds.). *Uddannelse for en menneskelig fremtid. Gerd Biestas pædagogiske tænkning*. Aarhus: KLIM.

Larsen, S. N. (2017b). 'Know thy impact' – blinde vinkler i John Hatties evidens-credo. In: J. Bjerre et al. (eds.). *Hattie på dansk. Evidenstænkningen I et kritisk og konstruktivt perspektiv*. København: Hans Reitzels Forlag.

Larsen, S. N. (2017c). What is education? – A critical essay. In: A. Bech Jørgensen et al. (eds.). *What Is Education?* Copenhagen: DUF, Problema. www.whatiseducation.net/wp-content/uploads/2017/09/what-is-education.pdf.

Larsen, S. N. (2018a). Formålet med at uddanne sig er ikke at honorere givne læringsmål (review of John Hattie and Klaus Zierer. *10 Mindframes for Visible Learning: Teaching for Success*. London and New York: Routledge 2018). *Information*, 24(3). www.information.dk/moti/anmeldelse/2018/03/formaalet-uddanne-honorere-givne-laeringsmaal.

Larsen, S. N. (2018b). A critical essay on the exercise of critique: On the impossibility of reconciling ontology and epistemology. *Danish Yearbook of Philosophy*, 51.

Larsen, S. N. (2019a). Blindness in seeing – a philosophical critique of the *Visible Learning* paradigm in education. *Education Sciences*, 9(1), 47.

Larsen, S. N. (2019b). Hvordan det begrænset synlige blev det virkelige. In: D. Dalum Christoffersen & K. Stender Petersen (eds.). *Er der evidens for evidens?* Frederiksberg: Samfundslitteratur.

Larsen, S. N. (2019c). Imagine the university without condition. *Danish Yearbook of Philosophy*, 52.

Larsen, S. N. & Pedersen, I. K. (eds.). (2011). *Sociologisk leksikon*. Copenhagen: Hans Reitzels Forlag.

Lortie-Forgues, H. & Inglis, M. (2019). Rigorous large-scale educational RCTs are often uninformative: Should we be concerned? *Educational Researcher*, 48(3), 158–166.

Luhmann, N. (1998). *Die Gesellschaft der Gesellschaft 1.* Frankfurt am Main: Suhrkamp Verlag.

Luhmann, N. (2002). *Die Erziehungssystem der Gesellschaft.* Frankfurt am Main: Suhrkamp Verlag.

Luria, A. R. (1976). *Cognitive Development: Its Cultural and Social Foundations.* Cambridge, MA: Harvard University Press.

Marsden, J. (2019). *The Art of Growing Up.* Australia: Macmillan.

Marsh, H. W. & Hattie, J. A. (2002). The relation between research productivity and teaching: Complementary, antagonistic, or independent constructs? *Journal of Higher Education,* 73, 603–641.

Marx, K. (1976/1867). *Capital: A Critique of Political Economy.* Vol. 1. Harmondsworth: Penguin, New Left Review.

Marzano, R. J. (2018). *The Handbook for the New Art and Science of Teaching.* Bloomington, IN: Solution Tree.

McGraw, K. O. & Wong, S. P. (1992). A common language effect size statistic. *Psychological Bulletin,* 111(2), 361–365.

Meyer, G. (2016). *Lykkens kontrollanter.* København: Jurist- og Økonomforbundets Forlag.

Mitchell, D. (2007). *What Really Works in Special and Inclusive Education: Using Evidence-Based Teaching Strategies.* London: Routledge.

Moon, J. A. (2000). *Reflection in Learning and Professional Development.* London: Kogan Page.

Moulier Boutang, Y. (2011/2007). *Cognitive Capitalism.* Cambridge: Polity Press.

Musgrave, A. (1993). *Common Sense, Science and Scepticism: A Historical Introduction to the Theory of Knowledge.* Cambridge: Cambridge University Press.

Nietzsche, F. (2009/1889). *Twilight of the Idols, or, How to Philosophize with a Hammer* (Götzendämmerung, oder, Wie man mit dem Hammer philosophiert). Oxford: Oxford University Press.

Nuthall, G. (2007). *The Hidden Lives of Learners.* Wellington: NZCER Press.

Pedersen, O. K. (2011). *Konkurrencestaten.* København: Gyldendal.

Peters, M. A. (2013). *Education, Philosophy and Politics: The Selected Works of Michael A. Peters.* London: Routledge.

Pfost, M., Hattie, J., Dörfler, T. & Artelt, C. (2014). Individual differences in reading development: A review of 25 years of empirical research on Matthew effects in reading. *Review of Educational Research,* 84(2), 203–244.

Plato. (1989). *Cratylus–Parmenides–Greater Hippias–Lesser Hippias.* Loeb. Cambridge, MA: Harvard University Press.

Polanyi, M. (1962). Tacit knowing: Its bearing on some problems of philosophy. *Reviews of Modern Physics,* 34(4), 601.

Popper, K. (1945). *The Open Society and its Enemies.* New York: Routledge.

Popper, K. (1979). *Three Worlds.* Ann Arbor: University of Michigan.

Popper, K. (2002/1953). *Conjectures and Refutations: The Growth of Scientific Knowledge.* New York: Routledge.

Porter, A. C., Polikoff, M. S. & Smithson, J. (2009). Is there a de facto national intended curriculum? Evidence from state content standards. *Educational Evaluation and Policy Analysis*, 31(3), 238–268.

Purkey, W. W. & Novak, J. M. (1996). *Inviting School Success: A Self-Concept Approach to Teaching, Learning, and Democratic Practice*. Florence, KY: Wadsworth.

Rawls, J. (1971). *A Theory of Justice*. Cambridge, MA: Harvard University Press.

Ricoeur, P. (1995a). *Oneself as Another*. Chicago: University of Chicago Press.

Ricoeur, P. (1995b). Ethical and theological considerations on the golden rule. In: M. I. Wallace (ed.). *Figuring the Sacred, Religion, Narrative, and Imagination*. Minneapolis: Fortress Press.

Rømer, T. A., Tanggaard, L. & Brinkmann, S. (eds.). (2011). *Uren pædagogik*. Aarhus: Klim.

Rømer, T. A., Tanggaard, L. & Brinkmann, S. (eds.). (2014). *Uren pædagogik 2*. Aarhus: Klim.

Rømer, T. A., Tanggaard, L. & Brinkmann, S. (eds.). (2017). *Uren pædagogik 3*. Aarhus: Klim.

Rorty, R. (1989). *Contingency, Irony and Solidarity*. Cambridge: Cambridge University Press.

Rorty, R. (1999). *Philosophy and Social Hope*. Harmondsworth: Penguin.

Rosa, H. & Endres, W. (2016). *Resonanzpädagogik: Wenn es im Klassenzimmer knistert*. Weinheim: Beltz.

Rousseau, J. J. (1979/1762). *Emile, or On Education*. New York: Basic Books.

Safranski, R. (2003). *Wieviel Globalisierung verträgt der Mensch?* München: Carl Hanser Verlag.

Sartre, J.-P. (1998/1943). *Being and Nothingness*. London and New York: Routledge.

Schön, D. A. (1983). *The Reflective Practitioner: How Professionals Think in Action*. New York: Basic Books.

Scribner, S. & Cole, M. (1981). *The Psychology of Literacy*. Cambridge, MA: Harvard University Press.

Scriven, M. (1991). Pros and cons about goal-free evaluation. *Evaluation Practice*, 12(1), 55–62.

Sheets-Johnstone, M. (1990). *The Roots of Thinking*. Philadelphia: Temple University Press.

Simmel, G. (1910/1908). How is society possible? (Wie ist Gesellschaft möglich?) *American Journal of Sociology*, 16(3), 372–391, November.

Sinek, S. (2019). *The Infinite Game*. Penguin.

Skovmand, K. (2016). *Uden mål og med – forenklede fælles mål?* København: Hans Reitzels Forlag.

Skovmand, K. (2019a). *I bund og grund – reformer uden fundament?* København: Hans Reitzels Forlag.

Skovmand, K (2019b). *Folkeskolen – efter læringsmålstyringen*. København: Hans Reitzels Forlag.

Sloterdijk, P. (2013/2009). *You Must Change Your Life*. Cambridge and Malden: Polity Press.

Snook, I., O'Neill, J., Clark, J., O'Neill, A. M. & Openshaw, R. (2009). Invisible learnings? A commentary on John Hattie's book – '*Visible Learning*: A synthesis of over 800 meta-analyses relating to achievement'. *New Zealand Journal of Educational Studies*, 44(1), 93.

Sperry, D. E., Sperry, L. L. & Miller, P. J. (2018). Reexamining the verbal environments of children from different socioeconomic backgrounds. *Child Development*, 1–16.

Szumski, G., Smogorzewska, J. & Karwowski, M. (2017). Academic achievement of students without special educational needs in inclusive classrooms: A meta-analysis. *Educational Research Review*, 21, 33–54.

Tayler, C., Ishimine, K., Cloney, D., Cleveland, G. & Thorpe, K. (2013). The quality of early childhood education and care services in Australia. *Australasian Journal of Early Childhood*, 38(2), 13–21.

Turkle, S. (2017). *Alone Together: Why We Expect More from Technology and Less from Each Other*. New York: Basic Books.

Vygotsky, L. S. (1997). *The Collected Works of LS Vygotsky: Problems of the Theory and History of Psychology*. Vol. 3. New York: Springer Science & Business Media.

Watkins, D. A. & Biggs, J. B. (eds.). (2001). *Teaching the Chinese Learner: Psychological and Pedagogical Perspectives*. Hong Kong: Hong Kong University Press.

Weingartner, C. & Postman, N. (1971). *Teaching as a Subversive Activity*. London: Pitman.

Westover, T. (2018). *Educated*. London: Cornerstone Digital.

Whitehead, A. N. (1959). The aims of education. *Daedalus*, 88(1), 192–205.

Wilmot, E. (1987). *Pemulwuy: The Rainbow Warrior*. McMahons Point, NSW: Weldons.

Wittgenstein, L. (1953). *Philosophical Investigations*. New York: Macmillan.

Young, M. & Muller, J. (2013). On the powers of powerful knowledge. *Review of Education*, 1(3), 229–250.

Zeichner, K. M. (1992). Conceptions of reflective teaching in contemporary US teacher education program reforms. *Reflective Teacher Education: Cases and Critiques*, 161–173.

Ziehe, T. (2004). *Øer af intensitet i et hav af rutine*. København: Politisk Revy.

Abbreviations

ABC	Australian Broadcasting Corporation
ADHD	Attention Deficit/Hyperactivity Disorder
AI	Artificial Intelligence
AIDS	Acquired Immune Deficiency Syndrome
AITSL	Australian Institute for Teachers and School Leaders
APA	American Psychological Association
C21st Skills	21st-Century Skills
DI	Direct Instructions
ECTS	European Credit Transfer System
EU	European Union
fMRI	Functional Magnetic Resonance Imaging
Gates-MET study	Gates Measures of Effective Teaching study
GPS	Global Positioning System
HALTS	Highly Accomplished and Lead Teacher(s)
MIT	Massachusetts Institute of Technology
NAPLAN	National Assessment Program–Literacy and Numeracy
NZ	New Zealand
OECD	Organisation for Economic Co-operation and Development
PISA	Programme for International Student Assessment
RCT	Randomized Controlled Trial
SES	Socioeconomic Status
SOLO	Structure of Observed Learning Outcome
UK	United Kingdom
UN	United Nations
US	United States of America
VL	*Visible Learning*

Glossary

Three-mode factor analysis, p. 7

This model can be used when you have three modes of data, such as when there are scores from tests administered using different methods (Likert, open ended, interviews) and different traits (self-concept, agreeableness, conscientiousness) – thus there are people x methods x traits; or scores administered to people over many times with ratings from self, bosses, and those who you supervise – thus there are people x times x different raters (see Law, H.G., Snyder, C.W., Hattie, J.A. & McDonald, R.P. (1984). *Multi-mode models for data analysis*. Praeger, USA. p. 687).

PISA tests, p. 31

PISA is the OECD's *Programme for International Student Assessment*; administered every 3 years, it tests 15-year-old students from over 80 countries and economies in reading, mathematics, and science (see www.oecd.org/pisa/).

Corwin, p. 10

Corwin is an independent, family-owned professional learning and publishing business based in California. Corwin has formed a long-term partnership with John Hattie and Janet Clinton to scale Visible Learning[plus] worldwide.

Skanderborg, p. 10

Skanderborg Municipality is a municipality on the Jutland peninsula in central Denmark that for three years implemented the Visible Learning[plus] professional learning program in many of their schools.

. . . to let this scriptural 'third' blossom, p. 18

Steen Nepper Larsen's attempt to emphasize that the paper (exam assessment, free essay, master thesis, etc.) in process (#3) first and foremost has to be fertilized and get a life, strength, and quality of its own right there between the writing student (#1) and the supervisor (#2), never forgetting that the student is not just destined and doomed to deliver and the supervisor to control in the world of academia.

Meta-analysis, p. 7

Meta-analysis is now a well-established form of synthesizing literature that involves finding a sample of studies, developing a single underlying continuum on which to compare results, using a metric to place effects or studies along this continuum (effect-sizes), and using moderators to explore in more detail the implications of these effects.

Popper's principle of falsification, p. 21

The Austrian-born English philosopher Karl Popper (1902–1994) argued that science progresses when we seek evidence to falsify claims or theorists; that is, asking, "What evidence would we accept that we are wrong?" and if we do not find such evidence then the theory survives.

See also: Fallibilism, p. 208

Effect-size, p. 19

An effect-size is a quantitative measure of the magnitude of a phenomenon. It can be calculated as the standardized mean difference between the two groups divided by the pooled standard deviation (e.g., between control and treatment group, or between a pre- and post-measure).

Freire, p. 28

Paulo Freire (1921–1997) was a Brazilian educator and philosopher who became the leading advocate of critical pedagogy and is among the most influential philosophers of education from this past century. His main work, *Pedagogy of the Oppressed*, should be compulsory reading for all involved in schools.

Nietzsche also said there was no such thing as 'immaculate perception', p. 31

The German philosopher Friedrich Nietzsche (1844–1900) had a chapter in his book *Thus Spoke Zarathustra* (1883–1885) arguing that the will and desire of the perceiver is critical to understanding their view of the world.

Telos, pp. 31, 218

Telos is an old Greek word meaning goal-directedness; teleology (telos + logos) is the basic conviction that there is a moving and targeting force in cosmos, nature, life, history, society, or language – often working behind the backs (i.e., under the conscious level) of human agents.

Reflective judgment, pp. 44, 45

The German philosopher Immanuel Kant's (1724–1804) famous notion of man's skills and capacity to reason and reflect critically in concrete situations in which they have to act or communicate but no strict rules for how to think and how to behave exist beforehand.

Owl of Minerva, pp. 45, 112

In retrospect – when we have learned from and qualified our experiences and sharpened our concepts and communicative and cognitive means – we might come to know the wiser, the German philosopher G.W.F. Hegel (1770–1831) claimed while he used the well-known narrative of Minerva's owl flying out in the sunset as the symbol of wisdom.

Hegel is the dynamic, dialectical, and relational philosopher par excellence, p. 45

The German philosopher G.W.F. Hegel (1770–1831) brings time, change, tensions, and conflicts into modern thinking, emphasizing how the human spirit gets transformed through its interaction with the world (e.g., via work, education, and state building).

Biesta wants to defend Emmanuel Levinas' logic of exteriority against learning regimes and constructivism, p. 52

The Dutch educational philosopher Gert Biesta (b. 1957) is inspired by and defends the French phenomenological philosopher Emmanuel Levinas' (1906–1995) view that the exteriority (the unknown, the extra-factual being) and, not least, the other human beings' otherness can never be grasped scientifically – and based on Levinas' humble 'logic', Biesta criticizes both what he considers to be the destructive traits of today's predominant 'learnification of education' and a wild-running and exaggerating constructivist approach to thinking (i.e., the idea that teachers and students are the sovereign creators of knowledge).

Biesta's idea that we should deal with things we do not know, the exteriority, the transcendental questions, ontology, and the impossible, p. 53

The Dutch educational philosopher Gert Biesta (b. 1957) claims that it is important that teachers, pupils, and students dare to cope with 'the beautiful risk of education' (= the title of one of his books) – that is, deal with fundamental questions of existence, meaning, and belonging and not just learn to reproduce what is already known (e.g., so-called facts and learning goals).

See also: Difference between epistemology and ontology, p. 323

Sloterdijk's concept of the endless second birth, p. 53

According to the German philosopher and anthropologist of practice Peter Sloterdijk (b. 1947), humans go through an endless second birth throughout life because we are not only what we are, once and for all – and in this connection it is important to acknowledge that we did not decide to get born in the first place ('the first birth') – but we have a tremendous responsibility when it comes to qualifying the second birth's content, form, and expression.

Abrichtung, p. 77

The German word for enforced socialization and upbringing that the Austrian-English philosopher Ludwig Wittgenstein (1889–1951) uses in his later writings in which he depicts how we come to live, embedded in life-forms that follow rules of language use by which we come to know the meaning of things.

Gadamer's concept of play (*gespielt werden*), p. 78

The German philosopher Hans-Georg Gadamer (1900–2002) does not think that the individual human consciousness nor the subjective reflexivity is the clue to our being in the world; instead we are played by (*gespielt werden*) the things we encounter (e.g., art works, texts, events . . .), which forces us to be engaged in processes of understanding and attempts to interpret the game of life.

See also: Hermeneutics, pp. 89, 111; Hans-Georg Gadamer, p. 111

Bloch, Adorno, Arendt, Sheets-Johnstone, p. 88

Ernst Bloch (1885–1977), Theodor W. Adorno (1903–1969), and Hannah Arendt (1906–1975) were German philosophers, and Maxine Sheets-Johnstone (b. 1930) is an American evolutionary anthropologist and groundbreaking body phenomenologist.

Teleology, p. 88

See: Telos, p. 31

Hermeneutics, pp. 89, 111

A theory and method of understanding and interpreting forms of communication, human actions, and artefacts, emphasizing that we never come to know or should strive for 'pure', universal, and eternal truths.

See also: Hans-Georg Gadamer, p. 111

Hans-Georg Gadamer: *Truth and Method*, p. 78

Gadamer (1900–2002) was a German hermeneutic philosopher, and his major work *Truth and Method* (*Wahrheit und methode*, 1960) stressed that we always meet the world, texts, acts, and artefacts as understanding and interpreting creatures, rooted in prejudices that we can change and challenge through questioning and interaction.

See also: Hermeneutics, pp. 89, 111

Rorty wanted to strengthen the eternal communication of mankind, p. 92

The American pragmatist philosopher Richard Rorty (1931–2007) claimed that philosophers have to do their best to contribute to and, not least, to qualify the eternal communication of mankind instead of detecting and 'preaching' eternal truths.

Pleonasm, pp. 95, 132

Even though a pleonasm is normally defined as the use of more words than are needed to express the meaning (e.g., a riding rider on a horse back) and therefore something you ought not to use, the conscious use of a pleonasm can be used both to create an attention towards an assertion and as a capability to demonstrate self-critique.

Phenomenology, critical theory, hermeneutics, and theories based on the importance of agency and reflexive subjectivity, p. 111

In order not to forget nor to objectify the existential, perceptual, bodily, thinking human subjectivity in its uniqueness, phenomenology (the study of experiences in a first-person perspective), critical theory (the profound critique of self-destructive logics in modern societies), and hermeneutics (see: Hermeneutics, p. 101) have a lot to offer the seeking soul and curious mind.

Klafki's concept of the double opening, p. 137

The German didactic and educational philosopher Wolfgang Klafki (b. 1927) states that learning processes 'get fuel' from the double fact that human beings open themselves towards the world and at the same time the world opens itself to them – and (t)hereby a fertile dialectical and transformative encounter logic takes place.

Ricouer's idea that the existence of the gift is the clue to mankind, p. 141

For the French philosopher Paul Ricoeur (1913–2005), the gift is much more than a physical object and a mean to impose power on other people; it is a way to intensify attention, strengthen bonds and narratives, and share everything from wealth, goods, and art to worldviews.

Ziehe and the educational *Fremdenführer*, p. 142

The German professor of pedagogy Thomas Ziehe (b. 1947) prefers the German concept *Fremdenführer* to the English translation guide, because *Fremden* equals strange/stranger and *Führer* is the leader and navigator; that is, the good teacher is a *Fremdenführer*, he or she opens the access to unknown fields and things in collaboration with curious pupils and students, implying that they go through identity-transforming processes through which they get the chance to be 'provoked' to become a little bit 'alien' and thereby new to themselves.

See also: Klafki, p. 137; The art of decentering, pp. 238, 243, 244

Simmel: *Wie ist Gesellschaft möglich?*, p. 162

The early, founding German neo-Kantian sociologist Georg Simmel (1858–1918) posed the German philosopher Immanuel Kant's (1724–1804) profound question "How is it possible to know something?" in a slightly different but completely new way: How is society possible?

Pedersen's *The Competition State*, p. 181

In 2011, the Danish political scientist Ove Kaj Pedersen (b. 1948) wrote a highly influential and contested book *Konkurrencestaten* (*The Competition State*) conceptualizing the role of the state doing the best it can to strengthen the survival of the competitive nation and the welfare state project in the age of globalization.

Fallibilism, pp. 184, 187, 248, 252

Every claim and statement stated in everyday language or based on scientific research can in principle be wrong (fallible) or be proven to be wrong. Therefore it is healthy for a self-critical and open society – and, not least, a scientific society – to practice, praise, and internalize an open consciousness of fallibilism (= *Fallibilismusbewusstsein* in German).

See also: Popper's principle of falsification, p. 21

Fuchs, de Jaegher, p. 191

Thomas Fuchs (b. 1958) is a German philosopher and psychiatrist and Hanne de Jaegher (b. 1978) is a German philosopher of mind and cognitive scientist, and these interdisciplinary and highly productive phenomenologists study and conceptualize how real people of flesh and blood interact, communicate, share intentions and attentions, and form intersubjective patterns.

See also: Phenomenology, critical theory, hermeneutics, and theories based on the importance of agency and reflexive subjectivity.

Madeline Hunter, p. 199

Madeline Hunter (1916–1994) created a model called the Instructional Theory Into Practice (ITIP), a professional learning program widely used particularly during the 1970s and 1980s, that includes seven steps: objectives (or success criteria); standards of performance (or expectations); anticipatory set (the hook to elicit engagement); teaching (input, modeling, etc.); guided practice; closure (review critical aspects of the lesson); and independent practice.

Purkey's invitational learning, p. 199

Developed by William Purkey and Betty Siegel, invitational education aims to create a more exciting, satisfying, and enriching school environment that intentionally *invites* people in schools to want to learn.

 Difference between epistemology and ontology, p. 323

An at least 2,500-year-old and utmost important distinction with implication and tremendous importance for philosophy, science, and everyday life – between what we know and can come to know (epistemology; for example, through production of science) and what is 'is' (ontology; that is, how being in the world is constituted).

Kant's perpetual peace, p. 220

German philosopher Immanuel Kant (1724–1804) was far ahead of his time when he wrote *Zum ewigen frieden* in 1795 and started to reflect upon the necessity of obtaining a perpetual cosmopolitan peace between fighting and competitive nation states and citizens 'loaded with' narrow-minded interests.

Plato's *Cratylus*, p. 291

Written by Plato 2,420 years ago, the dialogue *Kratylos* (Eng. *Cratylos*) can be read as one of the first language philosophical classics in the history of Western thought.

The art of decentering, pp. 238, 243, 244

If you manage to decenter yourself, you get at least three fertile options: distancing yourself from self-centered, strategic, and instrumental approaches to other human beings and the world; coming to reflect upon who you are and how you came to be thinking and acting the way you do; opening yourself to the unknown, unseen, and unforeseen.

See also: Ziehe and the educational *Fremdenführer*, p. 142

Ziehe, Kierkegaard, von Humboldt, p. 243

Thomas Ziehe (b. 1947) is a German professor of pedagogy, and his studies in education reforms, youth culture, and identity formation have had a great impact in, for example, Denmark. Søren Aabye Kierkegaard (1813–1855) was a Danish philosopher, theologian, and author known, read, and studied around the globe. Wilhelm von Humboldt (1767–1835) was a German philosopher, philologist, minister of education, and university builder (he founded Berlin University, today Humboldt University, in 1810).

Derrida, p. 243

Jacques Derrida (1930–2004) was a French philosopher who wanted to deconstruct Western metaphysics, emphasizing and defending the radical difference between what is (and exists in the world and in the texts) and what can be claimed about what is (e.g., by the scientist and the text interpreter).

See also: Difference between epistemology and ontology, p. 323

Malinowski, Margaret Mead, Mary Douglas, and Lévi-Strauss, pp. 267

Four prominent anthropologists in the 20th century. The Polish-born Bronislaw Kaspar Malinowski (1884–1942) is considered to be the inventor of the ethnographic fieldwork. The American cultural anthropologist Margaret Mead (1901–1978) had a tremendous impact while she managed to bring anthropological studies into wider public attention. The British social anthropologist Mary Douglas (1921–2007) wrote – among many books – the classic *Purity and Danger* (1966). The French ethnographer Claude Lévi-Strauss (1908–2009) is the 'father' of structural anthropology.

Adorno's credo, p. 290

In Latin, the first word Christian believers say when they pray is 'credo' (= 'I believe' in English), and even though the German philosopher and sociologist Theodor W. Adorno (1903–1969) was not a believer, he still maintains a profane 'credo' when it comes to philosophy: that it cannot be summarized.

Vivid, pluritopic, multilayered, and unforeseen, p. 306

Four words stating the vitality ('vivid'), the many places ('pluritopic'), the complex woven and pattern-rich forms ('multilayered'), and non-anticipatory dimensions ('unforeseen') we – John and Steen – have explored, touched, and mutually reflected upon during our long conversation in Melbourne.

Index

Note: Page numbers in *italic* indicate a figure and page numbers in **bold** indicate a table on the corresponding page